The Heart is Like Heaven

Lydia Maria Child
Courtesy of the New-York Historical Society, New York City

The Heart is Like Heaven

The Life of Lydia Maria Child

by

Helene G. Baer

Philadelphia
University of Pennsylvania Press

7422
Printed in the United States of America

For Mother, whose heart was like heaven

Acknowledgments

SO MANY PEOPLE SHOWED ME KINDNESS AND INTEREST WHILE I wrote this book that I wish the work were worthy of their expectations. Chronologically, my thanks go first to my dear teacher, Dr. Merle M. Hoover, who introduced me to American literature at Columbia University and to the unending joys of research. He and Mrs. Hoover gave me love, strength, and encouragement throughout the project.

Mrs. Arthur Cort Holden, bless her, permitted me to use her excellent library on women and, through her generosity, stimulated me to valuable methods of study and development of my enthusiasm for Mrs. Child.

Miss Margaret Hackett of the Boston Athenaeum, Mr. Clarence Brigham of the American Antiquarian Society at Worcester, Mrs. Marian King of the New York Society Library, Miss Mary Isobel Fry of the Huntington Library in California, Mr. Roland Baughman and Miss Cushing of Columbia's Special Collections, are among the many librarians who showed me how devoted and interested book people can be. I owe deep thanks to the librarians at Wayland, Mrs. Busser, Mrs. Bentley and Mrs. Lincoln, and to Mrs. Charles Morgan, Chairman of the Board of Trustees of the Wayland Library.

My friends Dr. Regina M. Duffy and Mrs. Henry S. Huber bore with "Maria" and labored over her with patience and good humor.

Professor Vernon Loggins, under whose critical eye I began this study, scolded and spurred me on and I thank him most wholeheartedly.

7

Dr. David Donald was most helpful in his research suggestions, especially those concerning the Child-Sumner relationship.

How can I begin to thank people such as Dr. and Mrs. Dunning of Englewood, New Jersey, who allowed me to examine the Hopper family papers and furniture while telling me priceless family anecdotes? Where are words to thank the Damon family of Wayland, and Miss Mabel Damon in particular, who permitted me several precious hours in her home among the souvenirs and letters Mrs. Child gave that family? Mrs. Edmund Sears of Wayland offered many valuable suggestions including the information that it was the Reverend Sears, whom my "Maria" so loved, who wrote "It Came Upon a Midnight Clear." Mr. Buckingham Sears of Camden, Maine, added delightful physical facts to the descriptions of the little brown house as it was in Mrs. Child's lifetime. Miss Elnora Curtis of Framingham gave me a wealth of detail on the Child family of Boylston.

Mrs. Newton Harris deserves a paragraph, perhaps a chapter to herself. She gave up her bedroom in Wayland in order that I might sleep in the very room which Maria and David used. Mrs. Harris let me poke and pry from shed to parlor, from floor to ceiling, from garden to orchard to let me feel at home—to let me *be* Lydia Maria Child.

My husband knows my satisfaction and joy in the way we together worked out some of the problems of authorship. On the day we found Maria's grave, I parted the overarching branches of bridal wreath and said, "Maria, I'd like you to meet Albert." He bowed to the little mound under the leaves and he said, "I am glad to meet you at last, Maria. I have been living with you for five years and it is really time we got together."

HELENE G. BAER

Contents

	Introduction	15
I	Welcome Home, Maria	19
II	Maine Lessons	25
III	The Pale Knight	36
IV	The Frugal Housewife	48
V	The Strings of Her Conscience	61
VI	Her Heart at Flood Tide	72
VII	Left Behind	83
VIII	Beet Sugar Bog	95
IX	The *Standard's* Call	110
X	Letters from New York	124
XI	The Demnition Grind	144
XII	Her Carriage Passes	162
XIII	Mrs. Child and Miss Fuller	177
XIV	Over the River	190
XV	Way Station to Home	206
XVI	Without a Cloak	216
XVII	Hiatus	225
XVIII	Moral Arithmetic	234
XIX	High Noon	247
XX	Yankees Brave and Dandy	255
XXI	The Sunset Crusader	269
XXII	The Rainbow Fades	283
XXIII	We Are the Living	299
	Appendix	311
	Bibliography	317

Illustrations

Lydia Maria Child   *frontispiece*

Maria's Knight   34

How Slavery Honors Our Country's Flag   70

The Firing of the *Mexican*   77

Croton Water Celebration   138

Letter to Theodore Tiebon   221

Lydia Maria Child at Age 63   267

David Lee and Lydia Maria Child   281

Mrs. Child at Age 65   291

Note to George Curtis   291

Placque in Beaman Library   297

We Are the Living   308

Will of Lydia Maria Child   311

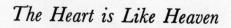

The Heart is Like Heaven

The human heart is like heaven; the more angels, the more room.

FREDERIKA BREMER

Introduction

EARLY ONE WINTER MORNING MORE THAN ONE HUNDRED YEARS
ago, a muffled roar exploded the quiet of a Boston street and
startled passers-by nearly lost their footing on the icy
cobbles. The watery lemon sun had barely found strength to
sweep a pale beam through School Street, and darkness hung
like a limpet in the corners. The date was January, 1861, and
the place, Tremont Temple.

Inside, Wendell Phillips stood facing his hostile audience
while behind him on the platform ranged his friends and
supporters, row on row, jammed together with faces tense
and hands clenched. The air was heavy with the smell of
wool, stale dust, and perspiration. An abolitionist meeting
such as this drew people of every sort—rich, poor, sympathetic, some murderously opposed, some who came out of
curiosity, but most who were determined to fight abolition
by any means and under mob leadership if need be. The
sour smell of fear was in this air, yet there was courage
too, in strange clothing. All but lost amid the rows of men
were fifteen women, fifteen partisans of Phillips who was to
speak at the Temple for the second time that week against
Negro slavery. Fifteen shawled and bonneted ladies and all
those furious men!

Eyes searched furtively and frantically for the police; the
mayor of Boston had promised that they would protect any
public meeting. But this time the police did not come; power-

ful forces had warned the mayor that his own future
depended on keeping hands off this antislavery beat. Mayor
Wightman had to think about himself; charity began at
home. So, with no official protection, Wendell Phillips came
forward to speak and pandemonium exploded. Prodded by
the gibes of certain anonymous fellows who shouted that
Phillips and his friends had caused the current trade
recession, the loss of jobs and mills whose wheels no longer
turned, clerks, bank tellers, small shop owners, all the "little"
people whose work had slowed or was altogether gone, made
a rush for the front of the hall. This was the "Broadcloth
Mob" in screaming, bellowing action. They howled from the
galleries, they tumbled in at the doors; and the Bell-Everett
rowdies, hired to stir up the trouble by so-called respectable
Bostonians, incited the Broadcloth Mob to do its worst.

Phillips' self-appointed bodyguard of a dozen friends lined
up before him, arms locked, while those fifteen women
cowered under their fringed shawls, moving their lips in
prayer. For a long moment it looked as though Phillips'
"noble head would be assailed by murderous hands," but
he, himself, hardly acted as if he believed it. He stood
unperturbed, every inch a "conquering angel," and his only
sign of emotion was his insistence upon standing in front,
not behind, his defenders. Olympian, with the gaslight form-
ing a halo around his handsome head, this aristocrat seemed
taller than his actual six feet two inches.

He began to speak and the din swelled. "Tell John
Andrew, tell John Andrew, John Brown's de-ead, John
Brown's de-ead," chanted the mob as they shuffled closer
and closer. Still Phillips stood, one hand lightly at rest on
the rostrum, the other relaxed at his side. He smiled slightly
and spoke to the newsmen in the front row. Chants and cat-
calls ceased. "What's he sayin? This here meetin's public.

Hey, speak up there!" shouted the crowd. Then for a full half hour they listened to Phillips' clear, melodious voice— the voice of the finest orator in New England. When he was done, there was silence.

The instant he moved back, though, hell broke loose. His friends of the bodyguard braced themselves again, aware that so few could hardly stand against so many. It was then that two of the timid ladies detached themselves from their perch high up beside the organ and climbed down to Phillips. He smiled and bowed as they approached, and offered each an arm. Then the three together moved slowly down the platform steps, out between the lines of hissing, snarling men. On Phillips' right walked lovely Maria Chapman, born organizer and feminine whip of the antislavery ranks. On his left was a plump little wren of a woman, chin up, color high, her only beauty in dark eyes and in her simple, motherly expression—Lydia Maria Child. She looked at those irate men as though they were naughty children to whom she might be kind if they behaved, and no one could guess how her knees shook under her long skirt.

The trio reached the outer door in safety but there were loiterers beyond who snarled as they walked past and were ready to pounce if the ladies deserted their charge. Consequently the two Marias walked him all the way home to Essex Street and the waiting arms of his invalid wife Ann; and though the two women quaked at every step, not once did the muttering crowd that followed them see them falter. The two ladies drew a deep, shuddering breath as Phillips closed his heavy front door and they allowed themselves to sag with relief for one blessed instant. Then they straightened their shoulders, bowed towards the onlookers as though they were at a polite reception, hooked their trailing skirts up out of the mud, and walked away.

"That small one—say, she don't look like she'd hurt a fly," said one ruffian to another. "Fer a fact, she don't; but them high muckymucks says to watch her. You can't never tell about them what looks like butter wouldn't melt in their mouth," came his answer.

There were some in Boston who believed that not only butter but fire and brimstone too would melt in the mouth or from the pen of Lydia Maria Child. Who in all of that city thought of her as simple and motherly? She, who had written the first effective antislavery broadside in the United States and lost security and social position because of it! She, who was denounced for her writings and her activities with the same scorching breath as William Lloyd Garrison! She, an insidious, tireless protagonist for freedom no matter what the cost! The men of the Broadcloth Mob knew all about her, and they knew that when she came forward to rescue Wendell Phillips, it was part of the pattern she had followed all her life. And upon her death, many years after this day in 1861, John Greenleaf Whittier wrote:

> It is no exaggeration to say that no man or woman . . . rendered more substantial service to the cause of freedom or made such a great renunciation in doing it.

I

Welcome Home, Maria

LYDIA MARIA FRANCIS WAS BORN IN MEDFORD, Massachusetts, on February 11, 1802. Her father, David Convers Francis, baker and real-estate operator, combined shrewd business ability with sympathy for his fellow man. It was from him that this youngest of his six children derived her fondness for reading, her antislavery convictions, and her quick wit. Yet Mr. Francis was enough of a man of his time not to show tenderness too openly to any of his children or friends; and while all duly respected him, the people *loved* his wife. The poor knew who would help them when their larders were empty or their woodboxes low. On Thanksgiving Eve, Mrs. Francis set out Indian puddings and spicy pumpkin pies for any comers to her kitchen. Often twenty or thirty—the wood sawyer, the washerwoman, even the peddlers—went on their way with fragrant bulging packs. The Francis children learned early to live simply themselves but to be generous to others. Mrs. Francis taught little Maria the selflessness which was to motivate so much of her life.

Maria was proud to have been born in Medford-on-the-Mystic, which boasted of having been the first town in New

England to shelter a fugitive slave. Even as a small girl, Maria's eyes smarted whenever she heard about that hunted man, Caesar, and the agonies he had endured until he found a haven in her town. Slavery had been outlawed in Massachusetts only six years before she was born but she heard her father fume that other states still permitted it and that he, for one, spurned the thought that one man could own another, whatever the color of his skin. Maria longed to hug him for sounding so right and brave and strong; and somehow, when his youngest burst at him affectionately, he never reproved her.

Her years in Medford were rich with the wonderful tales she heard. Some of her own uncles were among the heroes who lay in the burying ground down Dead Man's Alley. Her grandfather, Benjamin Francis, was one of the Yankees at Concord and had killed five British redcoats himself. Yet stories such as those were not to Maria's liking. She did not want to think about graves; wet paddy fingers seemed to run up and down her back. There was something awfully damp about death. But there were other grandfather stories she did like and when he taught her about the woods, the call of the bobolink, and the spot so secret where the wild ginger grew, she was enthralled. Together they found arrowheads left long before by the Indians, and mosses that grew on rock, tree, and brookside. And elderberries, blackberries, and huckleberries. And bayberry for candles and pennyroyal and sage and endless other herbs. Her mother's lessons were of a more domestic character. She taught Maria about a proper dooryard garden, marigolds, lobelia and hollyhocks, how to encourage flowers to flaunt their bravest color, how to store their seeds away for the winter safe from dampness and mice. Mrs. Francis had the prettiest garden in town. Flowers seemed to love her too.

The best days of all were when big brother Convers took Maria to watch the shipbuilders at work. Convers was careful to keep her out of the way of flying mallets or sailors' harsh words, and she retained the mixed fragrance of wood shavings and tar in her memory for the rest of her days. There were four shipyards to visit, one at each bend of the river. Best of all was a school holiday, the day of a ship's launching, a day to get away from the drudgery of ABCs and the piffly things that Marm Betty, Maria's snuff-stained first teacher, considered important. Poor old Marm Betty ran her Dame School as best she could while trying to forget the shame of having been caught one dreadful day by Governor Brooks drinking tea in her back parlor out of the spout of the pot! That episode had made Marm Betty shy of looking grownups straight in the face, but she was kinder to children than ever. Maria loved her old teacher and learned to read and write with her, but it was really Convers, six years her senior, who taught her most.

Convers was the dominant influence in her early years. He read everything to her and they talked it over. Though he teased her, she did her best to keep up with him, and her questions were likely to make him dream up fantastic answers rather than to have to admit that he did not know. When they read *Paradise Lost,* she asked him the meaning of "the raven down of darkness."

"That's easy," answered the superior male. "Can't you see? It's the fur of a black cat that sparkles when it gets stroked." He was pretty pleased with himself by that but it did not make a bit of sense to her.

Convers was his father's assistant in the bakeshop and every day after classes, he and Maria studied in the steamy, fragrant oven room. Mr. Francis' motto was, "Whatever you try, whatever you do, is worth doing well." Therefore he expected his son to be an expert baker. The Francis product was famous, as famous as the Medford rum which smelled heavenly but made strong men silly after a few tots. The Francis product was good for you—a cracker that was not a cracker at all but a sweet butter cookie made with great labor. It was misnamed "cracker" because the dough, while baking, had to be pricked at the sides to let the steam escape, which caused it to crack into equal halves when finished.

Often Maria begged Convers to let her push the doughy bits around the floor with his long-handled shovel, but he said she was too small and too fat and too ignorant. Despite her big brother's insults, life was very lonely for her when he went off to Harvard to study for the ministry and left her alone with the books they had read together. Her parents tried to lessen her loneliness by giving her a thick leather Bible in which they inscribed, "A reward due to merit and proof of parental affection," but while Maria studied the Good Book and learned long sections by heart, she felt that piety could not fill the void of Convers' absence. Even at that age, religion as she knew it just did not give enough.

When she was twelve, she learned the beginning of real sorrow. The eldest of her brothers and sisters were almost strangers to her, married and living away. Convers was at Harvard. Only Mary, slightly older than Convers, and Maria were left at home when Mrs. Francis began to waste away of a mysterious "lethargic affliction," a form of tuberculosis. The poor mother wanted desperately to help her youngest. Perhaps, as mothers will, she foresaw the dangers of an overgenerous, overloyal spirit, and a dash of romance that sometimes put her little daughter's practical self far, far away. In a reedy voice broken with long nights of coughing, the mother told her child: "When you are older, when

trouble comes to you, remember what I say. The Bible will
help you when all else fails, Maria. Turn to it for your
comfort. Help your father when I am gone. He will need
you."

The girl, distressed by what she could not understand,
ran out of the room. She could not bear to look at her
mother's flushed, thin face or at the veined claw she held
out for a sip of water. Maria hated her mother for being
sick and she hated herself for her own selfishness, but she
could not change either one. Her mother was going to die
like so many others and lie in one of those damp, mossy
graves and be food for worms. Ugh! The world was a gray,
ugly place.

Four months after the funeral came another blow. Mary
Francis asked her father's permission to marry Warren
Preston and move away to the District of Maine. Maria
and her father would be left alone in the big brick house
on the corner of Ashland and Salem streets—Maria and this
man who practically never showed affection to anyone. Now
Maria understood why her mother had asked her to be
loving to him.

On the day of the wedding, Maria was miserable. Instead
of needing her, everyone acted as though she were in the
way. While Mary put the spices in the wine punch, the
young sister slipped out of the house and ran down to her
secret cave by the river where she brooded all day without
a thing to eat, sure she would starve before they came to
find her. She longed to have anyone, anyone, even her Aunt
Lydia whom she loathed, come to look for her, but no one
did. Out in the channel the current moved swiftly, but here
under the trees it was quiet and dark, and she stared into
the depths and saw shadows behind her reflection. She was
afraid, afraid of the loneliness of that big house with only

her busy father for company. "Mother, Mother, why did you leave me?" she sobbed.

She dawdled by the water until Mary and her bridegroom had left for Norridgewock, Maine. Then she went home, half hoping that her father would pay enough attention to her to scold. Dusk was falling and a lighted lamp stood in the window. Her father sat in front of the fire, head bowed, waiting for her. She came in timidly. He looked at her, his face lighted in a tender smile, and he opened his arms. He greeted her as he would greet her for another fifty years.

"You're welcome home, Maria."

II

Maine Lessons

AFTER MARY LEFT, LIFE SETTLED DOWN INTO A SLUGGISH
tide. Had Convers been at home to play and read with her,
had Mr. Francis concentrated less on making money, had
there been one close friend in whom Maria could confide,
she would have felt less desolate. It was a cold winter, and
up and down the hills of Medford the icy roads cut through
her boots. She took a perverse pleasure in her sore feet; her
father, she sometimes thought, would not have noticed if
she left bloody tracks in the snow. Of course, if she had
been a fugitive slave, he would be the first to see and to help.

The neighbors clucked their tongues disapprovingly at
Maria's shabbiness. Her father was a busy man and she,
they said, was too big a girl to be a sloven; but the truth
was that Mr. Francis' lack of encouragement made her
that way. He never praised her for a good dinner, though
he was quick to comment on a failure. When he came in
evenings he always asked about her doings of the day, but
after that he hardly spoke at all. The fire burned low as
they sat together, but it was only by the subdued tone in his
usually stern voice and the gentle kiss he gave her for
good night that she knew he really loved her.

25

The spring of the year was no better. The wildflowers she picked shriveled and withered for lack of water. By summer the garden was ragged and ill-grown no matter how hard she tried to follow her gentle mother's instructions. The hollyhocks were scraggly and the lilies lacked in fragrance what they made up in leggy growth. The pinks, ordinarily the most prolific bloomer of them all, seemed to have lost the will to live.

Miss Swan's Seminary, where she had gone since the days of Marm Betty, was a bore. Stilted education was not for this girl who had reveled in the flights of Milton's Satan and his band of fallen angels. Who would want to bother with Webster's *Speller* or the *Young Ladies' Accidence* after dreaming over *Love's Labour's Lost?* The seminary was no answer to her problems.

Meanwhile changes had occurred in the town. The date was 1814 and Medford felt the pinch of Mr. Madison's war which had already dragged on for two years. Medford ship-yards no longer thrilled the children, for they were ghostly places with never the tap of a hammer to break the silence. Shipping was at a standstill. The unemployed sat around complaining in the taverns while new shoes and oil lamps and butter churns stood gathering dust in the shops. Mr. Francis listened to the talk at Simpson's over his tot of rum and decided to sell his business while it had a value. No sooner decided than done; he sold his bakery for a fat price, along with the house his children had been born in, that "honest" house that eventually became the first home of the Medford Historical Society. What to do with his twelve-year-old daughter was now the question. She needed a home and sympathetic guidance such as he knew he was incapable of giving her. Her nose was never out of a book, and she had picked up such odd ideas from her reading that her father knew she would never fit into a pattern of conventional young ladyhood. Maria did as she pleased without considering the proprieties. He wrote to Mary for help.

Mary promptly invited Maria to come to Maine to live, and Maria was so happy to be wanted that she forgave her brother-in-law for marrying Mary in the first place and began to pack before she finished her letter of thanks. Treasures went in and out of her old carpetbag a dozen times until she realized that little-girl keepsakes had better be left behind. This was to be a new life; so, like snakes in the spring, she must shed the old skin. But with the responsibility of the move before her, she remembered her old friends. She took special pains with a basket of provisions for Marm Betty, whose school fees, ninepence payable each Monday, were not enough to keep her in firewood. The prosperous families in town took care of Marm Betty out of affection and Maria knew that her mother would have wanted her to carry on the tradition. For her parting gift she tied up the basket prettily with ferns and small bags of herbs, filled it with good things she had made herself, and brought it down to Marm Betty's cottage between Steve Lincoln's cobbler shop and the Brooks mansion. She could not stay long, for she had one more visit to make—to Miss Lucy Osgood, daughter of the Second Church minister. In a second basket, with a bow on its handle, Maria carried her kitten as a gift for Miss Lucy, who had to cope with Religion and its problems every day, all day, and might be glad of some simple, unquestioning, cat companionship.

Duty done, Maria ran down to her secret pool by the river for one last look at the spot where she and Convers had fished for alewives, shad, and bass. She was much too excited to stay there quietly and watch her old friend, the snapping turtle, lumber out of the muck. Instead she raced across town to watch the boys hop on and off the boats as they went through the locks of the Middlesex Canal. Then she remembered one more sentimental pilgrimage, a stop at the spot where her eldest brother, James, had three times dug for buried treasure without finding it. An old sea captain had whispered his secret to James years before, but no one had ever succeeded in digging it up. Maria poked around for a few minutes and then ran home to finish her packing.

One fine morning, with nine other passengers, she boarded the bus for the five-mile trip to Boston. She paid her fare of thirty-seven and a half cents to the driver and listened to his instructions about the change she must make at the city depot for the stagecoach to Maine. And then, with a small bag of belongings and a large stock of memories, Lydia Maria Francis set out for Norridgewock, Maine.

Life with the Prestons at Norridgewock was anything but lonely. The homesick young bride was made happy by her little sister's arrival and new warmth flowed into the rambling clapboard house one block over from Main Street. The girls worked and sang tunelessly and the household chores were easily done. Mary and Warren Preston gave Maria the sense of security and love she needed, and she could not do enough for them in return. She knitted cozy hug-me-tights for the Preston babies as they came along. She learned to quilt in the rose, star, and double wedding ring pattern. When little Sarah Preston was born, she made the christening robe, its yoke embroidered in tiny fern fronds and the same motif in bands down the long skirt. Maria sat relaxed under the apple tree in the yard while she stitched the dress, and all the neighborhood children stretched themselves out on the sweet-smelling grass to listen to the stories she spun as she sewed.

Yet domesticity could not claim all of the time of a girl

so enthralled with books. Norridgewock was more than a backwater in the wilds of Maine; rather, it was an island of learning and culture. Four hundred families lived there, with homes dotting either side of the Kennebec. They were proud of their white-spired churches, their gristmill, their square meetinghouse, and their school which was taught by college students on leave. Maria went to classes and embarrassed the young teachers by proving that she knew more and had read more than they. Even so she would not give up going to school for fear of missing a class in French or German, which languages Convers was studying at Harvard, for she still did not want to fall far behind him. Latin presented a problem in that none of these visiting teachers would offer it to her. She wrote to Convers:

> I have long indulged the hope of reading Virgil in his own tongue. I have not yet relinquished it. I look forward to a certain time when I expect that hope with many others to be realized. I usually spend an hour after I retire for the night in reading Gibbon's *Roman Empire*.

Convers could not doubt that this determined miss would get her Latin one way or another.

Warren Preston's position in town made Maria's ambitions easier to achieve. He was the appointed librarian and owned two full shares, valued at three dollars each, in the library. Maria had the run of the books, and she strained her eyes with Homer, Johnson, and the *Spectator* papers. She daydreamed over the Waverley novels and she bombarded Convers by mail with questions about Byron, a subject nice girls were supposed to ignore. Her letters to her brother sailed on a high literary plane, for she knew enough now to pay him back for his teasing when she was small. The whole summer of her fifteenth year, she tried to convert him to her own irritation with Milton's attitude toward women. "Don't

you think," she wrote, "that Milton asserts the superiority of
his own sex in too lordly a manner?" While, superlative on
superlative, she praised the grandeur of her old favorite
Paradise Lost, she scorned the philosophy of its author, who
made Eve ever the humble servant of man. She read whenever she could, and at night she dreamed of books and of
writing them herself. Some day, some day, she too would
write.

For three months out of each year, there was little time
for such dreams. Norridgewock was the shire town, the
county seat of Somerset. Lawyers from a hundred and fifty
miles to the north and from all the surrounding countryside
came with their entire families when the courts convened.
The Prestons very properly entertained generously, and three
times a year Mary and Maria "redded up" the house from
cellar to attic until it shone. Septembers, Maria ran out to a
damp spot in the woods to gather scouring rush so that she
could make the pewter candlesticks sparkle; and though she
longed to loiter in the glory of the pines and to rest on the
fallen needles in a patch of sunlight, to sniff the woodsy
fragrance and to listen to the wind rustling among the
pointed treetops, she must hurry back to help Mary. On the
way she scooped up a handful of scarlet partridge berries
with their twin-leaved runners and a clump of star moss for
a dish garden for the kitchen windowsill. As she ran, she
marked the grove where most of the ladyslippers stalks stood
bare so that she could see them in bloom in the spring.

Back at the house there were pies to bake—quince, apple
or pumpkin; wild fowl and chickens to pluck; and spiced
cucumbers to lift from their brine. The Prestons, like most
Norridgewockians, used whatever was at hand, for they had
little extra cash for "bought" goods. The War of 1812 had
starved all of New England; but the backs and wills of Maine

men were strong, and there was fish in the river and game in the woods for the taking. Not even old George of England would have scorned a dish of broiled Kennebec salmon. Maria worked vigorously in the orchard to sort the "Macs" and the Baldwin apples the boys shook down from the trees, and she made rhymes about the squash and pumpkins glowing gold under their coarse green leaves. Just about the only items Warren Preston did buy was a bit of tea or coffee from the bright, rattling peddlers' wagons. The house was snug and smelled sweetly of apples, leather, and good wood fires; and winters, the deep snow kept off the wind. Sometimes the drifts piled above the second-floor windows and Maria made up stories for the children about living in an igloo.

Often, when the day's court session was over, men gathered in the Preston living room for an evening of talk. Maria shivered in the corner as far back as she could shrink without missing a word of the conversation. She had to hear all they said about law and politics, war and secession. For there was talk of secession too. The British invasion of Maine in 1814 had come within fifty miles of Norridgewock and there were plenty of families between that point and the Preston house who had gone over to the enemy and who now clamored to have the District of Maine get out of the Union. The majority, though, remembered that their fathers had been Minutemen at Concord or had manned the redoubts at Breed's Hill. They would not go back to English rule even though the Congress of the United States allowed the war to drain prosperity from New England. As the demijohn of rum circulated, as voices rose, Maria heard the men shout, "Let those who like 'em, swear allegiance to the Georges of Hanover; we'll stick by our George from Mt. Vernon."

Come spring, off went Maria to the woods again. Some of her exciting days were when she visited the bark cabins of the Abnaki Indians six miles up the Kennebec at the village of Old Point. Some girls—most girls—would be afraid to go off alone, but teenaged Maria was filled with noble spirit and as she made friends with the red men, she saw them not as sellers of sweet-grass baskets nor as rum-sodden wrecks to which contact with the white men had reduced them, but as stalwarts of the forest, lordly fishers and hunters, members of a great historic race. She used her time to explore, to weave new tales with old as these people told them to her, and she stored bits of day-by-day living in her mind with the nuggets she treasured from books and the grandfather tales of long ago. The Indians liked this girl who brought small gifts for their papooses and who wanted to learn how they did their beadwork and basketwork.

One day Norridgewock was stirred by excitement. Boys on a squirrel hunt came upon a giant oak which had been turned over by a Nor'easter. Beneath the torn roots and green with mold lay an old bronze bell. The boys tried to pull it out, but the roots held firm as though to protect it from irreverent hands. The boys ran back to town through the sunlit afternoon and the sweet-scented bracken. "Buried treasure, there's buried treasure in the woods," they yelled. Heads poked out of doors and soon, despite the hot day, a stream of people were on their way to see the wonder. The boys danced ahead forgetful of the prickling of their linsey-woolsey shirts. A shower of gold and scarlet leaves floated gently to earth as they pushed through the brambles to show their find. "Do you suppose," Maria wondered aloud to Warren Preston, "it could be Father Râle's bell?"

The story of Father Râle recorded the bloodiest page in the annals of Norridgewock. The priest had lived with the

Indians, hunted, fished, and prayed with them in their own language while he led them toward God. Nevertheless the British believed that he taught them less holy lessons; that he, a Jesuit, incited the Abnakis against the Iroquois tribes and their allies, the British soldiers.

On a day in 1722 the good father called his followers to prayer in the little log chapel. The mellow tones of the chapel bell reverberated through the gold and azure day and stole the silence from the pines. During the litany, the Iroquois ignited the pine needles around the chapel and in one instant flames cut off any chance for Father Râle and his people to escape. They died as they prayed together.

The bell fell into the wreckage. A few nights later, some Abnakis who had missed church on Sunday crept back to salvage the bell. They inched it out painfully; their mocassins crushed the charred bones of their brothers into the ashes. They carried their booty deep into the woodland and buried it. Weeds and brambles soon covered the ruins of the chapel and the story of Father Râle's bell became a legend, half-believed, always honored.

Now at last the legendary relic might be found. Maria strained to see as the blacksmith climbed into the hole under the tree and with his mattock hacked off the first of the roots. The tool struck the side of the treasure with a hollow thud and scraped a long green scar in the mold. Others jumped in to help and onlookers shivered as the old story came to life. They eased the relic out, levering it edge by edge, and they brought it to Norridgewock on a sledge and hung it from a stout beam in the courthouse. History claimed that the bell had the sweetest tone with which bronze could sing. Someone pulled the rope and the bell spoke. But what was this—this dull, sepulchral clang? Was this the welling for which their ears had strained? Had fire, the purifier,

Maria's Knight

deadened the bronze? The sound shadowed the air like a bad conscience, and the superstitious murmured that it was the voice of Father Râle warning against strife, bigotry, and hatred. That was a memorable day in the little Maine town, one that Maria, for one, would never forget.

Years passed, with the court sessions marking off the seasons. Suddenly Maria felt that she had grown up. Two months after her eighteenth birthday, she wrote seriously to Convers and without a single literary joke. She had imposed herself on the Prestons long enough and now she wanted freedom to think for herself, to work as she chose, and to fall in love if the right man came along. She wrote:

> I can't talk about books or anything else until I tell you that I leave Norridgewock and take a school in Gardiner as soon as the travelling is tolerable . . . I hope, dear brother, that you feel as happy as I do. Not that I have formed any high-flown expectations. All I expect is that, if I am industrious and prudent, I shall be independent.

Characteristically she had decided on the step before she asked his approval. She was young to set out for herself, but, as her father had recognized years before, conventional objections could not keep her from the course she chose. When Maria made up her mind, nothing else mattered.

III

The Pale Knight

MARIA BOARDED IN GARDINER WITH THE HEAD OF THE
school and his ailing wife. The schoolmaster was an urbane
man with a smattering of knowledge in many fields and a
manner which made superficialities seem important. He
dazzled his new assistant by his apparent preference for her
company and her youth, and when he offered her guitar
lessons while his wife pressed eau de cologne to her brow as
she heard them plink and plunk, Maria felt that she was
moving in truly sophisticated paths. Her sense of humor
and honesty made her admit to herself that guitar or any
kind of music lessons, for someone unable to carry a tune,
were pretty funny.

From the first, Maria had no trouble with her own pupils.
The nature lore her mother, her grandfather, and the
Abnakis had taught her crowded into her lessons; and tales
of the Revolution, learned at Medford, were as exciting to
her students as they were to her. Scott's novels too. Ivanhoe
and Nathan Hale rode side by side in the rich tapestry she
spread. She showed the children that chivalry still lived in
the color and glory of the legends of America.

Maria made friends easily. People talked freely to her.

She was quick to mend a kite for a boy or to help his mother salt down a batch of beans. People liked to talk; she was ready always to listen, to think over the conversation later and put it, like the beans, away for future use. She wanted to learn about anything and everything, and she reported to Mary that Gardiner ladies were more fashion-conscious than the matrons of Norridgewock, that the Paul Revere bell in the Christ Church steeple rang its nine o'clock curfew far too early for the enterprising to get through with all they wanted to do, that the average income of Gardiner folk was really high, that an ambitious citizen had built an icehouse on Gray's Wharf—the first such in all of New England—but that the spring floods had washed it downstream. She told about the boats on the Kennebec, side- and stern-wheeled, and that there was talk about establishing a Gardiner Lyceum. There was so much doing in the prosperous town.

Yet the schoolmaster tried to keep her interests centered at home. Encouraged by her progress on the guitar, he next suggested that he teach her to draw in the mornings before class time. To his astonishment, she refused, with the excuse that those early hours were all she had for reading. Her answer piqued the gentleman; he shrugged when she told him of her preference for Milton, Shakespeare, and Scott, and he loaned her Locke, Kant, and Swedenborg to confuse her and make her turn to him for elucidation. He set a wily course to win her heart through books, but Maria immersed herself in the new philosophy rather than in him. How different she found Swedenborg from Milton or from the narrow patterns of the church; how broad the vision of Locke, how rich the stimulation of Kant. Her age and her loneliness— for, despite brave words, she did miss the family—made her a ripe target for philosophical unrealities.

Convers, who by now was an ordained minister and held

a Unitarian pulpit at Watertown, Massachusetts, worried that Maria's religious faith might waver. He apparently did not realize how far from orthodoxy it already was, but he cautioned her particularly against becoming a partisan for the theories of Swedenborg the mystic. She answered:

> You need not fear my becoming a Swedenborgian. I am more in danger of wrecking on the rocks of scepticism than of stranding on the shores of fanaticism. I am apt to regard a system of religion as I do any other beautiful theory. It plays around the imagination but fails to reach the heart. I wish I could find some religion in which my heart and understanding could unite.

Convers wisely recognized the mysticism that pulsed beneath her practicality and her youth. She was floundering out of her depth and he must give her an answer. He had recently married Miss Abby Bradford, and he and his bride dutifully and lovingly invited Maria to leave her post in Maine and to move in with them. Whether Gardiner and independence no longer seemed glamorous, whether the schoolmaster overestimated his charm and frightened her, whether it was the prospect of living with the brother she adored, Maria was quick to accept the Watertown invitation. Convers and Abby, with whom Maria established a friendly but never easy relationship, did their best to make her comfortable, and Maria was delighted once more with the opportunity of proximity to Boston and Cambridge and the intellectual stimulation she craved.

The Francises were constant hosts, and Maria acted as their junior hostess. Convers' excellent library and encyclopedic mind attracted many thinking men although his critics carped about his "all-sidedness." Convers was socially and politically conservative but his theology was liberal, a combination that some of his visitors considered "paralyzing to controversy." He straddled issues and withheld opinions even while eliciting them from others. But not so Maria. Guests found the young sister, fresh from Maine, delightful. She never hesitated to argue a point but dived in whenever she felt impelled to disagree. She would not mind her tongue but allowed it to speak her mind. According to her lights she was merely being honest when she denounced sectarian bigotry and restrictive convention. Theodore Parker, slightly younger than she, said he would always be grateful to her for her frankness during those evenings and for her "cheering words to a young fellow fighting his way to education."

The Maine schoolmaster pursued her to Watertown on frequent trips to Boston, but by now Maria knew that she could sail free on her own, with no middle-aged, married Romeo to teach her how to sing. She sent him packing. Convers was a popular teacher as well as pastor and he gladly discussed literature, art, as well as theology with her. He theorized on lessons for the Indians and discussed a book he was writing on the works of John Eliot, apostle to the red men. Emerson, Whittier, and Convers went deep into Indian lore; Maria added the bits she had picked up from the Abnakis while Emerson made strange and wonderful pronouncements until the loftiness of his talk made her feel stifled. She burst out, "All your theories do not come to the heart of the matter. An uneducated man can more safely trust to his conscience than his understanding. You must see that, can't you?" She felt that it was terribly important for her to have an answer, that her approach, being more immediate, was the more practical. Thanks to her demands, the argument started over, but this time young Emerson foundered in a morass of doubt. Conscience over understanding? This was a knotty problem.

However much such discussions appealed to Maria's intellect, they did nothing toward solving her own religious dilemma. She wondered if her impatience with theologic doctrine was caused by the reading she had done in Maine. Perhaps, now that she was away from that influence, a closer association with the Unitarian church might help. Toward that association, she asked Dr. Osgood, her old Medford pastor, to baptize her "Maria," not "Lydia," a name she disliked because of the aunt about whom she felt the same way. Her parents, it was true, had chosen that "Lydia" but now the "Maria" was entered on the parish ledger. Somehow or other she thought that the simple act of baptism would wash her doubts away, but it wrought no miracle for her and she was as upset as before.

The thing to do was to keep busy. Quickly bored with being a mere ornament in her brother's home, she opened a girls' school in Watertown. Her teaching methods shocked the parents but delighted the girls, since she allowed them to play rough games like battledore and shuttlecock and did not care if their hair flew wild as long as they really enjoyed the exercise. She actually ridiculed the girls, who minced and simpered in proper lady style, and she praised them for any act of independence. Mothers winced when they heard about these modern ideas and wondered how far Miss Francis dared to go. Miss Francis soon provided an answer.

One Sunday after her brother's morning service, she picked up a copy of the *North American Review* and riffled restlessly through its pages. Sunday really was the dullest day! An article by John G. Palfrey, author of the *History of New England*, caught her eye. It underscored the rich, colorful romance that ran in a golden vein through American history, material ripe for a novelist's pen. How exactly that fitted her own thinking! She threw down the book and paced back and forth.

The idea of writing was not new to her, but she was uncertain about subject. Should she yarn of battles, ancient monuments, forest green? Of farmers, witches, Indians? Indians. . . . Of course, Indians. All at once there was no doubt. She dashed to Convers' desk and with trembling hand scratched down the words that tumbled through her mind. The story burst full-blown onto the page. She finished her first chapter on that same Sunday afternoon and completed the rest of the novel, *Hobomok,* in six weeks. Hobomok, her hero, had a white wife, widow of a white husband. Indian and bride had a baby and would have lived happily ever after if that earlier spouse had not returned. Though the wife preferred her forest lord, he gave her and the child up to the man who said he had a prior claim. Honor must be served and this was a noble savage. It might have been from Maria's story that Tennyson later took the theme for *Enoch Arden.*

Maria's knowledge of Indians had been limited to the talks in Convers' study, her explorations with the Abnakis, and her reading of Cooper and Charles Brockden Brown. She was aware of Scott's influence on Cooper, who had transferred the valor and glory of the knights of old to the wilds of America. With no intent to imitate Cooper, *Hobomok* too stressed the nobility of the moral man, a nobility which rests in the conscience, not in the color of the skin. Her plea for tolerance outweighed her sentimentality. Convers no longer feared that his sister had lost God; her book proved how deeply she loved Him.

Cummings, Hilliard and Company published the book in 1824. They announced its author as "An American," as nonrevealing an identification as could be found. Not even

Lydia Maria Francis, unconventional as she prided herself
on being, dared to admit that she, a lady born, had written
a book. It just was not done in her circle. Yet the secret was
soon out and Maria became Boston's fad. Genteel mamas
prodded their beruffled and beribboned daughters to assure
them that it was acceptable to be a little "different." A deluge
swamped publishers' desks—a sensational change in a
society which might laugh or cry over Maria Edgeworth
and Fanny Burney but which carefully covered the works
of Madame de Staël with brown paper and marked the
plain cover, "Cookbook." With *Hobomok,* Maria, one of
Boston's own, became society's darling.

Once started, she went straight on, and her next book,
The Rebels, which she finished within a year, established a
new literary trend. In this one, for the first time, actual New
England history became the setting for a novel in which
Maria recounted some of the events that preceded the
Revolution. James Otis' speech in Faneuil Hall which Maria
wrote for this book was quoted and "elocuted" until the
public convinced itself that these were Otis' actual words
by which he had aroused the colonists against their English
overlords.

That same year, 1825, Lafayette was to come to Boston as
part of his American tour and Maria was so much in favor
that George Ticknor asked her to help receive the old
general. When that venerable hero kissed her hand at the
reception, she vowed she would never wash the imprint
away. She described the event in a small book, *Evenings in
New England,* and she wrote to Mary Preston about it, "My
little book has met with more unqualified success than
Hobomok."

Maria was only twenty-three and it was fun to be successful and popular, to wear pretty clothes out of her own earn-

ings, to hear compliments from everyone from an old French gallant to fops like Nathaniel Parker Willis. Not that she believed herself beautiful. Her nose was a bit long and she pressed her lips tightly when she was excited or concentrating on a writing problem, so that even now, tiny little lines were etching themselves in a frame on either side of her mouth. But her eyes and broad forehead made up for the rest—deep, dark eyes set far apart. Alexander's portrait of her caught the essence of her youth and charm. Brown hair parted in the center hung in gleaming ringlets behind her ears. A plain blue dress with white ruffles at elbow-length sleeves and low neckline set off her round neck and arms.

Admirers were not lacking, men who would not have given a second glance to the simple schoolmarm from Maine, the girl she had been only three years before. One of these, a writer of airy whimsies, more sophisticated than she, undertook to flatter her into believing that she was cherished. He was an attractive, popular fellow, which made her feel gay as she saw the envious looks of the other girls when he walked by her side on the Common. But she noticed that no matter how deep her conversation, he kept his own eyes wide open to tip his tall beaver to any socialite who happened to pass. Even though she recognized his superficiality, she did not want to give up the fun of his escort.

One day he said to her, "I hear that you are a religious girl but I am sure it must be a mistake. You are too fine to give yourself up to such humdrums." She was furious. Whatever her own feelings about religion, they were her own and no one else's affair. Yet in his very arrogance he was so, so attractive. She swallowed her temper, watched him bow to the next Boston bluebloods, and sighed.

She was headed for trouble. The debonair young man, still a college boy at heart, kissed and told, as he had about

his escapades at Yale. Maria's friends lost no time in inform-
ing her that she was merely a collector's item to him so that
she might as well forget the fast beat of her heart for this
particular young man. His boast, they said, was that it was
no harder to kiss the foremost lady writer of the day than
any of the girls at New Haven. Maria simply froze and said
nothing, but those little lines around her mouth deepened
and she showed a new maturity.

Not long afterward a new, more serious friend came to
her, a sympathetic young lawyer, David Lee Child, whom she
met at the home of the Curtis family. David was fine and
kind and she felt at ease with him, at ease for the first time
since her humiliation. She invited the young lawyer to visit
her, where they walked and talked for hours in Convers'
lovely rose garden and discovered their mutual liking for
reading, intensive research, and for the freedom that meant
most to them .

David was an idealist. Born on a small farm in West
Boylston and educated in the district school, he had studied
by candlelight after the day's chores were over in order to
be able to teach. While he studied, while he dug, plowed,
and furrowed, he dreamed of ways to better a sick world.
In 1822 he gave up teaching of the classics at the Boston
Latin School to be secretary to the American consul at
Lisbon. A year later he joined the Spanish army to fight
against France "in consequence of my love of liberty and
my abhorrence of fraud, cruelty and despotism." If he, one
American, could help to prevent the return of Bourbon
tyranny over Spain, he was willing to give his life for it. By
a strange quirk of fortune, David's long fight for freedom
actually began in the neighborhood of Don Quixote's fabled
tilting, and pale David Child henceforth was frequently

compared to the tilter. People love the Don Quixotes of the world, but they sneer at them a little.

Back in the United States, David had studied law with his uncle, Tyler Bigelow, of Watertown. It was then that he and Maria met. She listened raptly to his tales of adventure. Later she wrote in her diary, "He possesses the rich fund of an intelligent traveller without the slightest tinge of a traveller's vanity." He told her that the farmers in Spain still used the plow described by Virgil, and she confessed her old dream to read Virgil in the original. He offered to translate any classical passages for her or to teach her Latin or Greek. This was a new form of wooing— generous, stimulating, and how different from that other silly dandy. Yet she sighed.

Meanwhile much of her time was taken by the editing and publishing of the first periodical for children in the United States, the *Juvenile Miscellany*. Its ninety pages, most of which she wrote herself, came out every two months. All those nuggets of conversation, history, legends that she had heard as a girl, quizzes, acrostics, digests of articles she had read, short biography and original stories found their way to this little magazine with its index carefully printed on its back. The "Bell of Father Râle" was one of the stories she told. The magazine was immediately successful and Maria wrote to Mary, "The *Miscellany* has been very kindly received. It seems as if the public was resolved to give me a flourish of trumpets, let me write what I will." She need not have been so modest. The *Miscellany* was praised even by so severe a critic as Margaret Fuller with whom Maria had recently become friendly.

Convers took his family away for a trip in the fall of 1826, and Maria was left in the empty, echoing parsonage. Much as she wanted privacy to write, she needed love and companionship all the more, now that she began to know how pleasant it was. She wrote to a friend:

> I come home from school, tired to death with nouns and verbs and I find the house empty, swept and garnished, with not a single indication of animated existence, except the cat who sits in the window from morning till night, winking in the sun. That is to say when the sun is to be winked at, for the whole of this week, the skies have looked like a tub of cold suds.

She felt as hollow as the house, and the social life she might still have had bored her. She was teacher, editor, author, and belle, and it was not enough. She wrote out her attitudes and her selfanalysis in a small book called *Emily Parker, or Impulse, not Principle.* The title page stated that *Emily* was "intended for young persons" but the young person for whom it undoubtedly did most good was Maria herself. Her story was in that little book, just slightly disguised. The schoolmaster and the fop were there—and the idealist. David Child emerged and enlarged under her microscope—David the idealist, the contrast to the Gardiner guitar player and the dashing Don Juan.

David called on her at the parsonage and never had his charm so beguiled her. Suddenly her fingers itched to trim the edges on his frayed coat; her heart fluttered over the loose button on his sleeve. She who only came up to his shoulders longed to protect him from a harsh and practical world. Never one to hesitate when her course of action was clear to her, she decided to board for the winter with a Madame Canda, a fashionable French teacher, the reason for the move ostensibly to better her French "in order to hold my English tongue." Of course it was mere coincidence that David's office was practically around the corner—and that he too would board there.

She forgot to study French that winter while he read law cases to her or wrote his speeches for the Massachusetts State Legislature by her side. Well-meaning friends warned her that David deliberately "forgot" to send bills to his poorer clients but that only increased his luster in her eyes. She confided to the journal: "He is the most gallant man that has lived since the sixteenth century and needs nothing but helmet, shield and chain armor to make him a complete knight of chivalry." His almost ascetic appearance stirred her as no man's had before. She who had doubted that she would marry at all was singularly appreciative of dreamy David. Margaret Fuller had called her particularly honest and natural. But was she either now? Vacillating, she was not sure that she could really care enough for any man to share her life with him. The warnings of friends chilled her, yet was it not strange that every one of the ladies who met him fell under his spell just as she had? What was there about the man? And he had lots of friends on his own, influential men who relied on him to give their law cases or their political speeches real meat.

She did not ask for advice—not she. She would make her own decision as to whether David was merely an antidote for other men who had tried to dominate her, whether he would truly be the second half of her self as Swedenborg had outlined a good marriage to be. Of course, such thinking was rather premature, since then as in all time, it was polite to wait until she was asked. Yet she felt how the wind veered, and if she thought well of it, she would do a bit of blowing in the right direction. Still she doubted, and wrote to Mary, her sister: "Nature never intended me for anything but a single life and I am not going to quarrel with her plans." That was plainly her last word on the subject—until she saw David again and, in the face of his helplessness, her resolution crumbled.

IV

The Frugal Housewife

ONE EVENING IN SEPTEMBER, 1827, DAVID RODE OUT TO
Watertown on his trusty steed Thalaba. Because her family,
like her friends, disapproved of the young lawyer as a husband, Maria met him at the Curtises'. Twelve-year-old
George Ticknor Curtis spied on their interview through the
staircase banister and he told later that David had looked
frozen with fright as he proposed at last. The lover's face
tautened as Maria answered neither yes nor no, but as long
as she did not laugh at him there was hope. For four hours,
while that child on the stairs never missed a word, David
pleaded his cause, and four times he left her to go outside to
pacify his tethered horse. George probably exaggerated to
make a good story better, yet David too may have been
uncertain that marriage was right for him. The horse made
a convenient excuse to escape, but something, those dark
eyes of the girl on the horsehair sofa, drew him right back.
At any rate, at one in the morning he melted her resistance
and she agreed to become his wife.

The engagement announcement shook the family. Her
sisters-in-law bobbed their heads and brother James's wife,
old shrew that she was, murmured, "Through the wood,

through the wood, and find a crooked stick at last." All of them fussed at her for choosing this drifter instead of a man more settled in a profession. They condemned him for being a visionary even while they admitted his charm, and they enraged Maria by quoting something that an outsider had told them, that David's sense of business was about equal to "cutting stones with a razor." His efficiency in defending any derelict with no money for lawyer's fees did not impress them, and they warned little sister that he would never notice if his own or her boots went without cobbling. Not that David was ever unkempt. He looked tall and distinguished in his shabbiest clothes; and his pallor wrung, while his smile won, ladies' hearts.

Maria simply blew their criticisms away and relied on her Swedenborgian theories which had taught her to look for a man who, like her, believed that to live without charity was to exist without love. Moreover, she was sure to be practical enough for both of them. Swedenborg showed her that David's idealism was not a flaw but a sign of near perfection, and she preferred her knight as he was, quite without armor. She gave David a copy of *The Rebels* as an engagement present.

They planned a small wedding and invited only the near and dear, but Maria was sad because Mary Preston and her family could not come down for it from Norridgewock. Maria had to pour out all her bridal rhapsody by mail. She told her sister about gifts and plans and clothes.

> My mantua maker has been here a week. I have a claret-colored pelisse lined with straw-colored silk made in the extent of the mode to make anyone stare, one black-figured levantine silk and one swiss muslin.

Riches indeed for a girl whose taste verged on the simplicity of a Quaker.

They were married in Watertown at eight o'clock in the evening on Sunday, October 19, 1828. The bridegroom's dark coat accentuated his pallor, but the bride, gowned in India muslin with scrolls of white satin, was as lovely as could be. Her eyes were luminous and her mouth soft as she promised to love, honor, and obey. She looked directly at David as she made her vows and was sure that they were joined for a lifetime of truth, good, and bliss; and David saw that she was beautiful. The wedding guests toasted the bride with wine and nibbled at the thirty-five pounds of cake Maria had ordered from the baker.

Festivities over, the Childs drove to a tiny house in Harvard Street, no more than a mile from the heart of Boston and quite near David's office. The bride wrote to her sister that the house was "a proper little martin-box, furnished with very plain gentility." Maria's simple taste was part home training and part caution which stemmed from her awareness that budgets and David were poles apart. Her foresight was soon confirmed, for most of David's erratic income as lawyer, legislator, and journalist (he became editor of the *Massachusetts Whig Journal* during that year) was gone before she saw it. What he earned, he loaned or gave away outright.

Maria did not really mind. She was earning enough for both of them and she realized that he did only what he had to do. She put a few dollars aside for the future without comment and saw to it that their home was as gracious and welcoming as it could be. What fun to polish and fuss over her own home, to display her wedding gifts, to hang prisms in the window, and have a kitten on the hearth! Beautiful Emily Marshall, a legendary New England beauty, had sent stellar lamps with pretty etched globes which shone as brightly as Emily herself among ordinary girls. One of the lamps stood in the center of the writing table so that Maria could share its light with David as he wrote editorials for the Whig party. David was enraged at the election of Andrew Jackson to the Presidency in 1828. Jackson stood for all that he, as a rabid Whig, detested—a man violent, arrogant, impatient of schooling and careless in his selection of office-holders. He seemed to be against the banking interests of the East and certainly unsympathetic to Henry Clay's favored internal improvements at national expense. It was Jackson who first made Maria concentrate on politics and the personalities behind them. In a sense it was this cognizance of Jackson that began a redirection of her life.

David wrote to Henry Clay on the 14th November, asking for an explanation of Jackson's election. David was aware that his fellow New Englander, defeated President John Quincy Adams, was an austere, tactless character, devoted to his country but with no flair for winning public favor. Henry Clay, Adams' Secretary of State and one of the most astute politicians America ever had, had been unable to improve Adams' image as a candidate no matter how he tried. During the campaign his oratory was magnificent but unavailing. He closed his ears when Adams' supporters gossiped about General Jackson and his wife, Rachel. He apparently made no effort to leash his cohorts in their castigations of the Jacksons' uncouthness and he repeatedly stressed the point that Jackson was a military man who was ignorant of the affairs of state. But Adams lost to the hero of New Orleans.

When John Quincy Adams lessened his chances to succeed himself as President by making derogatory remarks about Thomas Jefferson, David felt that *he* must take action or many of the pro-Whig Southern votes would be lost. He combed the country for information which would sway the balance toward Adams and sent it to Clay for distribution.

Clay's reply arrived within a week and David gnashed his teeth in fury while tears ran down Maria's cheeks as she read the long letter aloud:

CONFIDENTIAL

Washington, November 20, 1828

Dear Sir:

I have duly received your letter of the 14th inst. Events not known at Boston at its date, but a knowledge of which has been acquired here, demonstrate the . . . of Mr. Adams' election and the success of General Jackson by a considerable majority. It is known that the latter has received the votes of Ohio and Kentucky, probably Indiana, and I should not be much surprised, after all that has occurred, if he gets that of Louisiana also. It is useless to indulge in the expression of mortification and regret on account of the inauspicious event. It has filled me with more than any language could convey. Ardently devoted throughout a life which is now not short, to the freedom of my fellow man, nothing has ever heretofore occurred to create in my mind such awful apprehensions of the permanancy of our liberty. I most devoutly pray they may not be realized.

The duty enjoined by patriotism and philosophy is submission to what has become inevitable. We must bear with fortitude a calamity which we have done all that honest men and sincere patriots could do, to avert. Whilst there is life there is hope, and henceforward we should exert all our energies to preserve those great principles of liberty and of policy to which our best exertions have hitherto been zealously dedicated. Such is my own determination, and I am happy to tell you that since the event was known, I have enjoyed a degree of composure, and a buoyancy of spirits, which I have not known for many weeks before. If you had possessed the information which has reached us, you would not, I think, have made the suggestion of the declining of Mr. Adams, and bringing out a new candidate. Such a measure on his part would expose him to ridicule, if not contempt. Calamitous as I regard the election of General Jackson, any attempt to defeat his election, at this time, would be still more calamitous. It would be the signal of instantaneous civil war. Electoral Colleges which have been constituted with an express understanding to vote for him, would not vote for another, and could not, without dishonour and disgrace. Believing that you would not have made the suggestion if you had known all that we do, I shall exercise my discretion in not forwarding the letter you have transmitted me for Richmond. I think the bare suggestion of the project calculated to do mischief, and that if it could be supposed to originate with the great body of our friends, it would attach to them a lasting prejudice.

I regret extremely that Mr. Adams should have excited such feelings as you describe, by his comments on the letter of Mr. Jefferson. Although I thought them unnecessary and unfortunate, I sincerely hope those feelings may be softened if not eradicated.

I am well aware of the friendly feelings for me which prevail throughout New England's. They excite my profound gratitude and whatever may be my future lot, they will always constitute a source of the most pleasing reflections. It would afflict me if I believed that I should never be able to visit again that interesting quarter of our Union. When I had that happiness, now more than ten years ago, friendly impressions were made on my mind which can never be effaced.

> I am, with great respect,
> H. Clay.

It was hard to settle down to their usual quiet routine that evening. Even the sight of her charming room, replete with loving remembrances of her friends, failed to reassure her. Yet, for David's sake and her own peace of mind, she tried to soothe him and gradually he became less agitated.

"It is not easy to be philosophical as Mr. Clay suggests, is it, dearest? I suppose we must submit to the inevitable, but not forever, not forever. There will come a time in spite of General Jackson."

Maria sighed and spoke tenderly. She certainly did not want David or his writings to be the instrument of civil war. She had begun to think as badly of Jackson as did her husband—or Clay. But she had a story to write for the *Miscellany* and her bridegroom must allow the atmosphere to quiet down or they would not eat the following week. The magazine had to be done. Usually it was restful to write with David beside her in their "martin-box" house. She looked around again. What a nice place this home of theirs was. No matter how stormy the future, she and David would keep their home and sanctuary. The things they had been given as wedding gifts would give it flavor and permanency, the plated candlesticks and a snuffer on a tray on the mantelpiece, and the butter knife and cream ladle with which she set the table even if no butter or cream were on the menu. She said that these pretties gave an air to the room.

Other friends had sent more practical if less durable gifts: a keg of tongues from Mrs. White, whose daughter would one day marry James Russell Lowell; and a jar of pickles from the Thaxters. The prisms in the window flashed rainbow colors over the drab walls, the kitten purred, and Maria was sure that life could not have been better. And so it would have been if David's openhandedness had not driven them into debt. Instead of putting Maria's small savings out at a decent rate of interest, those went first to cover his promises of help to a complete stranger whose notes that David had no right to sign in the first place; but Maria's savings not being enough, they had to borrow five hundred dollars from Mr. Francis to cover the rest. All this only seven months after the wedding, and how the sisters-in-law must have chortled. Maria would be headstrong and marry, would she? Maria herself was humiliated by the loan from her father and the realization that the family predictions had been only too true, but she refused to let the money poison her relationship with her husband. He was wonderful, endlessly wise in ways she knew nothing about, and witty, and she would not permit any speculation that theirs was less than a perfect marriage.

It was during this first year that she wrote the *Frugal Housewife* for "those who are not ashamed of economy." Her own tribulations undoubtedly gave the book its authenticity.

Its unvarnished, homely style flavored its recipes, and its hints, "odd scraps for the economical," helped to extend any budget. Experienced housewives nodded approvingly at this: "A little salt sprinkled in the starch while it is boiling tends to prevent it from sticking; it is likewise good to stir it with a clean spermaceti candle." And at this: "Pepper, red cedar chips, tobacco, indeed almost any strong spicy smell is good to keep moths out of your chests and drawers but nothing is so good as camphor." And how did a new bride know this except by having looked into someone else's kitchen? "Always have plenty of dish water and have it hot. There is no need to ask the character of a domestic if you have ever seen her wash dishes in a little greasy water." This could have been a private hit against those carping sisters-in-law who did employ domestics. Certainly Maria had none in her "martin-box."

There were numberless cookbooks and household manuals on the market but the *Frugal Housewife* caught the public fancy. It was read in fashionable boudoirs, in farm kitchens, and in the trademan's cottage; and any country girl who came to town to buy a length of silk for her wedding gown was likely to bring back the *Housewife* as well. When Maria pronounced that preserves were useless and "extravagant for those who are well," readers simply crossed preserves from their household lists. Nor did they dispute that "green peas should be boiled from twenty to sixty minutes according to their age." Personal experience taught her, and she passed on the information that beef chuck at four or five cents a pound made as tasty a roast as sirloin.

For faded wardrobes she suggested that bee balm steeped in water made a lovely rose dye, while saffron or the outside scales of onions gave good yellow. Birch bark, peach leaves, and the purple paper in which sugar was wrapped were each useful for color. With ingenuity and the help of Maria Child, anything fit for the dustbin came to life. Brides had Maria to thank when their husbands praised them for their housekeeping.

Reviewers praised her book—all but Willis, the versifier dandy, who continued to keep himself aloof from the grubbiness of the practical world. Willis poked fun at Maria's statement that "hard gingerbread is good to have in the family; it keeps so well." He jeered that if the gingerbread were good in the first place, it would not be there to keep; and he had nothing else to say about the book. But Willis and his sneers were a long way from her present life; and though he might prick, he could not really hurt her, and the public in general gave her nothing but praise. Again she wrote to Mary, "My *Miscellany* succeeds far beyond my most sanguine expectations. That is people are generous beyond my hopes." It was the same about the *Housewife*. The *North American Review*, highest literary authority of America, said:

> We are not sure that any woman of our country could outrank Mrs. Child. This lady has long been before the

public with much success. And well she deserves it, for in all her works nothing can be found which does not commend itself, by its tone of healthy morality and good sense. Few female writers if any have done more or better things for our literature in the lighter or graver departments.

Maria was a terribly exacting editor for her *Miscellany*. Rather than compromise on quality or time schedule, she wrote much of the copy herself. When William Cullen Bryant was late with a promised contribution, she wrote to him that she was very sorry but that she had filled the space with a poem of her own, "Lines to a Fringed Gentian," a Wordsworthian bit that included these lines:

> Thus buds of virtue often bloom
> The fairest mid the deepest gloom.

Bryant's poem was put aside for future publication. She had not the forsight to know that while her piece was sweet, his would gain posterity.

Between times, she wrote her third novel, *First Settlers of New England,* and compiled some of the *Miscellany* pieces into a thin volume, *Souvenir of New England.* Then she edited the *Coronal,* the best of her published verse and stories. She hadn't much respect for her own poetry but her uncritical critics insisted that some of it ranked with the best of its time and her "Marius Amid the Ruins of Carthage" appears to this day in anthologies. Her story, "Adventures of a Raindrop," was often credited to another author then still virtually unknown—Nathaniel Hawthorne.

Not even her closest friends could understand how Maria covered as much ground as she did: writer, editor, head of the literary department of the newspaper, *The Boston Traveller,* one of three superintendents for a girls' school on Dorchester Heights, and homekeeper for David. If she skimped on any of her activities, it was never one which concerned him. Guests came as often as they were invited— wangled invitations, in fact, for her dinners of rack of lamb, cod dressed in herb sauce, brandied cherry pudding, and homemade beer, each dish as beautifully arranged as it was good to taste. But not even the stoutest, most energetic spirit can work endlessly without suffering for it, and Maria grew thinner and more pinched until David, who could not leave his law practice or his editor's chair, urged her to take a quiet holiday alone at Phillips Beach. She was no sooner there than she longed to be back, and wrote to him:

Dearest Husband:

Here I am in a snug little old-fashioned parlor in a rocking chair and the greatest comfort I have is the pen-knife you sharpened for me just before I came away. As you tell me sometimes, it makes my heart leap to see anything you have touched . . . I went down to a little cove between two lines of rock this morning and having taken off my stockings, I let the saucy waves come dashing and sparkling in my lap. I was a little sad because it made me think of the beautiful time we had when we washed our feet together in the mountain water- fall. How I do wish you were here. It is nonsense for me to go a-pleasuring without you . . . my private opinion is that I shall not be able to stand it for a whole week.

She got home as fast as she could and they decided that living in the hubbub of town put too heavy a burden on her nerves. Boston's close-built houses, the seventy-five thousand people who thronged the streets and markets, the noise and bustle of roving, be-earringed and bedaggered sailors, of the high two-wheeled carts that clattered up and down the cobbled hills, the babble of thousands of immigrants and street vendors who sold anything from thimbles to rutabagas, and the loss of the last aspects of rurality by the banishment of cows from the Common, made her long to breathe fresh air and sleep through quiet nights. Even the inducement of running water which gushed through log conduits all the four miles from Jamaica Pond, could not keep her in the city; and though it meant that she would herself have to make a great many things including soap which the shops in town easily provided, she was ready for the move.

In the latter part of 1832, the Childs found a house that was just right. It was in this small home on Cottage Place in Roxbury that Maria realized her greatest happiness. Everything she had ever hoped for was hers, except a child, and if one had come to her then, life would have taken a different turn. But nothing else lacked, for David was her all and, for the moment, even he was in a better position financially as a Boston justice of the peace. Mr. Francis lived nearby on Dorchester Heights, near enough to visit them or for them to go to him frequently. She could write without interruption, and when her fingers or back cramped she had only to step to the door to watch the clouds shift or rainbow lights come shimmering through the rain. Or work for an hour in her flower and herb garden while the peepers announced the spring. Or hear the high, thin call of the cedar waxwing.

When she did have to go to Boston, she trudged the full three miles along Washington Street instead of paying twenty-five cents for stagecoach fare. She could always rest at the Boston Athenaeum on Pearl Street at the end of the trek because she had held a complimentary privilege at the library ever since she had written *Hobomok*. The Athenaeum was distinctly a man's organization, and outside of Hannah Adams, the eccentric historian, Maria was the only woman accorded that privilege. Members asserted that ladies were barred because their full skirts made it dangerous for them to navigate the narrow, spiral iron stairs; but either the plain dress of Miss Adams and Mrs. Child lulled their fears or the gentlemen respected the "men's minds" of these two ladies.

Maria used the library extensively, for it carried newspapers from anywhere in the United States or Europe provided the editorial policy was conservative. The ledger for 1832 still carries the list of the books Maria borrowed to take back to Roxbury, a long list headed by the words: "Mrs. D. L. Child—free by vote of the Trustees until further order of the Trustees." Elizabeth Peabody, who was given a six-month permit at the Athenaeum, thought herself lucky to get even that, but Maria for the moment was Fortune's child. The *Housewife* had sold out in ten editions in America alone and more in France and England, her *Mothers' Book* and her *Little Girls' Own Book* had gone through several printings. Margaret Fuller, not yet a writer though already a great talker, saw Maria examining a copy of the English edition of the *Mothers' Book* in the Athenaeum reading room and commented that the author deserved all the honor fame and hard work had brought her.

Back in Watertown several years earlier, Maria and Margaret had studied the lives and works of Madame de Staël and Madame Roland, writers relatively unappreciated in the New World. At the Athenaeum, Maria continued her study of the impact and influence of these Frenchwomen and made them the first subjects in a series of five books on the history of women. She called her series *The Ladies' Library*.

Again the books sold, almost as well as the previous ones, and again she was praised as a pattern of womanhood, the ideal of her generation, though a few perceptive readers began to wonder whether something more serious was brewing under her sweetness and light. Could it be that this model of propriety was faintly sounding the tocsin for the emancipation of women?

V

The Strings of Her Conscience

VISITORS FLOCKED TO COTTAGE PLACE: WHITTIER, THE SHY, handsome Quaker poet-journalist with political ambitions and an eye for pretty women; Theodore Parker, learned young preacher who refused to let his delicate constitution bar him from almost constant study; William Ellery Channing, saintly minister "whose intellect was the conscience of New England"; verse-scribbling Frances Osgood, who interpreted the meanings of flowers and whose name would one day be linked with that mad genius, Edgar Allan Poe. And the Lorings, the Curtises, the Sewalls, the Shaws, and frequently the children of brother James Francis, who, though he disapproved of her husband, liked being kin to a celebrity. When Maria was in a working mood, she barred guests; but work done and company come, she served them in fine style. Her masterpiece in the food line was her "Alamode Beef," stuffed with bread, suet, herbs, nutmeg, pounded cloves, the yoke of an egg, and a pint of claret poured over at the last. The guests sopped up every drop of gravy with her fluffy dumplings. David's pride in her inspired cooking revealed itself in the way he drew out her chair, in the tender triumph of his eyes across the table,

61

in his extra attention to the friends who most generously applauded her. The linen so smooth and white, the silver gleaming, Maria served her intricate banquets as casually as though she employed a staff of experienced servants. Dinner over, she whisked away the plates with no interruption in the conversational flow. What a manager she was; everyone said so.

She washed dishes with Plato or Diderot propped up over the sink and plenty of that admirable hot water to do the job right. When she mended, David read the latest depositions which came before him as justice of the peace. More and more of these concerned parcels of slaves who, though born in the North, had been shanghied into Southern bondage. There were shocking tales of children wrenched from their mothers' arms and of the pleas of these mothers to bring back the child before he died at forced labor in the South. Many of David's editorials in the *Massachusetts Whig Journal* reflected his horror of slavery and the threat it posed for national security.

How could Maria remain immune from his uneasiness? She had heard slavery condemned by her father when she was a child. Now Whittier and the rest talked for hours of what could be done to solve the problem. Yet why would a girl, newly married, publicly acclaimed, with a home that she called her "little Eden," why should this bride jeopardize security, literary and social position to go out of her way to bring the wrath of Boston upon her head? Why? There could be but one reason, the same one that would carry her through more than forty years, some of them very lean and uncertain. Maria Child loved her husband passionately and devotedly and she would do anything to arouse in him a response equal to her own. If the one way to reach his innermost core was to join him in reform, it would become her way, for she had to have his full love. Was David Child, the man so attractive to women, incapable himself of great physical passion? Was he no more than a passionate intellectual? Whatever there was, his wife had to have it.

She listened with intense concentration to his stories of the bereft mothers. "Oh David, it can't be as bad as they say. They must be exaggerating," she insisted. Whereupon David read an affidavit which had only that day been presented to him.

My friend, G——, an honorable man, was in North Carolina recently and actually saw a female slave who complained of illness and couldn't work, struck a dozen times with a paddle. Two hours afterward she was delivered of a dead infant.

The impact of this made Maria rage to ferret out the facts of the full case against slavery.

David was one of fifteen men who formed the New England Anti-Slavery Society on January 6, 1832. He went along with the group although he objected to some of the more violent constitutional provisions for the new society which dedicated it to the immediate rather than the gradual emancipation of the Negro. David preferred to educate the Negroes and make them ready for their freedom before liberation rather than loose a mad, ignorant horde on a troubled country, but William Lloyd Garrison, David's friend and colleague in the *Journal* office, insisted on immediacy. It was on that dreary January night when the wind howled and the snow swirled that Garrison declared:

We have met tonight in this obscure school house; our numbers are few and our influence is limited. But mark my prediction: Faneuil Hall shall ere long echo with the principles we have set forth.

The shivering group of men then and there pledged themselves to the cause; Garrison's thunderbolts set them afire.

Maria listened again as she had in the Watertown study, in the Norridgewock parlor—listened while the arguments swirled around her, and built up a case against slavery on her own. She read historical tracts, pamphlets, and essays. She fumed over the stated belief of the South which was that its attitude had not much changed from that of a Southern delegate to the Constitutional Convention of 1787 who sneered that it would always be possible to make peace with the North "for a hogshead of tobacco." In other words, that the North would accept anything as long as trade and money were involved. Maria borrowed books and records from the Athenaeum Library and became convinced that she too must join the abolitionists. Garrison was the beacon among the riptides of antislavery. Many years later, in speaking of him, she said, "He got hold of the strings of my conscience and pulled me into reform work . . . I could not do otherwise so help me God."

The Athenaeum's original "two barrels of books," the core of its collections, had been augmented by John Adams' great library and other acquisitions until, in this year of 1832, it contained over thirty thousand volumes. Other libraries were closer to Cottage Place but the advantage of free access and borrowing of such riches made it worth Maria's while to take the trip. The librarians allowed her to keep the books as long as she liked rather than to abide by the house rule of a limit of three for a month. Her taste, according to that ledger, changed during this period. Where formerly she had read French, German, or English plays, poems, and histories, she now took Brougham's *Colonial Policy*. Instead of Moore's *Anacreon*, Bower's *Life of Luther*, Stanley's *Lives of the Philosophers*, she requested

Smith's *History of Virginia* and tracts on the islands of the Caribbean. She read every issue of *Niles' Weekly Register* with its lurid accounts of the barbarous treatment of slaves. Had a perceptive trustee glanced over her ledger page, he would have been shocked; but no one seemed to notice the pattern of her borrowing, and parents went on reading the *Miscellany* to their children and quoting phrases from the *Girls' Own Book* to make their daughters behave.

Yet it was here in 1833, in this retreat for gentility, in this fortress for the elite and the elected, that Maria took the first steps toward her *Appeal in Favor of That Class of Americans Called Africans,* the first hard-hitting, important antislavery book in America. Garrison's *Thoughts on Colonization* and Whittier's *Justice and Expediency* stirred scarcely a whisper compared to the tornado which erupted as a result of the *Appeal*. Maria expected this upheaval. In the preface she had written:

> I am fully aware of the unpopularity of the task I have undertaken but though I expect ridicule and censure, I do not fear them . . . Should it [the Appeal] be the means of advancing even one single hour of the inevitable progress of truth and justice, I would not exchange the consciousness for all Rothschild's wealth or Sir Walter's fame.

There it was, the gauntlet. She was committed to a cause for which she and David were of one mind and heart. If anything could bring her closer to the man she loved, this was it. Yet she could joke, serious though the subject might be. "Wait until they read further," she said to him, "and see what a woman who should be tending her own cookstove has to say on so unwomanly a subject."

David's answer was the one she craved. "I suspect that your cooking could probably convince any slaveholder that corn bread from your kitchen tastes better than anything their slaves could make; you've done a great and courageous thing, my dearest."

The *Appeal* began with a history of slavery from the time of Portuguese Prince Henry who exchanged ten Moorish prisoners of war for ten African Negroes. He in turn sold these Negroes for a fat sum, which set off the beginnings of the African slave trade. Maria's history related the spread of that trade following Columbus' discovery that while Spaniards made poor laborers in the New World, the Africans were mighty useful. She told of the horrors of the slave ships, of thumbscrews and shackles and pressure bars endured by the wretches. She and David experimented behind closed shutters at home to see and feel exactly what the slaves endured during transportation.

The next section of the book was a kind of sermon in that it described the brutalization of the trade's effect not on the slaves but on their masters who repaid faithful service with negligence and death. She taunted the owners for believing that anyone could prefer to be owned rather than to be free. Her style was terse and unsentimental. Step by step she erected an indictment to show how, morally and economically, slavery weakened the Union. Why should one part of the nation pit itself against the other instead of the two pulling together for mutual strength? Why could not cotton or tobacco be grown by white labor or with the use of mules and horses rather than just with enslaved human muscle? She pointed out that free labor worked more willingly and productively than slave. Prosperity would come to North and South alike if the example of Barbados was to be followed, an island in which slavery was at an end.

She made certain that readers of both sexes would read her book by punctuating the statistics with pathos. She called on God to condemn the criminality of one man's owning of another. The Union, she dared to say, under the conditions that existed between North and South, was worthless. "If the Union cannot be preserved without crime, it is eternal truth that nothing good can be preserved by crime." Blind business interests, North and South, were equally at fault. Northerners, she said, reminded her of the man who on being asked to pump a sinking ship replied that he didn't have to since he was a paying passenger. Were Northern tradesmen stupid or lazy?

Had she ended the book on that more or less objective note, the public might have accepted it as a curiosity written by a woman, and waited for her next novel or poems. Instead, Maria went further by floodlighting the basic canker between whites and Negroes. She said:

> In regard to marrying your daughter, I believe the feeling in opposition to such unions is quite as strong among the colored class as it is among white people. While the prejudice exists, such instances must be exceedingly rare because the consequence is degradation in society. Believe me, you may safely trust to anything that depends on the pride and selfishness of unregenerated human nature.

The threat implied by her text, though denied by it, could not be ignored. Mother hens and their timid daughters huddled closer to their empty principles, and menfolk said, "If that woman were a man, we'd tar and feather her." An unobtrusive little volume in a dark green cover had raised a maelstrom.

Old friends turned from Maria or crossed the street to avoid seeing her. *Miscellany* subscriptions ceased. The Athenaeum trustees did not officially recommend withdrawal of Mrs. Child's privileges, but one spokesman made it clear to her that she was no longer welcome. A prominent lawyer, later to become the state's attorney general, was so incensed by the *Appeal* that he lifted it with tongs and hurled it through a window. Edward Everett Hale, then eleven, heard the book denounced at home, and shocked by a display of it in the window of the Old Corner Bookstore, could not decide if he would risk punishment for throwing a stone through the glass. He satisfied his honor by making a rude noise for each copy he saw there. Then he squashed his cap square on his head and ran home to tell his parents, who gasped at William Ticknor's lack of taste in giving the work his window space. The Hales, like many Bostonians, shuddered to think that a lady had dared to call a black man an American. They argued that if the Lord had really intended men to be equal, He would have made them all one color.

Maria nerved herself to accept abuse and criticism for the sake of her belief in freedom for the Negro, but the forced ending of the *Miscellany* seared her spirit. Too much of herself had gone into the editing of that little magazine. Her editorial in the final issue took the form of an open letter to her young public:

> After conducting the Miscellany for eight years. I am now compelled to bid a reluctant and most affectionate farewell to my little readers. May God Bless you, my young friends, and impress deeply upon your hearts the conviction that all true excellence and happiness consist in living for *others,* not for *yourselves.*

In those simple words, Maria Child set forth her creed by which she lived and would continue to live—for *others,* not for *herself.*

On the practical side—and in her family someone needed to be practical—she asked that "compilers of books are respectfully requested not to use articles in the Miscellany, as the editor wishes to reserve that privilege for herself." There was no copyright law to protect her against the theft of her work. Yet it was the sentimental rather than the financial loss of the *Miscellany* which hurt and she needed David's love to soothe the sting.

Shunned by former friends and neighbors, forced to live more frugally than she had dreamed possible, removed from the happy, approving corner of the world she had made for herself in her writing, she still found reason to be satisfied. David was closer to her than ever. The old friends who remained loyal and the new who came to her as result of her brash undertaking praised her to her husband and bound him to her.

The Reverend William Ellery Channing walked all the way out to Roxbury on a hot sunny day, with his heavy cloak over his arm in case the weather should change, to thank her for writing the *Appeal* and helping him to crystallize his own feelings on antislavery. As Maria said to David, "Poor Dr. Channing seemed as exhausted by the walk as stimulated by the book and I think they more or less canceled each other out." Which wasn't quite fair since Dr. Channing said subsequently, "The reading of it [the *Appeal*] has aroused my conscience to the query whether I ought to remain silent on the subject." It was a tribute to Maria that this great minister-orator, often called the most brilliant theologian in Boston, credited her with his change of heart. Ten years later the book would have the same effect on Thomas Wentworth Higginson.

Her most noted "conversion" however was Wendell Phillips, the twenty-two-year-old aristocrat, just out of Harvard Law School and six feet or more of handsome, polished, intellectual manliness. On an evening visit to the Lorings, he picked up the *Appeal* to read it with a lawyer's concentration. What he read "obliged" him to become an abolitionist. Years later, in writing of this incident in an

How Slavery Honors Our Country's Flag

autograph book, Maria headed it, "How a very Small Mouse Helped Gnaw Open the Net that Held a Great Lion." Phillips became a great lion, indeed, second only to Garrison in the fight to end slavery, and Maria gave him the initial impetus.

Her work unleashed other lions too, less pleasant ones who gnashed their teeth and growled their dislike of interfering reformers. They tore her apart. Reputation, security, literary prestige were gone and with it the last of David's respectable law practice. Maria realized by the insults thrown their way that she had flicked the conscience of America. She wrote:

> The zeal of a few seems to counterbalance the apathy of the many . . . posterity will marvel at the hardness of our

prejudice on this subject, as we marvel at the learned and conscientious believers in the Salem witchcraft. So easy it is to see the errors of past ages, so difficult to acknowledge our own.

Maria did not need to call upon courage to buoy her up. Life was threaded with excitement. No sacrifice was too great for the right. She would not retract. Her heart was light, her husband ardent, her head was high.

VI

Her Heart at Flood Tide

THE ANTISLAVERY MOVEMENT BROUGHT MANY PEOPLE together who would not otherwise have enjoyed a mutual interest. There were Quakers like the wealthy Motts—James and Lucretia; and the venerable philanthropist Isaac Tatem Hopper. There were the Grimke sisters, who had turned their backs on the luxurious South Carolina plantation where they had been born because their mother refused to free her slaves; and the Tappans, Lewis and Arthur, New York silk merchants and founders of the conservative New York *Journal of Commerce*. And the ministers, the Channings, Mays, and Theodore Parker as well as Whittier and the "learned blacksmith," Elihu Burritt. Eventually the lists would swell with giants such as Emerson, Lowell, and Greeley. Garrison's insistence on immediate emancipation was a deterrent to many cautious, thinking persons who favored a firm Union, but the feeling was growing that Union without freedom, as Maria had said, was worthless. Even moderates among the abolition ranks realized that though Garrison was almost too much of a firebrand, he was still the leader whom they must follow.

As might be expected, a number of foolish ones used the

72

cause as a chance to ride hobbyhorses of their own. Ezekiel Rogers, editor of an antislavery newspaper, used his columns to denounce smoking because he could not bear tobacco himself; and Abigail Folsom, whom Emerson nicknamed "that flea of conventions," interrupted every speaker on the claim that she was exercising her right of free speech by shouting Biblical quotations that had little to do with the case. At one such meeting Wendell Phillips and two others, annoyed past patience with her, put her in a chair and carried her straight out, whereupon she called from her perch, "I am better than my Master was; He had but one ass to ride; I have three to carry me."

Garrison's singleness of purpose stirred his followers to admiration though his irascibility stung them. True, Henry Ward Beecher said that Garrison was "one of the most unfortunate of all leaders for the development of antislavery feeling," and true too that many lukewarm abolitionists objected to his despotic pronouncements. He was harsh where he should have been gentle and the whiplash of his pen spared no one. Slavery must go! The *Liberator's* first issue sounded the clarion:

> I am aware that many object to the severity of my language. . . . I will be as harsh as truth and as uncompromising as justice. On this subject I do not wish to think or speak or write with moderation. . . . I will not equivocate . . . I will not excuse . . . I will not retreat a single inch— and I WILL BE HEARD.

No wonder the cautious ones worried.

The Garrisons lived in Roxbury, not far from the Childs. Helen Garrison, whom her friends called "Peace and Plenty," was a fulfilled and happy woman even though she, even more than Maria, knew what scrimping meant. Garrison might be the "prophet of emancipation," but he certainly did not make money by his prophecies. He earned about seven hundred dollars a year to feed his wife and numerous children, but neither his wife nor youngsters suffered from the sarcasm he darted at his followers in the cause. The Garrisons had a gay and happy home, and Helen Garrison's only real concern was that her husband took no care of himself. Fortunately for her peace of mind, and without his knowledge, a bodyguard of loyal Negroes followed him each night as he walked the lonely road to Roxbury.

He needed that protection. Maria had seen the mob tear off his trousers, smash his glasses, and stretch a rope around his neck as he came out of the Anti-Slavery rooms on Washington Street. She quivered in fear, but Garrison had not shown a tremor as he walked "head erect, calm countenance, flashing eyes, like a martyr going to the stake full of faith and hope." Fanatically he believed in such martyrdom, but his friends felt otherwise and managed to rescue him just in time by spiriting him to the Leverett Street jail, where he stayed until another supporter drove him out of town in a cart like a sack of potatoes. It was scenes like this that made abolition wives fear for their husbands but work harder than ever themselves for the Cause.

Garrison, like many visionaries, was not a man of business sense. When millowners and Northern bankers argued that they needed cotton in order to retain prosperity for New England, he refused to listen. He snapped, "Then let's not raise any more cotton if it has to be grown by a race in bondage." Amazingly it was David, the dreamer, who had a more practical plan. "Why can't we find substitutes for the crops that slaves raise? Especially if we can prove that they are cheaper to grow."

"Oh, David, what a wonderful thought!" his wife cried. "What will we do first?"

Together they studied statistics and tables to see where the need was greatest and how they might best use their information. First they must conclude which crop was hardest on the slaves and whether any experiments for a substitute had already been started. "There are cotton, rice, indigo, tobacco, sugar," mused David as he ticked them off on his fingers. "Sugar. I wonder how much has been done on that. You know, it takes an enormous toll every year because it is so difficult to grow, Maria."

Sugar might be the answer. David read articles on Belgian success in the extraction of sugar from beets. Beets grew in New England. Why not try to extract right here? He began to experiment at home, messing Maria's kitchen, charring her pots, without a word of complaint from her. They were in this effort together and she cleaned up after him smiling. He borrowed money from his Bigelow cousins for further experiments, but it was not enough for so complicated a problem. He ought actually go to Belgium, he said, to study it thoroughly. Maria listened and smiled again, unruffled by the word "travel." Where would he get the money? Her activities no longer brought them much income, for her editing was limited to the *Oasis,* a small antislavery annual, the precurser to Mrs. Chapman's *Liberty Bell.* For the moment the rest of her writing did not amount to much.

As to other activity, she was a director of the Boston Ladies' Anti-Slavery Society, though ordinarily she had no patience with doings that segregated women from men. She had told Lucretia Mott tartly, "I have never entered very earnestly into the plan of female conventions and societies. They always seem to me like half of a pair of scissors." Being a half-implied separation and personally, very personally indeed, she wanted only to be the essential part of a whole. Yet, whether she appreciated these ladies' societies or not, they thought well of her, for one day a packet, wrapped in several thicknesses of soft paper and sealed with wax, arrived for her. Inside was a gold watch with a silver face and gilded hands. Admirers from Lynn and Salem had sent it to her with the inscription:

Mrs. Child

The true, the noble unapproachable

who made the first appeal in behalf

of the American slave.

August 8, 1835

Maria loved that watch and many times, during the dark years that followed, she touched it as it hung on her breast and felt the warmth of the reassurance it gave her. She was rather ashamed for her peppery answer to Mrs. Mott. No present, except the love rings that David had given her, had ever pleased her more.

Convers, her brother, tried unavailingly to warn her against the radicalism she had shown. He was proud of his part in having molded her mind but, true to his own straddling nature, he urged her to be prudent. She answered:

> You ask me to be prudent and I will do so as far as is consistent with a sense of duty; but this will not be what the world calls prudent. Firmness is a virtue most needed in times of excitement. . . . I have examined the history of the slave too thoroughly and felt his wrongs too deeply to be prudent in the worldly sense of the term.

Prudent! Married to David, whom Harriet Martineau once described as a Boston sensation because he defended Negroes at law. It had been through David that Noyes Academy, of which he became a trustee in 1834, opened its doors to Negro students. How on earth could Maria be prudent as her brother meant it? And so the next adventure proved.

The Firing of the *Mexican* by Ruiz, the Carpenter

In 1832 a Salem crew had come limping home with a story that horrified all hearers. The American brig *Mexican* had been set upon by the Spanish *Panda*. John Battis, one of the survivors, wrote an account of the attack. Theft, murder, and arson made convincing if awesome reading. The *Panda* got away.

Two years later the pirate crew was caught by a British man-of-war, hauled into a British admiralty court and then remanded to the United States under British escort as a gesture of international good will. Five of the pirates had turned state's evidence in England and the guilt of the *Panda*'s crew seemed incontrovertible. New England was thoroughly aroused and crowds cheered the British sailors, as their ship the *Savage* hove to at the wharf, and jeered at the pirates, who, chained to the deck, spat and gestured obscenely toward the land. Double the usual number of guards escorted the prisoners to the Leverett Street jail while good Medford rum flowed freely for John Bull's navy.

In spite of the Battis story and all accusations, David Child saw gaps in the evidence against some of the pirates. The story was already two years old and John Battis, who had been knocked unconscious by a blow on the head during the attack, necessarily had omitted many details. Memory is tricky and sometimes convenient to the subconscious and David suspected the motives of some of the witnesses, who were determined on vengeance. The case was incomplete; the pirates must have a fair chance to prove their innocence. The Childs talked it over while Maria washed up after supper, and David decided to act as the pirates' counsel— free, of course. It never occurred to either Maria or her husband that championship of these ruffians would damn the Childs all over again in Boston's eyes. Maria, who loathed the concept of capital punishment and called it "legalized murder," was as eager to help to avoid a hanging of the prisoners as David was.

On the day of the trial, the men shuffled into court, chained in pairs. They stood in the dock, eleven downcast, fearful prisoners and a twelfth who bared his teeth madly at anyone who dared to come near him. Judge Story of the United States Circuit Court took his place on the bench. Lawyer Child and his partner, George Hillard, struggled to break the case against the pirates, but witness testimony undermined every point they brought up. It was difficult to controvert a story of blows, of knives "ground sharp at the point like daggers," of the flames set by the pirates aboard the *Mexican* after all valuables had been stolen. David still insisted that full evidence was missing and at last he was able to prove that some of the accused were not even aboard at the time of the attack. He also made the point that the *Panda,* by mathematical calculation, could not have reached the spot on the recorded date if she had left Rio de Janiero, her last port of call, on the day registered in her log.

For twelve hours, while he summed up, David did not rest but stormed, pleaded, and finally won a case for five of the men. On the sixteenth of December Judge Story sentenced the remaining seven "for the crime of pirates and felons and that each of you be severally hung by the neck until you be severally dead." Sentence would be carried out in March. The twelfth pirate, he of the bared teeth, fell foaming at the mouth as the verdict was pronounced and a doctor pronounced him insane. The judge granted the madman a stay of execution and he was carried raving from the courtroom. As for the other six, only Presidential pardon could save them. Who would go to the President on such an errand?

David and his partner had to stay close by in case fast action was needed to stop violence on the part of an ugly-tempered mob that might not want to wait until March to see the pirates hang. No escape was possible for the con-

demned, since the jail was of stone reinforced with iron
binder rods and in the hollowed walls lay huge iron cannon
balls.

The lawyers also acted as supervisors to see that their
"clients" were decently fed on the usual prison diet of fresh
meat and bread and "skilly," a nourishing broth made of
beef stock and thickened with Indian meal. A doctor was
on call if any prisoners showed the slightest sign of illness,
the idea no doubt being to keep them well enough to hang.

Facts being as they were, the trip was up to Maria; and in
dead of winter, bundled up until only the tip of her nose
showed, she took the stage to Washington. Once there,
Attorney General Butler made an appointment for her at
the White House. The wind whipped her coat and brought
brilliant color into her cheeks, but she paled as she was
ushered into the scowling hawk-eyed presence of that fire-
eater, Andrew Jackson. She wondered for a moment why
she had to be the one to broach this delicate subject of mercy
to the hostile man before her. But she knew well enough:
for David; and her face softened as the President waited
grimly for her to start her plea. She took a deep breath,
anxious to do her best. She explained that those poor men
back there in jail had no wives to plead for them and that
was why she was here. As James Russell Lowell would say
of her in his *Fable for Critics,* "Her heart at flood tide
swamps her brain now and then."

She fell on her knees to the President and begged his
mercy, not for the prisoners but for the sakes of their wives
and children. She explained about the inconclusive evidence,
the lapses of memory, and the heroic efforts her own David
had made; but the granite face of Jackson did not soften.
How was she to guess that the cause was lost before she
came and that Jackson knew a side of it that prejudiced

him entirely against pardon. Before her visit he had received an anonymous letter which read:

You Damned Old Scoundrel:

If you don't sign the pardon of your fellow men now under the sentence of death, I will cut your throat whilst you are sleeping. I wrote you repeated cautions, so look out or damn you, I'll have you burnt at the stake in the city of Washington.

Your Master.

You Know me.   Look out.

The hero of New Orleans was unlikely to be intimidated by wild threats such as this nor would the tears of this female abolitionist move him. He was sick of the whole affair, and when Maria's sobs continued, he began to puff. She was too persistent—a nuisance, in fact, despite her literary fame and eloquent eyes. His craggy features were purple as he crashed his fist to the desk and snarled, "Enough, madam, enough. By the Eternal, let them hang!"

Maria's mission was a failure. Strangely, only one pirate, the *Panda*'s mate, de Soto, won a Presidential pardon through the intervention of his beautiful fifteen-year-old bride. Her sobs did soften the heart of Old Hickory. (Years later de Soto admitted that he had indeed been aboard the *Panda* and that his subsequent respectability, could never make up for his guilt.) The other five men were hanged in the dusty jail courtyard on June 9, 1835, after refusing absolution from a Spanish priest. The madman, last to go, swung alone on the gallows in September. He had the distinction of being the last pirate ever to be executed in Boston.

The usual criticisms were hurled at Maria for her part in the affair, but when the case reached the history books, years later, Wendell Phillips said, "It was she as much as her lion-hearted husband who, at their own cost, saved Boston from the crime and infamy of murdering twelve pirates before they had even a mockery of a trial."

The story of the pirates was done. It was time to get back to the business at hand.

VII

Left Behind

MARIA HAD A NEW BOOK UNDER WAY, A FORMIDABLE PIECE
of research, in which she traced the history of women from
ancient times onward in order to prove their equality with
man. The *History of the Condition of Women in Various
Ages and Nations* came out at a time when women were
beginning to protest against laws that prevented them from
owning or administering property, even that which they had
earned or inherited. To want to hold anything independently
was considered unladylike or downright fanatical in certain
circles where it was held that woman's place, as ever, must
be at home. Since most women studied only domestic
subjects after the grammar school grades, the outcry against
these restrictions had been relatively limited as well. Women
such as Lucretia Mott and Angelina Grimke, who spoke
publicly against the status quo, were unbelievably hardy;
but when Frances Wright, that exotic, redheaded exponent
of free love, free education, and free press exhorted her sex
to break loose, she frightened liberal ladies themselves and
made them want to creep back under male protection.
Curiously, these feminine reformers pointed up the theory
that the emacipation of woman correlated closely with

emancipation of the slave. There must be freedom and equality for all.

Maria in her usual independent way worked the problem out as she saw fit. Though she was frequently asked to address meetings, she refused. It was not in her nature to be flamboyant like Fanny Wright, that "Beelzebub in petticoats," nor as eloquent as saintly Mrs. Mott, but Maria's forte was to study, sort, and analyze facts in order to present them in a logical pattern most likely to interest a reader. When her book with its ponderous title appeared, she had letters from ladies of all kinds and degrees who thanked her for clarifying much that was new to them. How they could go through that compilation of endless fact, how they took that long, humorless dose without gagging, was certain proof that the women had a strong yearning for freedom and wanted to know what they could do about it.

Yes, there were letters and readers but not enough to pay the bills, especially for David's beet-sugar project. The way to make money was to sell to a wider public, to forget reform and concentrate on romance. With a guilty sigh she retreated into the rainbow land, back to the Golden Age she had reveled in as a child. In 1836 she published *Philothea, a Story of Ancient Greece*. It told of the days of Pericles, of the indescribable luxury of Aspasia's court and of Maria Child's love of beauty, and it revealed a side of her that the *Frugal Housewife* had denied. It reached toward the purple and fine linen which her life pattern had taken from her. She dwelt lovingly on silver robes, precious vessels, and the glorious sculpture of Phidias; she exulted in the music, gardens, and jewels; she rambled through a complicated plot; but her inmost self called out from every page.

Reform simply could not be entirely absent from any work of hers, however much she might luxuriate. History praises Aspasia, Pericles' beloved, for her political wisdom as well as her beauty. Notwithstanding Aspasia's influence, she could not change the law that prohibited women from having legal rights. It had been much the same in ancient Greece as in nineteenth-century America, a condition that Maria and her cohorts were bound to alter. In *Philothea* Maria fought for woman's equality through the glamor of pagan artistry, and at the same time satisfied her personal quality of aesthete and reformer.

Philothea brought her back into the field of popular literature but not as successfully as she had hoped. She was too deeply branded with the antislavery cross for her former readers and those who knew of her activities to be accepted now as a mere romancer. It had been her hope, when she offered the book to Park Benjamin, the publisher, that its mysticism would attract people to it. In her preface she said:

> This volume is purely romance; and most readers will consider it romance of the wildest kind. A few kindred spirits, prone to people space "with life and mystical predominance," will perceive a light *within* the Grecian temple.
>
> For such I have written it. To minds of a different mould, who may think an apology necessary for what they deem so utterly useless, I have nothing better to offer than the simple fact that I found delight in doing it.

"Light within the Grecian temple" indeed. There were many who thought they understood that "light," but to each the interpretation might be different. Philothea, the maiden, was the voice of reform, of conscience, of inner, philosophical wisdom. Maria told Mr. Benjamin that she thought readers would be amused to "see how crazy a person may be and yet be able to cook her own dinner," but perhaps she overestimated her powers of dissembling, or the public felt that a book about a courtesan lacked conscience. It did not sell well. Prim and proper Sarah Josepha Hale took satisfaction in the fact that "the bitter feelings engendered by the strife (antislavery) have prevented the merits of this remarkable book from being appreciated as they deserve." Yet every critic admitted that it was a remarkable book, especially for such an untraveled country mouse as Maria Child.

Those who knew her well realized that her moods shifted as quickly as the rainbows in the sky and that, after that long pull on her *History of Women,* a change of pace had been absolutely urgent. Besides, as she remarked to her friends, "Like the ignoramus in the Old [Greek] Drama, I can boast, 'Though I *speak* no Greek, I love the sound on't.' " Which meant, in another sense, that David loved and spoke Greek and what he loved attracted her. He, that patient man, was more stable emotionally than she. She complained once to her friend Mrs. Silsbee of Salem, "I wish that David were more mercurial or I less so." Maria was bored with a smooth emotional life; she wanted to keep it stirred up. She cried over the beauty of a buttercup and she cried if her baking did not rise as it should. She tore through her housework in order to sit and watch an ant colony for a half hour to rush inside and write about it for a children's story. All of this showed in *Philothea.* In the preface to the first edition, Maria described a dream.

It was the spring of the year and off in the distance, the sun glinted on the river and a flotilla of fairy ships rode the tide. Splendid marble statues stood on the decks. As the dreamer watched, a raucous voice shocked her. An old crone in a checked apron called out, "Ma'am, I can't afford to let you have that brisket of beef for eight cents a pound." Maria ran to David with her dream and he patted her shoulder while he explained that the first part was dreamed by Philothea and the second by the Frugal Housewife, and forever after Maria was to wonder if he smiled just a little as he said it.

But *Philothea* revealed something else, which if David recognized it must have hurt him deeply. A century later, Van Wyck Brooks called the book a "virginal vision" and he may well have been right, for while David nourished Maria's mind and partially satisfied her "nesting" impulse, she wanted to savor life to the full. He fed her Plato. She loved both David and Plato—but where was the ecstasy?

Inadequacies of a material sort loomed over them constantly. There never was enough money to pay Mr. Francis the interest on that loan of his which by now had nearly been doubled. Maria asked Park Benjamin for an advance on the Grecian romance and assigned the copyright to her father with the hope that sales might pay off that old incubus. Unfortunately, Mr. Francis was growing forgetful and did not keep account of the payments as they arrived. When James, Maria's eldest brother, checked the record, the Child debt stood out as large as ever.

James never knew how to behave toward his sister and her impractical husband. In the early days of her success, he acknowledged her proudly and named his third daughter for her, but times had changed. Whatever must people think, that he was brother to a radical, determined, penniless abolitionist? It probably was her poverty that bothered him most. James was a sturdy Democrat, a hard worker, a believer in solid comfort and a full stomach. He ran a model farm and he waited until newfangled tools proved themselves before he bought them. He took no chances—no, not he! He did not want his fine lot of sons and daughters contaminated by the horrid example of the Childs who had not a dollar put by for the future. James preferred less rather than more intimacy with his unpredictable relatives, at least as long as David was around. Those wild ideas about beet sugar were far afield from the plans of a conservative Massachusetts farmer.

David cared not a snap for what James thought. He pursued his will-o'-the-wisp of the sugar beet and talked about studying Belgian methods of raising the mangel wurzel over there. Then suddenly, instead of helping with the sugar beet dream, the Anti-Slavery Society decided to send the Childs to England. George Thompson, the British abolitionist who had recently barely managed to escape from pro-slavery mobs in America was most anxious to have the Childs come to England to study conditions there. The Society was to pay their expenses and at first Maria was jubilant. Traveling excited her. But then the Frugal Housewife side of her came to the fore. They would need clothes and medical supplies for which the Society would not pay. The cost of those extras would put them further into debt. Their trip was canceled. Maria wrote to Loring that she thought that people who were in good health and able to work ought to avoid "entering on the charity list if they can."

Instead, with a brave show of inconsistency and Quixoticism, they decided to join Benjamin Lundy's free labor settlement in Mexico. They had made friends during a short stay in Philadelphia that winter and these friends now banded together for the Mexican venture. The Childs set about to throw every available asset into it to join them. Unencumbered, they would go forth to change the lots of the poor Mexicans. Maria wrote to Loring to sell her pictures and bibelots for whatever they would bring. She offered to assign to Loring and her father, and through her husband

as the law directed, the copyrights to the *Oasis,* the *Housewife,* the *Girl's Book, Family Library* and *Philothea.* She
insisted that no amount of discouragement could dissuade
them.

But something did. Probably it was the prospect of being
associated with as unstable a character as Lundy. The settlement plan fell through just as had the trip to England and
once again, David's thoughts were beamed on the sugar beet.
Maria wrote to friends to raise money for the trip. Inconsistent again? Yes, but she could never say no to David. Of
course she planned to go with him, but when the Society
had to add to the little the Childs had collected—in order
to have enough for David alone—Maria knew despair. Was
this to be the end of her first real home since her mother's
death? She cried over Cottage Place and its memories. David
was necessary to her, physically, emotionally—even mentally. He was husband and child to her and she could not
do without him. She was not meant to live alone. There was
danger in it.

Yet David was the knight of old who must search for
his grail and go as he must. Tormented by the prospect of
emptiness without him, she did her best to keep her grief to
herself. He knew though; David always knew.

The little home in Roxbury was the first sacrifice to the
beets. Maria sighed over each ell and dormer and wondered
if ever again she could feel so attached to a warm "nest."
Here was the window David had hinged so that the cat
could jump in and out while Maria wrote; and there, the
racks he had built for their books, the prisms he had hung
at the window, and the ingenious arrangements of pipes and
drains to make dishwashing easier. Bidding good-bye to this
beloved home, Maria wished others would carry the burden
of reform and leave David alone to her. He apparently felt

the wrench less or the responsibility more. He faced the future with optimism, she with a sigh.

Once again the family hinted that he did not know what he was doing, and though secretly the poison of doubt was working in Maria's heart, she answered with facts. Beet sugar had been discovered in 1747 by a German chemist, but few people recognized its potential until about seventy-five years later. Napoleon had been one of the wise ones; he encouraged its development when France was threatened by England's naval blockade so that French farms could supply sugar formerly grown overseas in the West Indian colonies. David was sure that Northern farmers could grow a similar crop to discourage the slave-grown cane crop of the South. The seed and fertilizer experiments in Belgium were the important ones for him to study.

Maria promised that she would not cry when they reached the pier in New York even though Belgium seemed farther off than the moon. She could not look at David's face, for he was now as woebegone as she. She bustled about, poking in the portmanteau where she had stowed their favorite remedies for colds and fevers, powdered wild cherry and sage. She showed him the lists she had pinned to the insides of his coat to remind him not to take, as a tonic, a yeast poultice intended for open sores, instead of hop vine tea. She was sure he would poison himself without her. Heart in his eyes, David told her, "I wish for your sake I were as rich as Croesus," and she, carried away by the pain of parting, answered, "You are Croesus, for you are king of Lydia." David carried that answer with him throughout his life and it compensated for much that came later.

Meanwhile, as they waited for the ship's whistle and chatted with friends, a bailiff appeared with a threat to sue for debt. The last of Maria's bravado crumpled and she collapsed onto the baggage sobbing. Could nothing ever go right for them? Must even this horrible separation take place without dignity? The Tappan brothers came to the rescue, paid the debt, and brought Maria to her feet for a last hug from her pale knight. He sailed away and she was left to drift with the tide for the next year and a half alone.

For several months Maria stayed with David's mother on the farm in West Boylston. She was fond of her kind mother-in-law because the elder Mrs. Child had such "honest shoulders" and because being with her seemed to bring David a little nearer. It was the old story of Ruth and Naomi, "Thy people shall be my people." There was not much money on the farm but Maria was as happy as she could be, husbandless. She called the farmhouse her "little paradis des pauvres," but paradise palled or else she felt herself a burden, for soon she moved on to James's farm at Natick.

Spring that year was bleak and uncompromising. It was late when the fiddleheads uncurled their fuzzy fronds and the spring glories hid their pink and white under last year's leaves until Maria despaired of them altogether. The seasons were so out of order that she wrote: "What a misnomer in our climate to call this season Spring, very much like calling Calvinism religion." Neither of which held comfort for her. Harsh weather or no, she walked in the woods for hours as she had in Norridgewock long ago and poked under stones, in brooks, and around the trees for the herbs which interested her, the wild ginger, black oak bark, wild carrot, pennyroyal, and the pipsissewa which old people had told her was so good for any number of achey ailments. To be alone with nature was a restorative from James's robust demanding family.

Frequently she went to Boston for a conference with her publishers or to talk antislavery with friends. James allowed no mention of such radicalism in his house, and if she had not kept her ideas to herself, he would have let her know that his house was full to bursting without her, a lone battered sparrow of a sister who contributed little but sighs for her feckless husband. He did not count the number of nights she sat up with the children when they ailed; that was to be expected of any woman. James and his wife were sure that a few children of her own would have put Maria right; but they doubted that her poor stick of a husband—well, on all counts, David fell short of Francis standards.

All in all, that spring was miserable but James's house was the only home she had, and it gave her a place to write the short stories which sold readily to the *Boston Book* and other periodicals. Potboilers, they spilled out one after another—stories of good little girls as opposed to their more beautiful but ugly-souled sisters, stories of good, kind moral fairies and ugly, materialistically minded gnomes. Stories of adventure into far-off places which satisfied her Philothea side a little.

She was working on another book as well, a dour one that reflected the Frugal Housewife in her, and her lopsided, self-pitying state of mind. This was *The Family Nurse,* a simple compendium of first aid and home nursing with homeopathic remedies. If there was one thing that Maria really hated, it was nursing, and she did this book as if she were wearing a hair shirt for penance. She had not wanted to write it. As she said in the preface:

> For many reasons, the preparation of this work has been an arduous and disagreeable task; . . . Still I should take undue credit to myself if I professed that the usefulness of such a book was my strongest motive. If any other than very practical works would sell extensively, I fear I should still be lingering in more poetic regions.

The style of her writing made it clear how she felt, enough to make a sick person sicker, but so were some of her medicines. Imagine anyone afflicted with nervous spasms being forced to drink a concoction of skunk cabbage and molasses. Think of giving a sick baby a syrup made of steeped purple violets and sugar as a laxative. Best of all, or worst, depending on whether literary or medical standards are the measure, this:

> Two pounds of the seed vessels, freed from seed, may be sliced and boiled about an hour in fifteen quarts of water; strain them by squeezing strongly and boil it down by one half. Lastly add four pounds of sugar, and let it simmer a few minutes. This syrup is an opiate of uncertain strength, and should be used sparingly until tested by experience.

This nostrum was made of the seeds of white poppies— opium, to be exact.

The *Family Nurse* sold one small edition and this only because she had written it. It was the "shortest lived" of any she ever wrote.

She went to New York in 1837 for a Women's Rights convention. Again she, as a Massachusetts delegate, was asked to speak, but her answer was that she would do the writing and let someone else try to compete with Lucretia Mott, the announced major speaker. If Northern businessmen disliked anything more than antislavery, it was the movement for Women's Rights. Goaded by eloquent Mrs. Mott, or Mrs. Chapman, or the subtle propaganda of a Mrs. Child, mill girls might rebel and demand an end to economic slavery. Then who would turn the spindles to weave the cotton grown by the slaves of the South? It was fine, argued the businessmen, to talk of raising wages for mill hands and to free the Negroes, but these muddle-headed idealists did not consider that high-sounding theories could kill the nation's prosperity. Panic was already in the air. The merchants tossed in their beds at night while they tried to plan how to stop these mad reformers.

Maria meanwhile was not nearly as involved with Women's Rights as her conscience, that awful compulsive conscience of hers, should have pressed her to be, for she had a reason, stronger than any other for being in New York. David was coming home. Mrs. Mott's eloquence made little impression on her, for her heart was on the ship that was carrying David back to her. She forgot his easy-going, unruffled inadequacies. Mind and body, she yearned for the life that now at last they would be able to build together.

VIII

Beet Sugar Bog

THEN DAVID WAS THERE AND THEY WERE HOMELESS. WHERE to go? The Ellis Gray Lorings, friends from Roxbury, came forward to help. Loring had been one of the group who with David and Garrison had formed the original antislavery society back in 1832. He, rather than David, was Maria's business adviser and lawyer and, aware of the Childs' financial vacuum, he and his wife offered them a temporary home.

It was a lean time with the nation in the grip of the Panic of '37, and while thousands starved, others like the Childs came through only with the help of friends. The Lorings not only fed and housed David and Maria but lent them four dollars for David's new boots, for he, characteristically, had come home ragged to his wife. The Lorings' and their little girl Nony's kindness was the only thing that prevented Maria from being smothered by her resentment in feeling so beholden. She had awaited David's homecoming with such elation, but now, on reflection, she realized that after nine years of marriage she still could not count upon her husband to support her. As she knitted stockings for Nony, she asked herself again and again why David could not be

95

as up and doing for her as for his sugar beets. She yearned to be alone with him but he, though he said he felt as she did, was too busy giving lectures on his European experiences to do anything about finding them a home. Maria's emotions and needs came second. Bursting with thwarted love, she diverted her drive toward the Cause.

The records for 1837 list David as an honorary, non-supporting member of the Anti-Slavery Society, which accepted him gladly with or without dues; nonetheless when the Lovejoy Fund was being collected, Maria insisted on making a cash contribution and, at goodness knows what sacrifice, scraped up one precious dollar. The fund was to be a memorial to the Reverend Elijah Lovejoy, shot down in Alton, Illinois, while defending his antislavery press from mob destruction. Maria called the shooting plain murder, but as usual Boston's reaction was mixed. Those opposed to abolitionism deplored the violent death of a minister, but pacifists were equally horrified that a minister had offered armed resistance. Both sides ignored the fact that this was the fourth time Lovejoy's presses had been destroyed and that he had tried to guard not only his private property but the right of free speech in America.

When a hundred petitioners requested the use of Faneuil Hall for a memorial meeting, the authorities first refused to allow it on the ground of possible violence, but later they agreed to permit it as long as the gathering took place at eight in the morning when presumably attendance would be light. They were very much mistaken. A huge crowd ranging from determined Lovejoy partisans to just as determined anti-abolitionists packed the hall. Attorney General Austin, the same gentleman who four years before had hurled Maria's *Appeal* through the window with tongs, spoke first. Austin termed the martyred Lovejoy "presumptuous and

imprudent," and added that the minister had died "as a fool
dieth, marvellously out of place." Austin himself was doing
much as he said of Lovejoy, speaking "marvellously out of
place," for he lacked good taste in calling the dead minister
a fool, and *he* was a fool for putting himself in a bad spot
to precede the next speaker, none other than Wendell
Phillips.

The applause for Austin had risen to a roar as Phillips
reached the rostrum, stood still with no attempt to quiet the
crowd, and let his height, his impeccable poise, and his
dignity work for him. At last, the noise bubbled away and
the crowd heard that voice which "resembled the penetrating
mellowness of the flute and the violin rather than the blast
of the bugle." He warmed up slowly, feeling his way from
emotion to logic and back. "I hope," he began, "I shall be
permitted to express my surprise at the sentiments of the
last speaker—surprise not only at such sentiments from such
a man, but at the applause they have received within these
walls." The crowd began to shuffle with embarrassment.
They listened intently to his maiden speech in historic
Faneuil Hall, the first of many during which his life might
be threatened, his good name attacked, or rotten vegetables
hurled at his proud head. "Presumptuous!" he mimicked
Austin, "presumptuous to assert the freedom of the press
on American ground! Who invents this libel on his
country?" They cheered, they threw their caps in the air,
they shouted, and the James Otises, the Sam Adamses—
his oratorical predecessors—must have beaten their ghostly
hands together with the rest.

There were a few women at the meeting and someone
later told Maria Chapman that their presence "gave the
meeting the air of a Women's Rights affair—it hung out
false colors." Of course Mrs. Chapman did not object,

because to her, Women's Rights and abolition were marching side by side. Lovejoy's death became a milestone in
abolitionist progress, a peg for propaganda, a searching
examination to see where the constitutional system gave
men the right to defend life and property when the legal
guardians of the law had failed to do so. Even Emerson
emerged from his study to protest the Lovejoy abomination,
but he soon turned back to his contemplation of philosophy
to recover his orphic calm.

While Maria supported Phillips and wrote her antislavery
pamphlet, *The Evils of Slavery and the Cures of Slavery,*
David wrestled with the problems of the beet. Maria wrote to
philanthropic acquaintances to try to interest them in the
new farming. Beets do best in deep, rich, sandy soil, but
they can grow wherever corn is planted. She therefore tried
Gerrit Smith, who lived in the corn belt, to see if he would
donate $50,000 for land and machinery in Illinois. Smith, she
hoped, would back a project so highly recommended by the
Eastern antislavery groups, but Smith refused. At last, in the
spring of 1839, Maria's father made a suggestion.

Mr. Francis was a strangely restless man. In twenty years
he had moved thirteen times. Now he offered to live with
his daughter even though David must be thrown in as part
of the bargain. The old Medford baker agreed to lay out
$3,000 in lieu of leaving it to Maria in his will. This money
was a long way from $50,000 but welcome nonetheless, and
in short order the Childs bought a farm in Northampton, one
hundred rocky acres for $1,000 and probably worth a half
of the price. There was no proper house on the place, only
a crude shanty of two rooms and a lean-to, but Maria was
in high spirits. This would do as a start and the balance of the
money her father had promised could be spent as they
needed it. That spring they moved to a house that was

barely a shelter and a family life that was doomed from the start by its lack of privacy; and so started the new beet sugar industry in the United States.

The weather was dispiriting in itself. It rained or it snowed and the mud never had a chance to dry. It snowed in April as David worried and Mr. Francis muttered an old man's warning. The fields were too wet to plow but plowed they must be before June or the year would be lost. Rain loosened the stones which made them easier to raise, but it washed out the topsoil as well. Day after day David trudged home, mud clinging to his boots, his clothes wet through, his pessimism deep enough to darken any hope. Mr. Francis scowled at him and turned away while Maria started at the mess on her clean floor and felt that nature had joined the conspiracy to make life dreary. The rain poured on.

In May the skies cleared and though it was cool, fruit blossoms were unusually abundant. With the return of the sun, Maria's cheerfulness came back, and with it activity to make the shanty into a real home. She wrote a friend:

> We expect to whitewash it and build a new woodshed . . .
> I intend to half bury it in flowers, the hyacinth bean. I value
> them because they grew around my door in Cottage Place
> where I spent the happiest years of my life.

Whitewash for the walls, flowers at the door and home at last. So she thought. She explored the woods for hepaticas and spring glories, and later on the spotted pipsissewa with its tiny blush-pink bells gave her a true taste of spring. Here and there a rose ladyslipper swayed on its stem or nodded respectfully to a jack-in-the-pulpit. She pushed aside the carpet of brown leaves to find an earth star or a rare ebony fern for her wild garden. She sniffed the rich smell of swelling earth and felt strong stirrings in her. It was good to be alive and in New England.

Then Philothea shook off her misty cloak and turned into
the Frugal Housewife. The land was paid for but the beets
absorbed money, as did the repairs for which Mr. Francis
had forgotten to pay. The trouble those beets made! No
wonder some people called them the Scarcity Root. David's
mopes over the work he had contracted for were bad
enough, but her father's insinuations that they were squeez-
ing money out of him deliberately were unbearable. The
machines David had ordered in Europe, cash on delivery,
rusted on the dock in New York. Mr. Francis finally gave
enough for those machines, but the rest of the debts accu-
mulated, with only Maria's poorly paid writing to dribble
them down. Hardest of all, whenever she put out her hand
to comfort David, she felt her father's eyes upon her.

During this bad time, James Francis' disapproval hung
heavy over the Northampton venture. He made it clear that
his father's financial help to David was out of order, that
David's silly theories on crop rotation outraged him, that
to leave fields fallow for a season was merely a further
indication of David's shiftlessness. James was wrong; David
was not shiftless. He had seen fields in France where wheat,
grown near the sugar beet, was easier to thresh, while the
quality of the grain was better. Moreover, if corn were
planted on alternate years with the beets, it too improved.
Root crop, surface crop. He was a scientific farmer who put
what he studied and learned into practice, since he had been
a farmer's son before he became a scholar. There was one
point which clinched James's arguments, though, and that
was that David didn't have enough money to pay his own
hired hand.

With so much against her, Maria still managed to pay
off her debt to the Lorings, seventy dollars for four months'
board plus the four dollars for the boots. Pride demanded no

less, for even the sympathetic Lorings wondered about David's practical sense, and Maria had accepted as much patronage as she could. She loved her man; he had only to look at her in a certain way for her to melt—and if he looked seldom, it only made her the more eager for those times.

David was attractive even begrimed with mud. Farmers and financiers might call him a bad risk but there were plenty other solid citizens who respected his outlook on politics and history, and the ladies found his courtliness irresistible. Many evenings after a back-breaking day, he met with friends to discuss current national problems such as the pros and cons of the annexation of Texas. His in-laws would never have recognized this forceful speaker for the dreamy ne'er-do-well they thought they knew. He argued that if Texas came into the Union, slavery must spread there to give the South extra power in the Congress, which would bring on a civil war since Northerners would not stand for unfair voting rights for an unrepresented population. According to the way the voting went in 1837, Negroes were counted as so many heads with no voice. They were merely ciphers to protect the sugar, cotton, rice, and tobacco interests and to spread the noxious system further. David felt that Texas annexation was explosive, and when John Quincy Adams needed material for his plea to Congress to keep Texas out, he turned to David Child.

Thanks to his European trip, David knew more about international aspects of the Texas nettle than most people and could expound on the speed with which England would jump to divide the United States by inflaming public opinion and then by grabbing the Texas plains for herself during the excitement. Would America, postulated David, be stupid enough to make way for a new British colony to the north of Mexico? A member of the French Chamber of Deputies had told David that America's prestige in his country had suffered because of the continuation of slavery, which the French called a blot on American national honor. With Texas, there would be more of the same.

In any country but this, abolitionists who advocated the overthrow of existing national systems would have been burned at the stake like that fanatical monk Savonarola, but not here in the land of the free, where freedom must come to all. At the local taverns, David pressed his points against apathy toward slavery, but he talked to self-interested bigots whose enterprises depended on the trade with the South. One innkeeper, whose summer guests were mainly Southern, told Maria, "I dislike slavery as much as you do, but then I get my living by slaveholders." People like that man were hardly likely to throw away their livelihood as idealists of the Child type had done. Maria knew the man had a family and saw his dilemma for she answered, "Thou art an honest devil and I thank thee for not being at pains to conceal thy cloven foot."

Northampton's toleration toward slavery was a mounting irritation and sometimes David had to play loudly on his accordion to drown out the voice of a slave auctioneer who was visiting one of the neighbors because the sound of that voice made Maria sick. She found it ironic that the most professedly religious men, the deacons of the churches were the least sympathetic to abolition. "Love thy fellow man." Words, just Sunday words. She wrote to Convers:

> If I were to choose my home, I would certainly not place it in the valley of the Connecticut. It is true, the river is broad and clear . . . but oh, the narrowness of man.

Rigidity of spirit—strict Calvinism—was both binding and blinding to her. What these valley men needed was a deep inward self-investigation to see if their principles met with the standards they mouthed. They needed to search their souls.

Yet her own life hardly gave her time for that personal introspection she prescribed so freely. When she was not cooking, cleaning, carrying water or wood, she tried to keep peace between her father and husband. She had lost the heart to write her pretty-pretty stories. Now her output was limited to antislavery pamphlets and poems or tales with a sermon touch, and one poem in particular that had a kind of glory, just enough iron to save it from being maudlin. She called it "Lines—to those Men and Women Who Were Avowed Abolitionists in 1831, '32, '33, '34, and '35." Two of the stanzas read:

> Now the whole land is filled with light
> And converts come like dew,—
> God grant the torch may burn as bright
> As when our names were few!

> In sooth, it somewhat grieves my heart
> That the world is coming in,
> With its polluting, prudent art
> Of compromise with sin.

There she stated her disgust with "prudence" and compromise, with the Johnny-come-latelies to the Cause who would join now that the way might be less lonely and less perilous. She who had sacrificed for reform could be acid as wormwood over the easier way. David often said that Maria was "as direct and energetic as a locomotive under high pressure of steam" and there were times when she, like that locomotive, came close to exploding.

As the months passed she no longer jumped to David's defense as quickly when outsiders smiled at his experiments.

She was seeing him more as others saw him, a scholarly farmer-historian who had drifted in and out of the state legislature, the Washington lobbies, the practice of law—and now, beet sugar. If David had been less gifted or more egotistic, he might have made his mark; as it was, he knew too much to think he knew everything, and the more he studied, the less he earned.

One day while Maria sewed with Mrs. Lyman, the Mayor's wife, the two ladies had a revealing conversation. Mrs. Lyman asked, "Can you tell me the latest thing your husband is engaged in?" "Indeed I can," answered Maria. "He is carting stones for the railroad at ten cents a load." For a moment Mrs. Lyman's needle hung poised; then she sewed and said, "My dear, if your husband has got hold of any innocent occupation by which he loses only ten cents a load, for heaven's sake, encourage him in it." The implication was clear but Maria could not say a word. Even though it was disloyal to allow such criticism of David, she was too tired to defend him, too sick and tired to dream up one more way in which to disguise him as a hero. She knew that Mrs. Lyman, despite her sharp words, found David entrancing. He might not be much of a provider for his wife, but he was in demand as a dinner guest wherever he went. Mrs. Lyman in fact quoted him as her authority on international affairs, on the classics, and for his ready wit, and she had embroidered him a handsome velvet wrapper to set off his pale handsomeness. Maria did not worry over the gift, but took it as a slight tribute to her own good taste in choosing him. Yes, he might be a dreamer, a drifter, but there was something about that man.

By now Mr. Francis' innuendoes had become very pointed. He complained to the neighbors, "I deprived myself of home and comfort to help my daughter and all the thanks I get are bills, bills, and more bills." He implied that the Childs were sucking him dry. The neighbors gossiped as kind souls will who cannot keep their victims in ignorance of spicy tidbits, and the story fed itself back to the Childs. The reaction this time was enough to make the gossips gasp. Maria and David refused to take another penny from Mr. Francis, no matter what he promised and he packed up his things to leave for Boston then and there. He told them they could keep the farm for all the good it was and so at last they had the wretched place to themselves. The roof leaked but for once they did not care. After the first few days of tears and of blaming herself for her failure in keeping her father happy and comfortable, Maria began once more to try for the ideal home for an ideal marriage. Alone they could talk out their problems with no snuffling old man to hawk his throat or to breathe asthmatically on the other side of the plank walls. They could begin all over again.

Only it was not enough, this being alone with David whose mind was too taken with other interests to talk to her the way he had during their courtship days. She starved for intellectuality while he rambled on about fertilizers or Texas. Fortunately she could get to Boston occasionally for concerts and art and the conversations she craved. The carfare was extravagant, four and a half dollars for the more than a hundred miles of bone-shattering, rutted roads, but she and David sometimes drove in with the Reverend John S. Dwight, the new Unitarian minister whose church she seldom attended. Dr. Dwight did not condemn Maria for her absence from church services, for he was mightily interested in this new Transcendentalism that had Boston as well as his erring parishioner by the ears. The miles between Northampton and Boston shrank amazingly as Maria and Dr. Dwight discussed Goethe and Schiller and argued as to whether one should depend most on the experiences of the senses or upon intuition. When Philothea talked mystic philosophy, road bumps meant nothing to her.

Back in Northampton, when beets, dishcloth, and broom were too heavy, she straightened up with a long look at the little plaster copies of favorite statues she had bought in town or searched for the essence in Emerson's poems which had been published in *The Western Messenger,* or stood at the door of the shanty at twilight to watch the swallows wing home to their nests and David stride down the lane to her. It pleased her fancy that David came like the birds that fly unerringly to their mud-daubed homes and settle in with their mates. Still, the Transcendental touch was vital to her while beets and housework were a bore. She had neither energy nor audience for whom to make those delectable concoctions of the Roxbury days, and there was not much point, except for the purpose of self-discipline, to try to polish splintery floors which David immediately tracked with mud. The Frugal Housewife was heartily tired of that role. There was a good deal more to "being a woman."

Eventually the monotony at least broke when the Grimke sisters came nearby to live. The three women spent hours together discussing antislavery and Women's Rights, and gave Angelina Grimke plenty of fuel for public oratory. Angelina was an impressive speaker. In February, 1838, she had held the attention of the Massachusetts legislature for three days while she expounded abolition. Fear nearly undid her at the start and she admitted: "My heart never quailed before but it almost died within me at that hour." The fact that her sister Sarah was along to cheer her helped, because she added: "We abolition women are turning the world upside down, for during the whole meeting, there was sister seated up in the Speaker's chair of state." Maria too watched

Angelina, saw her courage strengthen as her speech went on and caught agreement dawning on the faces of some of the rock-bitten Massachusetts representatives. The crowd that came to hear Angelina on the second day was so enormous that the authorities limited the number of visitors to the gallery for fear that it might collapse. One member of the Massachusetts house of representatives suggested that a committee be appointed to "examine the foundations of the State House to see if it will bear another lecture from Miss Grimke."

Brother abolitionists pleaded with the Grimkes to confine their efforts to antislavery and leave Women's Rights alone. Sarah wrote a friend, "Brothers Whittier and Weld are anxious that we should say nothing on the woman question, but I do not feel I could surrender my right to discuss a great moral subject." Theodore Weld, Western abolitionist and newspaper man, worked so hard to convince Angelina to avoid Women's Rights that he ended up by proposing to her. They invited David and Maria to the Philadelphia wedding, a marriage which David nicknamed the "Welding." Angelina instructed her bridegroom to wear a "brown frock coat, white waistcoat and white or light-colored pantaloons, white stockings and shoes lower on the instep than those you usually wear." Like Maria, Angelina fussed more over her bridegroom's appearance than her own, which verged on Quaker simplicity.

Yet Maria did not go to the wedding—David had to stay at home to nurse the beets as usual—and to attend a wedding without one's husband is to cook soup without salt. As an apology for her absence, Maria wrote a wedding-present poem. Punsters had called Angelina "Devil-ina" or "Miss Grimalkin," but this was Maria's own play on syllables:

Can one who hears her clear and manly sense
Uttered in richly flowing eloquence
Or sees her eyes dimmed with repentant tears
To think of chains an injured sister wears—
Can such a one deny or doubt, think ye
She is in truth an Angel-in-a Grimke?

Soon after the wedding, David had a piece of luck that made him and his wife sure that the tide had turned. His work on the beets had won the recognition of the judges at the Massachusetts State Exhibition for 1839 and they gave him a silver medal for his raw and refined sugar. Then the Agricultural Society announced that they too esteemed his progress, in proof of which he would receive a cash award, amount unstipulated. Maria and David jubilantly planned for their glorious debtless future. They wrote their dreams on lists. Item 1: pay off Mr. Francis altogether and entirely. Item 2: the back salary of that poor hired man. Item 3: contributions for the Anti-Slavery Society and various others they had been too poor to help. Item 4: a real wedding present for the Welds. Item 5: presents for . . . oh, the list could be endless, for they were simply carried away by anticipation of generosity. The joy of that award. Suddenly they had never been more in love.

The official letter came on a snowy February morning. David was chilled through when he brought it back sealed from the post office and they opened it together with shaking hands. The letter praised David for his unrelenting, unremitting faithfulness to the beets. Enclosed was a "premium," a bank draft for one hundred dollars. David crushed the paper in his fingers. He took the list they had written in love and hope and threw it savagely into the fire. Maria could not comfort him. The disappointment was too bitter. The prize, the pot of gold, would make only a soft plop as it sank into the swamp of debt which their sacrifices and Mr. Francis' broken promises had flooded. They were stuck fast in their beet sugar bog.

IX

The STANDARD'S Call

THE MONTH OF NOVEMBER, 1839, WAS THE COLDEST IN twenty years and not even the old-timers could recall when, if ever, the ice had been so thick. Women shivered beneath their warmest shawls, and at the back of every range a pot of savory stew simmered. Men needed something hot when they stumbled in after shoveling the drifts that piled deep and blue on the roads. At the store, one heard of frozen travelers whose strength had nearly given out before a light guided them to a friendly kitchen. Farmers fingered the stubble on their chins and wondered if their cut wood would last the winter. Evenings they stood by the kitchen door and sniffed the air for snow, to measure the number of logs they would need to keep the fires going until more fuel could be gotten from the woodpile. It was impossible to keep out the cold even with blankets pinned over the windows to prevent drafts. Water froze in the pitchers only a few yards from the range, and to abandon the blessing of the stove, to go to bed under a mound of clammy patchwork quilts, was cold agony.

Maria shivered with the rest of the community but she was colder in her ramshackle house than most of her neighbors. Swirling storms beat in on the place; doors and windows rattled with each gust. Maria took hot bricks to bed every night and wished for a change in the weather. David had no time for improvements other than to his sugar-house, which left any carpentry up to Maria. Beets. Beets. Beets. All he talked, all he lived for, were those eternal beets. If only she could drag herself somehow out of this tangle where antislavery and David meshed her. She hungered for music, art, and spiritual conversation, while the freezing weather held her close to home, too cold even for a visit at the Lymans' or town meeting. She wrote to her friend, Miss Augusta King:

> Here I am well nigh thirty-nine years old and cannot for the life of me talk common sense . . . if I had been a flower or a bird, Linnaeus or Audubon, might have put me in some order. . . . One would think that being a woman were more to the purpose than either; for if to stand between "two infinities and three immensities" as Carlyle says (the two infinities being cooking done and to be done and the three immensities being making, mending and washing) if this won't drive poetry out of a mortal, I know not what will.

The Frugal Housewife was heartily sick of her role and the beets, and the winter might have beaten her at last; but chilblains or not, when Maria heard from the Reverend Dwight of Margaret Fuller's projected Conversations, she bundled herself into as many extra layers of woolens as she could find and off she went to Boston.

Dr. Dwight was one of the founders of the Transcendental Club to which Margaret belonged, so that he brought the news to Maria firsthand. He was concerned over both of the Childs' appearance. They were too worn with sacrifice and work and Maria, he felt, needed the relief of the Transcendental flights she enjoyed. "I think," she wrote to

Convers, "that was all he [Dr. Dwight] was sent here for and that the parish is paying for a missionary for me." Dwight's congregation actually appreciated him less than she did and complained that his sermons were too soft and that he did not have "the power of disciplined thought" required of a Northampton preacher. His "mild, transparent, amber light," as Maria described his style, could not satisfy a stronghold of rigid sectarianism. Had Dwight stressed Haydn and Mozart less and brimstone more, his "want of fluency in prayer" would have caused less complaint among the members of the congregation. For Maria, these very qualities were the ones that compensated for much of the valley stodginess, and she told Mrs. Loring that she had promised to "take flight with him from my washtub or dishkettle any time he would come along in his balloon." That was how it came about that he told her of the Fuller Conversations, another instance of his ministering to her soul "in seasons of great need."

Convers and Mrs. Loring wrote to her about it too, for all of intellectual Boston was buzzing with the Fuller plan. Lectures were of course nothing new, even lectures by women. Elizabeth Peabody had given hers in her "Historical School." Education was in fashion for everyone, education of a sort, at least, such as the "improvement societies" could provide for the spread of "Useful Knowledge," and short talks on natural history, geology, and the value of libraries. Edward Everett offered his on Greek antiquities. The railroads capitalized on the trend of lust for learning by advertising that "the cars" were convenient for out-of-towners to get a chance at real Boston education. There were popular Lyceum groups where discussions and declamations on Goethe and Carlyle were part of the usual program and the average price for a course of ten to fifteen such evenings was

two dollars; everyone—merchants, bankers and upholsterers'
apprentices—came to learn. Thought within thought in
intricate language was a passport to fame.

Sideshows flourished at the same time. Staid old Boston
sniffed and sneered that these attractions were for the
illiterate of no taste, but the promoters of the grotesque
exhibition in which a twelve-pound rat was featured, raked
in money faster than the lecturers on the Meaning behind
the Meaning behind the Meaning. Rats were a deal easier
to understand than Transcendental philosophy.

Margaret Fuller's Conversations combined showmanship
with erudition. She had always demanded and gone to any
lengths for attention, without which she was likely to
collapse with any one of several obscure nervous ailments.
As a girl she had deliberately banged her head against an
iron fender at school because the other girls were not enough
aware of her. Margaret was enough of the freak to intrigue
the curious and enough of the scholar to satisfy the pedants.
Her many friends feared and respected her and put up with
her arrogance. Maria said, "Margaret's egotism is a fault
much to be regretted. It mars the nobleness of her views and
of her expression. But it is the consequence of her father's
early injudicious culture. He never *allowed* her to forget
herself." Maria judged her, excused her, and yet admitted
that Margaret had the "most remarkable intellect I have
ever met."

It was more than intellect that drew people to Margaret.
Elizabeth Hoar remarked, "Her friends were a necklace of
diamonds about her neck . . . she was perhaps impatient
of complacency . . . and so her enemies were made." The
truth was that she repelled and magnetized at the same time.
Her physical idiosyncrasies annoyed, her emotional instabil-
ity drained, but the essence of the woman held them. Some,

though they could not say it to an ardent feminist, pitied her for her "man's mind" in a weak, womanly frame, but Theodore Parker was more explicit in saying that Margaret Fuller was "muscular minded." She was impatient with life and personal relationships; and without a normal outlet for her capacity to love, she turned inward and nearly consumed herself. Emerson, whom she met in 1836, for a time seemed to her a likely priest-confessor; but while he solved some of her literary problems, he only added to the volcanic emotions which raged inside her.

It was he, however, who introduced her to the Transcendental Club where she found opportunity to air her talent for talk. Most of the other members, Bronson Alcott, George Ripley, Frederick Hedge, and shy, little, happy Dr. Dwight were better at writing than at speaking. By being able to talk these gentlemen down, Margaret's tensions decreased though she frequently exhausted her fellow members with her demon drive to express herself. She was the only woman member at the time (Elizabeth Peabody followed). Although Alcott, Ripley, and the rest of the men professed to believe in equality of the sexes, their gallantry prevented their interrupting her, once she was astride any of her intellectual hobby-horses. For Margaret, though she knew that the use of too much energy gave her migraines, the joy of listening to herself was worth the cost and she swooped between heights of erudite, sparkling forcefulness and painful prostration.

Love of study and of scholars had first attracted her to Maria years before, in Watertown, where they had discovered a mutual interest in political philosophy, a rare bent for ladies. The two immersed themselves joyfully in John Locke's interpretation of the ideologies of Greece and Rome; they toiled over the obscurities of Goethe and analyzed the startling depth of Mme. de Staël. It was as a result of these

studies that Maria had written those five volumes of the
Ladies' Library about Mesdames de Staël, Necker, and other
feminine leaders whom she and Margaret found interesting.
Yet the true magnet was Goethe whose pronouncements they
took for their credo—the need to be one's self at all times.

Margaret, eight years younger than Maria, had been
jealous of Maria's marriage, and when as usual she over-
dramatized her feeling, Maria had had to scold and reassure
her. She wrote:

> My dear Margaret,
> The passion of love is very exclusive in a woman's heart;
> I acknowledge it—it ought to be so—nay, if it exist at all, it
> *must* be so; but do you suppose all other avenues of kindly
> feeling are shut up? I assure thee no! "I do not love Caesar
> less—but I love Rome more."

Now, ten years later, Margaret was the goddess of literary
Boston and Maria came to pay homage. The Conversations
for ladies were planned as a catharsis, a self-expression to
dispel fuzzy thinking. Perhaps Margaret sincerely expected
her audience to join her in speaking out, but as Charles T.
Congdon wrote in his *Reminiscences:* "Nobody else said
much when she was in a Delphic mood." Emerson, who was
fond of her in his own cold way, added: "In conversation
Margaret seldom, except as a special grace, admitted others
upon an equal ground with herself." As a master of words
she could even talk down Elizabeth Peabody, though that
kindergarten expert probably was unaware of it. Nevertheless Margaret hoped that this new series of meetings would
"systematize thought and give a precision and clearness in
which our sex are so deficient, chiefly because I think they
have so few inducements to test and classify what they
receive." Typically Bostonian, that classification, that
pigeonholing, despite the lady's attempt to be modern in her

thinking. She wanted to build up "the life of thought upon the life of action," a good round phrase that might mean almost anything but was an unconventional concept for lady if not Woman.

Miss Peabody offered the parlor behind her bookshop on West Street for the Conversations. "Lizzie" was now a member of the Transcendental Club and somewhat under Margaret's sway. There was no charge for the use of the parlor on West Street. Lizzie never asked and Margaret never offered to pay. Already the rendezvous of the Boston literati, Lizzie sold few books in the shop because her clients were too busy conversing to bother with mundane affairs of trade, that is unless Mrs. Peabody, her mother and practical member of the firm, was there to spur sales. Most of the time, Emerson, Alcott, Theodore Parker, Dwight, and the rest poked and browsed, talking mightily all the while. Hawthorne often came but mainly to visit Elizabeth's sister, Sophia. The shop, heady with Transcendental atmosphere, was nicknamed the "Hospital for Incapables."

Incapable though some of these thinkers were in money-making, they probed and tried for answers to practical as well as theoretical problems, answers which frequently turned out less practical than the problems. They evolved a plan to run a communistic farm where the labor would be furnished by the hands of the shareholders and the shares sold only to like-minded souls who were eager for intellectual stimulation through concerted effort. It was that same idea of "life of thought combined with life of action." There was acreage for sale out near Roxbury, a place called Brook Farm. The "Incapables" arranged for a real farmer to teach them how to plow, seed, and hoe and to take produce from the farm in lieu of wages. Would the plan work or would it turn out like Fanny Wright's fiasco at Nashoba, Tennessee?

George Ripley was enthusiastic, Hawthorne invested his few savings in the hope of stretching his money enough to marry his silly Sophia, and Emerson was frankly skeptical. When it came to facts, the young "sage of Concord" knew enough to hew out *his* philosophies in private. Platonist though he was, he could not believe in this community of thinking and living. The others raised their portions for investment somehow and prayed for success of their crops, literary and manual, to cover the deficit. The pinch of '37 was still on New England and writers would be the last to benefit by restored prosperity after years of depression. The Transcendentalists were optimistic over their solution for economic as well as intellectual drought.

For Margaret this was a type of thought *cum* action that held no appeal whatever. She was all for letting others milk cows while she went on talking, editing Emerson's new *Dial,* and doing some writing herself. Maria agreed with some of Margaret's reasons but with a different intensity; Maria had seen as much farm life as she would ever want and she, unlike most of the West Street habitués, could prove by the calluses on her palms how little time farm life allowed for creative writing. Besides, there was the matter of privacy above all. The boardinghouse where she and David stayed for the snowiest months that winter was community living enough.

On Saturdays the Brook Farm planners stayed away from the store, and, at high noon—in came Queen Margaret. Head slightly tilted, lorgnette raised, a handful of chrysanthemums trailing from her other hand, she nodded regally at her hushed and eager subjects. Few of them realized that the lorgnette was no prop and that she could not see without it. Nor did they know that a chronic spinal condition, result of bending over books since the age of four, made her hold her head in that awkward way. Margaret knew that she looked odd and she capitalized on her infirmities. They added to her stage presence and to the total effect of making her different from other women.

She conducted her Conversations for a selected few in the belief that, as Goethe posited, the perfecting of a few was preferable to the slight improvement of many, an autocratic point of view quite in keeping with Margaret's assumption of regality. The Saturday circle included Mrs. Emerson, Mrs. Loring, and twenty-odd other ladies plus Maria. Many a husband or father in Boston forbade his womenfolk to go near those Fuller lectures for fear of contamination with arrant feminism, a cursed gospel in a home where Man is master. Worse than that, they might be associated with the even more cursed gospel of abolition, be moved by it enough to pester the men about the plight of the Negroes, or worse. How right these conservatives were! Margaret, though she would have nothing to do with any organized reform movement, did preach that the mill girls at Lowell and the factory towns thereabouts were held in as grim a bondage as the slaves in the South, a thesis which hit the owners where they kept their hearts—in their pocketbooks.

Margaret set off verbal fireworks during her meetings. Her voice, harsh and nasal, alternately froze and warmed her listeners. She tossed out a theory on Greek art, mythology, or government or on current working conditions for women, then pounced on the next subject, immortality. Her gyrations dazzled her hearers and effectively stopped their participation, but her tactics were aided and abetted by her old friend, Maria Child, with whom much of Margaret's background in mythology and the progress in religious ideas had been learned. One of the areas which Maria did not abet was demonology, though this was Margaret's favorite. She wore a great carbuncle ring to ward off evil, made a serious study of the black arts, and spoke as though she were personally acquainted with vampires, to the dismay of the more suggestible of her audience, who stirred restlessly on their hard chairs and wished they might be anywhere but with Miss Fuller in the caves of the occult. Maria had to smile at this, the old Margaret up to her old dramatic nonsense, still in love with the limelight.

In that well-dressed circle, Maria stayed in the background, for the sixty-six cents each lecture cost her had been hard enough to find, let alone new clothes. Not that Maria really cared much how she looked, but even a woman of simple taste, when she knows that others pity her for an improvident husband, wants to put on a decent front and among these nicely accoutered ladies, she felt very shabby indeed. Harriet Martineau called Margaret's group the "Gorgeous Pedants," which was rather unfair since most of them in addition to being good wives and mothers led active, philanthropic lives and allowed themselves these lectures as a super, super luxury. Her intellectual prods stimulated them to a new self-evaluation and respect. One of them said, "Everything that Margaret said had the power of germinating in other minds."

If Margaret's pyrotechnics baffled the ladies on ordinary Saturdays, the one when Emerson came to serve as her foil floored them completely. Emerson presented his own series of talks, "The Present Age," in the evening so that he was free to look in on his protégé and find out why his wife and her friends were so impressed. He came and he too was conquered by her maneuvers and the use she made of the material she and Maria had dug up together. Those who heard both Emerson and Margaret were amazed by the contrast between his remote, chilly presentation and the warmth of hers. He the moon, and she the sun.

Maria, who would not have bothered to go around the corner to listen to Emerson for no charge, satisfied her Philothea self with Margaret's questings on the meaning of life or the oracles of Delphi. Weekdays, abolition claimed her, but Saturdays she reveled in the mysticism of the Transcendental world. The bond between the two women, the one who worked for the freedom of the slave and the other who sought to emancipate woman was strengthening. Margaret Fuller as representative of the "new" woman, and Lydia Maria Child in her unfashionable, unspectacular way were treading parallel paths.

Then the 1840 World's Anti-Slavery Convention was announced to be held in London and the Massachusetts Society asked Maria to be one of its delegates, with David to accompany her. The beets, however, came first and the Childs once more stayed at home in Northampton. Lucretia Mott, Maria Chapman, and the other American female delegates who did go, were humiliated to have their credentials refused and to be treated as ordinary visitors and relegated to the visitors' gallery off the working floor. When Garrison, who arrived after the meeting opened, discovered their plight, he sat upstairs with them and disdained the special seat of honor reserved for him on the speakers' platform. His behavior shook the confidence of his hosts and later, when Garrison and Phillips attended another antislavery gathering in Exeter Hall, neither was asked to speak for fear that they might bring up that provocative subject of Women's Rights. Garrison's championship publicly tied the two reforms together in America.

Maria read all about it in her antislavery paper and chortled. For the moment even the beets could not get her down, but her elation could not last. Those beets, those eternal beets! How they consumed time and energy and money! When David was digging or boiling or skimming, skimming and mashing and skimming again, he lectured on beets, beets, beets. Not immortality or music or the meaning of life, but beets. He and his wife almost never sat and read together. Only once in a while as she sat stooped over her mending would he stroke her hair and murmur, "Carum caput." His fingers were rough from the war with stones and mud but his touch was gentle and, for her, his touch was still enough.

It would have taken a more stable nature than her own not to despair, at the rate their debts swallowed up all she earned through poems and stories. No sooner did *Godey's* or the *Ladies' Companion* pay her than a creditor hammered at the door. At twelve dollars the full page (with tiny print too), even twenty hours of writing a day would not have paid the bills. Sooner or later something must snap. Then it came—an unlooked for, unexpected rainbow opportunity, an offer for David to edit the *National Anti-Slavery Standard* in New York City at $1,000 a year. An end to their trouble, an unbelievable piece of luck. But there were the beets, those nasty red globular fetters to the mud and the rocks of Northampton.

Maria shook herself. She had to be fair. David could not sacrifice his sugar, after all that work, to what might prove still another will-o'-the-wisp. She wrote to Mrs. Chapman:

> His soul has been almost worried out of him by want of funds and by delay after delay caused by cheap machinery, but he has made perfect sugar and finds his skill in no way deficient to the task he has undertaken.

She stuck by her man and his small success, but she cared even less for Northampton after this tantalizing glimpse of freedom.

Some weeks later, the editor's chair was offered to Maria herself at the same salary. She could not afford to refuse it for she rationalized that, by scrimping and saving most of that munificent salary, she and David might in one year clean the slate of their most pressing debts and start fresh. It took courage to be unconventional enough to leave her husband and become a newspaper editor alone in a great city, but Maria had never lacked courage to do what she wanted to. She almost convinced herself that she was not afraid when she wrote Convers:

> If I possessed your knowledge, it seems to me as if I could move the world. I am often amused and surprised how many things I have attempted to do with my scanty stock of learning. I know not how it is, but my natural temperament is such that when I wish to do anything, I seem to have an instinctive faith I can do it, whether it be cutting a garment or writing a Greek novel.

It was not the work but the loneliness she feared. Not to have David beside her when she woke in the morning, not to have him tease her back to good humor if she felt low or to be able to do the same for him, not to watch over him and see that he did not take cold. . . . Yet it was for love of him, to give him the chance to do as he wanted, that she would go to New York.

Before she left she went over every inch of the house to set it to rights. Ugly, crude, it was suddenly dear to her. She checked the chinks in the north wall and stuffed them with mud and moss as the Abnakis had taught her long ago in Maine. She knitted as many pairs of stockings for David as time allowed and sewed all his buttons on twice, just to be sure. She showed him the reserves of pickles and peaches and the hidden bottle of medicinal brandy for his rheumatics and where she kept the candles if the lamp oil gave out. He

followed her at every step, not that he needed to be told
where she kept things, but to have her with him as close as
possible. Maria was leaving him for the first time. His length
seemed to shrink into itself. He was a forlorn, defeated
knight. At last he knew what it meant to be left behind.

X

Letters from New York

THE RED BUDS OF THE MAPLES HAD BARELY BROKEN INTO
filigree when Maria left New England. Spring was her favorite season but go she must, away from David, from all she
held dear. On her way through Boston, she signed a contract
with the editor of the Boston *Courier* to do a series of weekly
letters on her impressions of New York. That contract, a
generous one, gave a fillip to her confidence in being able to
do a profitable job.

She came to the brawling port of New York in 1841 and
from the ship she saw the town, clean and bright, dotted
with green trees and white houses. The sun glinted on
steeples, windows, and roofs of glittering tin "as if the
Fire Spirits had suddenly created a city of fairy palaces." As
the vessel made its way through square-riggers, barks, and
brigantines to tie up at the dock, the peacefulness vanished
and "the din of crowded life and the eager chase for gain
. . . like the perpetual murmur of a hive" broke over her.
This bustling center was to be her home instead of the cool,
quiet woods and David's gentle hands at the end of the day.

The American Anti-Slavery Society had arranged board
and lodging for her at the home of Isaac T. Hopper, its

New York agent. He met her at the pier, a picturesque old man with black glossy hair and Quaker clothes like William Penn's and the kindest eyes she had ever seen. "Welcome to thee," he said as he pressed her hand, and she immediately felt less forlorn. A boy with a barrow trundled her baggage to a horse cab, shouting, "Keep de way clear. Clear de way!" The cab smelled of horse and dust and cracked leather, like the barn at home, but the ride was too exciting for her to be homesick. Mr. Hopper reminded her that Broadway from the Battery to Canal Street was the main business avenue and that the city was thickly settled all the way out to Twelfth Street, an amazing growth in the few years since Maria had been there. Children and pigs dodged the carriage wheels and the number of beggars seemed to have increased in proportion to the population because every time the cab stopped to let a horse car or another carriage have the right of way, she heard voices begging for a penny. City contrasts would be her first topic for the *Courier,* marble mansions and hovels, beggars and richly dressed men-about-town, the splendor of Broadway, and those snuffling pigs. She saw plenty in that first ride for a half dozen "letters from New York."

Maria resigned herself to loneliness because even the cheerful, sunny room at the Hoppers' where, she wrote Loring, she was "as comfortable as a poodle on a Wilton rug" could hardly make up for absence from home. But she had not expected harsh criticism of her editing from Garrison and Mrs. Chapman from the very start. She intended to do her best, but it would have been pleasanter if they had supported her, especially since they had given her a free hand to do the job as she saw fit. Without David's faith in her and her own satisfaction in self-martyrdom, she would have lost courage at the very beginning. The outgoing editor of the *Standard,* Nathaniel P. Rogers, had urged her to face the future bravely, "as did the Maid of Orleans," an exhortation to her liking, and her editorial answer reflected that she had taken it to heart:

> Such as I am, I am here, ready to work according to my conscience and my ability, providing nothing but diligence and fidelity, refusing the shadow of a fetter on my free expression of opinion from any man or body of men, equally careful to respect the freedom of others, whether as individuals or societies.

Chapman and Garrison had received her declaration of independence and for her there would be no compromise.

The Hopper house had the proper atmosphere for such courage. The family was originally Philadelphia Hicksite Quaker like the Motts. (The Hicksite branch took its name from Elias Hicks, who had worked vigorously against slavery until his death in 1830.) Mr. Hopper's neighbors loved and his enemies respected him. One of the family legends Maria heard soon after her arrival was of the day, a few years before, when Garrison was nearly mobbed in New York and Friend Hopper, who had come to hear him speak, took a three-legged stool and sat calmly watching while the mobsters fought the crowd that had rescued the abolitionist leader. No one hurt Friend Hopper, though he was well-known as an antislavery man, because his greater reputation among these people was for the kindnesses he had performed without regard to religions, races, or politics. Friend Hopper that day and always deplored the fact that proslavery wealth paid for the trouble-makers who started these mob scenes and insisted that the same influence which put brickbats into the hands of Irish immigrants was responsible for keeping them poor and ignorant.

Friend Hopper welcomed Maria as a kindred soul for he

had read some of her writings, heard of her sacrifices, and recognized in her a sympathy for her fellow man very like his own. Maria, for her part, quickly saw how his goodness infected his family, particularly his daughter Abby, the wife of James S. Gibbons, a bank teller who was also the *Standard*'s printer. The Gibbonses ate lightly so that James could give the paper his financial support, and their furniture had been mortgaged to keep the *Standard* afloat. They had suffered socially as well as dietwise for their antislavery principles. Abby's former friends of the Sewing Circle no longer would talk to her while she staunchly went to meetings to make warm petticoats for the children in the hospital on Randall's Island. The ladies did go so far as to oust her from the club but her sympathy for abolition removed her from *their* social climate.

Her father, Friend Hopper, and James, her husband, were in a worse position, for the Cherry Street Monthly Meeting of the Friends had threatened to "disown" any supporter of the *Standard*. Rogers, Maria's editorial predecessor, had written some outspoken criticisms of Quaker ministers whom he called proslavery in the paper and the Meeting had dismissed him for his brashness. The Cherry Street group held that Friend Hopper and Gibbons were partly at fault, although Hopper himself had never even seen the questionable editorial before it was printed. He and his son-in-law were disowned by the majority vote of their brethren, among whom, ironically enough, was a Quaker who made his fortune by manufacturing slave whips.

Many prominent Friends around the country protested the "reading out," and Lucretia Mott called it shameful that proslavery money should hurt so kind a man as Friend Hopper. She reminded Friends everywhere of that saintly John Woolman who, in 1750, had given up his thriving retail trade to work for the abolition of slavery. The Cherry Street Meeting did not retract.

When Abby heard of the reading out, she put on her bonnet and marched to the meetinghouse, where she took her seat quietly, waited until the minutes of the previous month had been read, and then rose. In a low but penetrating tone that could be heard in the farthest corner of the hall, she read her personal withdrawal from the Society. "I request that my name and the names of my children, William, Sarah Hopper, Julia, and Lucy be erased from your list of members; and from this date, I consider the connection which has hitherto existed between us to be entirely dissolved." She enunciated her reasons, particularly the unjust defamation of character of her father and husband. Finished, she handed the notice to the clerk and walked out with what monumental defiance only another devout Quaker could understand.

Interestingly enough, after disownment, Friend Hopper, whose feeling for the faith of his forebears could not be wiped out by the Cherry Street affair, continued to attend meetings in the same seat he had always used among the Elders. When someone hinted that the overseers were about to demand that he take a less conspicuous place, he retorted, "I expect they won't," and they never did.

This, then, was the atmosphere in which Maria found her home. Their self-reliance spurred her on, and when some readers objected to the feminist tone of the *Standard* since she had taken it over because feminism might destroy the family ideal, Abby and a growing number of partisans insisted that the paper had improved tremendously and that its increased circulation was proof in itself of Maria's position. Susan Hopper, Abby's sister in Philadelphia, wrote, "You can't know how much we enjoy the *Standard*. No man could have elevated it as Maria has. Bless her heart, the angels love her."

Maria herself was not sure about the angels but the Hoppers' affection was certain, and if the girls admired her, their brother, John, responded more emotionally. Accustomed to plain and sober ways, the presence of a celebrity in his house upset him. John had never dreamed of life in so rare an atmosphere. In the distinguished Mrs. Child he found a world, or thought he did, from which his simple upbringing had barred him. She brought music, color, poetry, and he did not notice the shabbiness of her dress, the darned tips of her gloves, nor the artful needlework on the patches of her cloak. Glamor had arrived at the house on Eldridge Street. For the second time in his life, John knew a certain different excitement.

Some years before, he had seen Fanny Kemble in a performance and, once enthralled, he could not stay away from the theater. He arrived home one night at a very unsober, un-Friendly hour to be confronted by his father. "My son, where has thee been?" John, a grown man in his twenties, feared and respected that direct eye and commanding tone. He quavered, "I have been to see Miss Fanny Kemble." The father's finger pointed at his son. "Has thee been to that place before this night, then?" "Yes, father, I have seen Miss Kemble sixty-seven times." In the face of that answer even Friend Hopper was lost. He sent the young man to bed with no more conversation, while he himself sat down to study over the problem, for he was terribly worried that John's light tastes might cause him to stray from the Quaker spirit. In the Hopper house even a piano was barred, so that this sixty-seven-time fall from grace was a real blow. John, it would seem, must be watched.

And now in 1841, John, a little older but still impressionable, was exposed daily to a celebrated author. When Friend Hopper's brass cowbell called the family to dinner, when it summoned a family conclave to discuss ways and means to raise money for the *Standard,* when Maria's solitary room with its airtight stove and Dresden transparencies stifled her with its loneliness, she and John were together. Circumstances fostered her friendship and dependence on him. As an abolitionist she had few friends in New York and even booksellers preferred her to take her own books elsewhere rather than let their conservative customers see her or her works on the premises. For the first eight months she never met a familiar face in the streets, and though the paper kept her busy, it could not fill all of her time nor still her longing for David. Time stretched endlessly and John was there, always helpful and almost panting to be of service. Does a woman ever lose desire, or is it buried deep within her subconscious until a fresh stimulus wrests it painfully to the surface? There were times when David seemed so far away that she could not see his face clearly in her mind; but John was here—now.

Not that he made any but the most respectful and helpful advances. It was he who pointed out the effects of New York's commercial doldrums and showed her the current bitter joke, the grand new Customs House at Pine and Wall Street, built to accommodate an expanding foreign trade that had decreased instead, leaving the building unused except as sleeping space for the beggars whom the City Watch ordered to leave its marble precincts. "Trade just doesn't exist, and everyone blames the antislavery movement," John told her. She knew why the wealthy including the Whigs felt so, because the price of cotton was down, stevedores were out of their shipping jobs, countinghouses had nothing left to count and, thanks to the abolitionists, the domestic demand for cotton goods was so far off that the mills had slowed down to throw thousands out of work as well. The Panic of '37 still pinched and the streets were full of hungry children. Even the "dandy workmen," as Harriet Martineau had called ordinary workers, had sold their "gay watch guards and glossy hats" for a piece of bread. Penniless, unemployed Germans, English and Irish flooded the city in their search for the gold-paved streets the sea captains had promised them, but instead they found disease and black misery and not an honest day's pay for willing hands.

John could do much for Maria, much more than the rest of his family, noble though they were. An unmixed feast of good works without poetry and music to lighten the dose and no sympathetic ear for her Philothean outbursts could not have sustained her. The cosmology of Swedenborg's angels was more important to her than the philosophy of John Fox. She missed the Transcendental ramblings with John Dwight and Margaret Fuller. She wrote to Loring: "There is no one here on that high plane. I must always look down, a weary task for one that loves to look upward and rise, so well as I do." John Hopper tried to be the answer to her need, though he could not achieve the heights she chose. Nevertheless his solicitude helped her, and without it she might have given up. It was impossible to remain unresponsive to his delight in being with her. Consequently most of their leisure hours were spent together and in letters home she called John, fifteen years her junior, her "dear, adopted son."

They went on a picnic to the Palisades with a packet of cakes and oranges and read the poetry of Lamartine aloud. They traveled by excursion boat to Grant Thorburn's wonderful botanical paradise on the East River. They ferried to Staten Island and Weehawken and took another boat ride to Rockland, where Major André had been captured by Revolutionary soldiers while carrying the papers entrusted to him by Benedict Arnold. They slipped out of the house early in the morning like truant children for these relaxations and were together all day, absorbing sound, sun, and emotion. They talked of their ideals and their hopes and came back by moonlight, each aglow with the other's appreciation. Back at Eldridge Street, Philothea would shed her moonlight veil and race upstairs to write out her stint for the *Courier*. Each of these trips made copy for her but it was an abrupt transition, this about-face to the workaday world.

Maria saw no danger in her intimacy with John, but both Convers and Ellis Loring cautioned her against indiscretion. She laughed at their warnings and reminded them that John was her "son," not her lover. Wasn't it natural for her to show gratitude for his courtesies, and couldn't they see that she might be thankful for his protection without compromise? Moreover, with Loring so far away, John had become her business adviser as well as her social escort and she would feel lost without him.

Naïvely she wrote Loring of a simple incident. One day when she was dreadfully low, John rapped at her door to offer her a small basket lined with grape leaves and filled with a melon and a few peaches. He disturbed her train of thought and she showed her irritation. "I am busy. I have no time for anything now. Please excuse me," she snapped. The misery in his face at her rebuff was reproach enough to make her cry, and John, horrified, turned and rushed downstairs in tears himself. This episode, she said, should prove to Loring how unfounded his fears must be, for how could she be emotionally involved with so weak a man? How could she indeed!

Maria made up for her harshness to John by giving him copies of her books charmingly inscribed, and she wrote her brother not to worry further. The incident was closed.

During the day her editorial duties took full time. *Courier* readers wondered how she found material for her "letters from New York." She gathered much of it walking to the *Standard* office, a mile and a half away over muddy, pig-infested streets into the Bowery, Chatham Square, behind the Hall of Records at City Hall Park, and into Nassau Street at last. On certain fine days when birds wheeled across the sky, a crowd gathered around a street musician to sing with him. Those were good days, but there were many more when there were neither birds nor music and all she saw was squalor, children with wizened faces and hacking coughs who sidled out of hovels to the east of Chatham Square to beg for a crust while merchant princes, wrapped in astrakan coats, ordered their coachmen to drive on. Maria gave her own dinner one day to a pair of little boys who lay sleeping in the gutter, their arms around each other to keep warm. Another day she saw two small sisters with one pair of shoes between them. While one wore the shoes, the other scampered in the snow, and vice versa. The sharing among the poor often seemed to Maria to be the one real religion, the one beauty that New York offered.

When the spring came she walked around the parks and stared at tiny patches of green until the spindly trees and dusty blocks around her melted away and she was back in her own New England. Then the cry of "Oysters, come git your fresh Blue Point oysters," broke her dream and she returned to "Babylon" with a thud. Sometimes she went to Washington Square to look at the handsome houses which bordered three sides while New York University stretched along the fourth. She was no part of this fashionable world of ladies dressed like walking rainbows in feathers, ruching, and bows; and their escorts were equally gorgeous with silk and velvet waist coats which, according to a style note in the *Tribune*, "glittered like a case of beetles in an entomological cabinet." Heavy gold chains spanned each manly chest and clinked as the gentlemen handed their ladies over pigs and puddles into gigs or phaetons for a pleasant day's outing to Murray Hill. Maria sighed a bit wistfully as she recalled her own gay outings on the Boston Common.

She rarely wandered north to St. John's or Gramercy Park because they were restricted to those who could afford a key which gave these owners as Maria wrote "a monopoly on sun and air." "But they are so pretty and none of the riffraff," countered one lady. "Do come, Mrs. Child, you must see how sweetly the children can roll their hoops." "Thank you kindly," said Maria, but did not go. The park at the Battery was free, however, to anyone who liked to walk there, and that spur of land in the moonlight held romance for Maria, especially when John was by her side. One morning they were early enough to watch the sun rise over the tip of Manhattan. The clean air invigorated them, and by turning their backs on the city to face the dawn, they saw open water and the green shores of Brooklyn with the light breaking over them. Off to one side rode a graceful ship, and as the day brightened they made out her name, *The Faery Queen*. For the moment all was gossamer and pearl and Maria's craving for the sublime satisfied. It was only later that they discovered that the ship had a cargo of dead hogs.

On summer evenings she and John listened to the music that floated over the stone walls of Castle Garden and once in a while, if they actually had a dollar between them, they managed to go inside where they could see as well as hear from seats well up on the sides of the amphitheater. The

Garden had hundreds of small tables where music lovers could sit for the concert and order ices during the intermission, but such luxury was not for reformers' thin pocketbooks. The music was the same, high or low seat, as it welled in the moonlight; and when Maria described these concerts, she apologized for her enthusiasm with the words, "There are three points on which I am crazy, music, moonlight and the sea." The Battery gave them all to her and brought her emotions closer to the surface.

When the gate of the Garden clanked shut after the concerts, she and her young friend sat on the promenade outside and mused over the days before the Dutch had bought Manhattan from the Indians. In those uncomplicated times there were no hordes of pale children nor jobless men who would remain unemployed and drunken unless they voted the right political ticket nor Negroes beaten down by the only kind of work open to them, the jobs the white men would not touch. Then, instead of stone ramparts, the green forest merged with the blue sea and white beaches stretched around the island like vanilla fluting on a cake.

Castle Garden itself had been old Fort Clinton, an offshore military protection around which the land had been filled in for the park floor. There were three gates now; the center one led directly into the Garden while one on the side opened onto Rabineaux' Floating Baths. For thirty-five years people had been paying twenty-five cents for exclusive dips in the filtered sea water of Rabineaux' barges. It was against the law to bathe in the open water, so that those without the quarter went bathless or trudged three or four miles up the beaches to the East River. Maria, who had neither twenty-five cents to waste nor time for beach excursions, took her icy sponges at home. She was a tremendous believer in bathing, though, and this was why she supported the Croton project in the columns of the *Standard*.

The chief reason for bringing piped water to New York was not so much for sanitary purposes as to lessen the number of fires, which often came close to burning down whole sections of the city. The Hopper house was almost reduced to ashes shortly after Maria's arrival. Fire broke out at three in the afternoon and by five, much of the familiar neighborhood was gone. Maria and the Hoppers worked with the bucket brigade until the heat forced them back to the heaps of personal belongings they piled in the street and now picked up to move to safety. In her letter to the *Courier* Maria commented:

> Our real losses are those where the heart is concerned. I am ashamed to say how much I grieve for my neighbor's little garden . . . the purple irises and yellow daffodils all trampled down under heaps of red-hot mortar . . . and the ailanthus which blessed me the livelong summer.

When someone called her foolishly sentimental, she flared:

> An autograph from Napoleon Bonaparte might sell for fifty dollars but if I possessed such a rare document, would I save it from the fire in preference to a letter from a beloved husband filled with dear little household phrases?

What the scoffers could not guess was that Maria helped that same neighbor to dig and replant the garden.

The fire in Eldridge Street was the last big one before Croton water gushed through the new system in October, 1842. The coming of the Croton was the most important local event during Maria's entire New York stay. It had taken five years to lay the pipes alone, an expensive procedure, but the protests that had followed each holocaust had finally goaded the aldermen into approval of the plan years after it had been suggested. By that time the city engineers doubted that the system could cope with the needs of an enlarged population, but the politicos would not condone an extra cent for water appropriations. They had their election to consider and were not too concerned over the bathing habits of future generations. The public clamor for water had its result in strange ways, such as the announcement of the new Astor House which advertised Croton water in every room, though the hotel's water tax would come to more than $500 annually. Water was a selling point.

Of course it was true that the Tea Water Pump, which was the main water supply for the city's poor, was near Five Points, the breeding spot of filth and epidemics, and that the Pump produced stuff too brackish to drink. The wells of the wealthy were not much better, because the liquid from these turned "ropy" an hour after being drawn, enough to make a sailor queasy. It just might be that the wells had been dug close to graveyards and that the water had a certain graveyard odor. Those who could afford it bought water from the carts that trundled in with hogsheads full each morning and Maria heard the vendors call "A penny a gallon, a penny a gallon," as she scribbled the last touch on a story before putting on her rusty bonnet for the trek to Nassau Street.

The day the Croton was due, the whole city turned out dressed to the nines. Maria found a spot close to City Hall Park to watch the parade. People were crowded ten deep to see the festivities. Even the little Irish housemaids who never had a day off were allowed this time of grace. The governor of the state, congressmen, mayors of neighboring cities, and foreign diplomats were all part of the show as they waved from their barouches. One person of importance

Croton Water Celebration

Courtesy of the New-York Historical Society, New York City

was missing, however—the Whig President, Tyler, whose switch to the Democrats had upset his own party considerably but who pleased those who had put him in office by absenting himself from this New York celebration, which was essentially a Democratic one. Church bells clanged, cannon boomed, and the crowds swelled as the floats lurched by. Each trade and profession had an exhibition of its own, and the printers showed a double entry. On one they displayed Benjamin Franklin's printing press, while on the other, a modern working press turned out copies of the ode which the Sacred Music Society was to sing on the steps of the City Hall.

Maria stood on tiptoe hurrahing for all she was worth as the Volunteer Fire Laddies passed, their dahlia-wreathed engines burnished and their uniforms smartly brushed and ironed. The crowd roared approval at a banner which showed Father Neptune in triumph over flames and at the gallant men who carried it, for, despite poor equipment, the fire fighters did a splendid job and had earned public gratitude. Then the aldermen themselves rode by, patting their nice full stomachs and preening themselves as if the cheers were for them.

As the parade went on, fountains especially set up for the day commenced to shower the parks and dusty squares and to freshen the air. The one at City Hall Park performed beautifully as the streams of water changed in shape from the Plume to the Maid of the Mist, the Dome, the Sheaf of Wheat, the Bouquet, and the Weeping Willow, sixty feet of liquid tumbling, twisting beauty. When the last float was past, the crowd surged toward City Hall for the singing of George P. Morris' ode, all seven verses of it in praise of the nymph Crotona. Morris' ode was expected to be good, for he was the author of the popular "Woodman, Spare That

Tree," but this time, classic allusion weighted every line and someone whispered that the verse was rather dry for so wet an occasion. Maria was not one of the celebrities or reporters who attended the feast after the singing, but one of them mentioned to her that the toasts all were made in water, the glory of the day.

The seven-mile parade had taken two hours to pass and Maria's feet had kept time as the bands thumped out their rhythms and the people sang, but she was relieved to have it over and get back to the *Standard* office and get her impressions on paper while they were fresh, tired as she was from craning to see over the shoulders of the people in front of her. Her copy was full of the fountains.

David came to New York later in the fall and teased her for her fountain enthusiasm. John joined in and Maria was pleased to see how well they got on. She was gay with two escorts, one her long-absent spouse, and when they were alone she could not be tender enough with him. David promised to build a fountain for her as soon as they had a proper garden of their own, and she hugged him for it though the practical side of her nature suspected that the day would be a long while coming. Yet he and John were right. She was in love with fountains, and her favorite was in the Alhambra Garden where a band played in rhythm with the cascade. "You see," she explained to her husband, "if you look at the light shining through the drops, you feel just as if you were immersed in a rainbow." David patted her hand and promised again that some day her rainbow would come.

Maria was not alone in admiring the fountains of New York which so obviously brightened the city. Willis had written a poem in praise of them and hard as it was for her to concur with anything he might say, she agreed that the glow from the lights of the Bowling Green fountain made

even a passing Dry Dock bus seem fairylike. However, a
dissenter called that same jet:

> A fountain that looked like a huge tureen
> Piled high with rocks and a squirt between.

Maria's *Courier* letter scolded the man for his ingratitude.
How could he fuss even if the object resembled nothing
more than a malformed fungus when the water was turned
off? It did spout when called upon, and swans floated on
the pond and deer nibbled at the grass in the park and gave
New York a cool quiet that was rare. Besides, argued Maria,
the ugliest of instruments often produce sheer beauty, and
to her this proved that it was beauty of the soul and spirit
which counted.

Once water was actually available in the town, there was
a scramble to be first to bring it into private homes. Pipes
and marble tubs with griffins' feet, the elegance of crystal
and dolphins' spewing streams were elaborations they simply
did not want to miss. Decorative mainly, because many
doubted the benefit of washing all over in winter, let alone
taking a real tub bath. If the Hoppers could have afforded
such geegaws, Maria, however, would not have used them
unless she were sick. She told Abby, "I seldom take warm
baths but when my system is very feverish and inflamed, I
find that nothing so cools and quiets me." Sarah Josepha
Hale assured the readers of the *Lady's Book* that a bath, of
course not daily but weekly, was good for them, big news
for the average city American who, though he changed his
linen frequently and used lots of lavender water, washed
all over only a few times a year. One of Maria's "Letters"
suggested that New York erect a huge cold-water public
shower to grant the privilege of health through cleanliness
to anyone.

The coming of the Croton gave her copy for the *Courier*

for weeks. She wrote privately to Loring that "if I must live in a city, the fountains alone would determine my choice in favor of New York . . . a beautiful city increasing every year in beauty." Obviously she had begun to feel more at ease even away from David. She admitted as much. "I will answer your question by saying that, though New York remains the same, I like it better. This is partly because I am like the Lady's Delight, ever prone to take root and look up with a smile in whatever soil you place it." When David went back to the beets there was still John.

Someone had to stand by to encourage her, for, fountains or not, her job on the *Standard* was becoming a "demnition grind." She must remind herself daily of her purposes in coming to New York, the Cause, and to be a "helpmate to David, my nearest duty." It was hard amid the bickering of the antislavery factions which became more acrimonious each month, and with the jealousy shown by her own newspaper staff, for her to pour out column after column in the flowery phrases expected of an editor. Whether the subject was Henry Clay and his American Plan, Dickens' *Christmas Carol,* or the modifications in the public-school system, she must garnish it with a paisley of adjectives and languishments. Maria wrote until her vision blurred, her fingers cramped, and her neck was wry. Then she took off on foot to search out more copy and wore her worn shoes still further because she could not afford horse-car rides. Once, when thirty-seven and a half cents had been her fluid capital for three months, the shoes went nearly through, a catastrophic forecast of no newsgathering and no job.

Garrison and his associates never did pay her salary as promised, and whenever a few dollars came from the Society for her, she heard mutters from the other *Standard* employees who implied that she was being favored because she was a woman. John Collins, her archenemy, coughed into the silver netting he wore to cure his chest complaint and hinted that he or any other *man* would have done better with the paper. He did not notice or care that her bonnets grew shabbier nor that for the first six months on the *Standard* her cash takings had totaled all of twenty dollars. Twenty dollars—and the promise had been a thousand a year. Now the first year was far behind and she and David were as much in debt and as far apart as ever. Her sacrifice would have counted for nothing except for the popularity of her "Letters from New York"—and John Hopper. Neither was enough.

She plowed forward, determined on success for the *Standard*. Firebrand abolitionists criticized her gentle editorial tone and demanded dagger thrusts instead of quiet guidance. She countered by explaining that rational exposition would lead more converts to antislavery than violent outbursts. Facts supported her thesis, since the paper's circulation had increased to four thousand a week. Yet the Chapman-Garrison faction added to the pressures already upon her by combining the *Standard* with the *Pennsylvania Freeman* of Philadelphia, which twice had been burned down over an editor's head. They expected her now to do twice the work for the same nonexistent salary, and she went on doing it in the hope of helping David and the Cause he cared for. Yet when Mrs. Chapman demanded more of "the bruising fire of wrath" in the Child editorials, Maria simply set her mouth and answered that she would write as she thought best, that she would stay clear of personal invective, and that while she would work hard, she would not change her policy "for king or kaiser." She had blundered blindly into this antislavery trap but, caught as she was, she would not let it beat her.

XI

The Demnition Grind

MARIA STUCK TO HER DESK AT THE "STANDARD," THOUGH at times her pen felt weighted with lead. But the "demnition grind" was not going to defeat her, not while she was able to lift pen to paper and write. She tried to keep her depression from those at home but it seeped through her letters, and their sympathy often came near to swamping her brave intention. She wrote to Loring one day, "Sitting alone in my chamber, a recluse in this vast city, I get run down and need an encouraging voice to wind me up at least once a week." Less than a week after came a letter from Gerrit Smith enclosing twenty dollars toward her salary, but it was the words that accompanied the money that acted as her "encouraging voice," for Smith praised her work for the *Standard* and told her that the paper breathed a "kindly spirit . . . since your advent." Since this was precisely her plan, she was pleased.

Such praise was rare, however. Even Wendell Phillips failed her now; when she wrote to him that her very arms ached with holding up the *Standard*, he countered by saying that her newspaper policy was too tame and that he could not make out why she was so "melancholy."

Where's all your spirit and what shall be done to prove that
Massachusetts who gives all the money and does all the work
for the Cause and quarrels enough to suit anybody but a
Connecticut pedlar, idolizes thee? Thou wert made for the
Standard and the *Standard* for thee. We *do* appreciate the
effort, and the self-denial which it costs you. . . . There, God
bless you, Standard-bearer; may thine arm not faint while
with such right good will Massachusetts holds it up.

Her failure to recognize his affectionate regard for her and
her labors proved how deeply she was committed to
despair. She denied that Massachusetts supported either her
or her arm and she doubted that anyone anywhere, except
for poor John, idolized her. Her self-pity swelled until she
doubted even David's love, for they had been so long apart.
His insolvency tied her to this miserable existence, and only
for him would she allow herself to be ground up for a
"cursed reform."

The woman was on the ascendant over the reformer.
Separation from David grew more bitter as the nineteenth
of October, their wedding anniversary, approached. She
determined to be with him even if it meant borrowing the
fare for the trip. Again she wrote to Loring: "It is better to
be dead outright, as not to have somebody to love and somebody you've a right to love." John Hopper was one floor
beneath her bedroom as she strained toward Northampton
and her husband, and Maria was a woman more than usually
affectionate and in need of her husband to counterbalance
the pressures of New York and make her whole again. She
tried to visualize David's face, but the image blurred and all
she could see was a tall, stooped figure with deep lines where
a face should be. She wanted him—she wanted to be alone
with him in that ugly shanty they called home.

There were too many pricks and prods in New York for

her to remain stable. Desperately she wrote again to Loring:

> What shall I do? The temptation is to quit reform but that
> is of the devil, for there is clearly more work for me to do in
> that field. I suppose I must go on casting a loving, longing
> look toward the star-keeping clouds of mysticism . . . while
> with busy hands, I row the boat of practical endeavor. I wish
> I were at one with myself.

Always the two Marias. She dreamed of stars and love until
a chill of mood thudded her straight to earth. Whenever she
could, she had sent Loring as her Boston attorney a few
dollars toward lifting David's burden of debt to her father,
and she had asked the lawyer to get a receipt each time from
Mr. Francis, because the old gentleman's memory was not
to be trusted and she would not want James ever again to
be able to say that the Childs had not tried to pay what they
owed. The nineteenth of October drew closer; no salary
and no story payment appeared, and she still needed the
carfare. She borrowed it at last from James Gibbons, wrote
enough editorial material for the *Standard* for her absence,
and set out for Northampton brimming with love and
excitement.

Home fell far short of her hopes. David was thin and worn,
the house more dreadful than ever, and she spent half of
her holiday in trying to straighten out both problems.
David's coats were out at the elbows and his toes poked
through his stockings and she had not time enough to go
out to the barn to see the new calves. Evidently David himself was beginning to live like an animal, what with neglect
of his home and self. He had used up most of the provisions
without laying in more for the winter because, like the grass-
hoppers, he never worried about the future as far as his
personal comfort was concerned. He just drifted. Maria or
someone else would see to his necessities.

How he had changed since she left! Nowadays, perhaps because he was run down and weary, he acted almost bored by her flights of mysticism or her accounts of the Hoppers. She blamed the farm with its vile odor of rotted beet scum, cooking sugar, and his odious routine for the loss of his affection. Was it possible that he was content to live out here with rough workmen and beasts—he, a scholar of the classics—while her need to seek beauty was as strong as ever? Had they drifted so far apart? She clung to the memory of Roxbury and of their courtship and tried to feel that nothing had changed.

She found a colored "goody" to clean, wash, and cook for him, give him one good hot meal daily and watch over the new stock of supplies so that he would not give them away. Then Maria attacked the house like a whirlwind. She stripped the rooms of the last ornaments rather than leave them to the dust, and her eyes smarted as she put her bits of wedding silver into a little horsehair trunk under the rafters. The stellar lamps, Emily Marshall's gift of long ago, went into a wooden case wrapped in an old flannel petticoat. David would probably not notice the ordinary oil lamps she substituted. Cobwebs streamed from the prisms in the window, but there were no rainbows. She unhooked each piece of glass, wrapped it in old *Standard* pages, and packed it in the lamp case. She hung David's winter clothes in the sun to air, brushed the seams of his one good brown coat, flung tiny bags of camphor and crumbled tobacco into every dark corner, scrubbed out the kitchen cupboard with soap and extra lye, and laid fresh newspapers on the shelves, opened doors and windows to the air on clear days while the cat and kittens were shooed off a pile of clothes she wanted to rehabilitate. By the time she left, the place smelled clean and sweet. Her burst of energy boosted her morale and she prophesied that she would not allow David to get into such a foul state again no matter what.

John was waiting on the pier when she got back, but the first sight of New York in November slush plunged her back into depression and re-emphasized her determination to shorten her exile from David. Those weeks at home had sharpened the ache of longing for her husband and her ambition to earn enough so that he could keep his horrid farm if that was truly his wish. She would simply have to bury her own silly dreams.

She almost forgot poor John's existence while, night after night, she wrote until her cramped fingers could not hold the pen. She met deadlines for the *Standard* and for the *Courier* while she wrote stories, articles, and essays for any periodical that would buy them. The sun barely glimmered on the rooftops before she was at work. Sleep was a waste of time; she barely took the necessary minutes to comb her hair.

There was one interruption that she never questioned. Every so often, when all the city was asleep, a knock on the front door brought her hurrying down the stairs. Whispers, muffled sobs, and the creaking of the cellar door echoed in the darkness. Sounds carry in the night. Alert and ready, she tiptoed down with a bundle of clothes and a packet of food to pass on to the shivering fugitives in the cellar. The Hopper house was an important link in the Underground Railway System, and in the flickering candlelight Maria and John helped to dress and disguise the wretched runaways for their rush to the docks where a ship would carry them to freedom. Maria forgot her own weariness during these hectic hours, and the danger shared brought her close to John once more. The emotional pit was yawning wide again but fortunately she was too busy to notice his mournful expression.

She seldom went to theaters or public functions any more

because, for one thing, the dramatic offerings were too sensational for her taste. The Bowery, for instance, presented a thriller called the *Gnome Fly,* in which the leading role, portrayed by a deformed man with the legs of a two-year-old and thick, muscular arms, alternated between the behavior of an ape and a fly. She did go to concerts, however, sometimes with John and sometimes with a new young friend, Edmund Benzon, lately arrived from Hamburg, Germany. Music could lift her right out of a mood, set her flying in the clouds, particularly when she was with a lover of German Lieder and of Wagner. Most lectures were too prosaic for her. When Emerson sent her tickets for his series at the Tabernacle, she returned them without telling the lecturer the reason, which was that she found fault with the unsubstantiality of his thinking, but she confided in her friends that she abhorred Emerson's "ghastly eluding spectres." She could not agree, at least with her Frugal Housewife side, on his insistence on Being rather than Doing. A fine pass she and David would have come to if she had lived only by Being. "If only," she complained to John, "if only Mr. Emerson would descend from his mental stilts! His essays are about as refreshing as soda water but quite as unsatisfactory." Another criticism was that Emerson had not so far committed himself to support abolition, and she considered his evasions unmanly. When he called on her with young James Russell Lowell, he did not once condemn slavery as evil and she therefore refused to go to his lectures no matter how popular they were with other people.

This was an irritable Maria, made more so by all the old reasons plus a few new ones, including a case of severe eyestrain brought on by overwork. Her eyes were so sore that she was waspish to those who had known only her gentler side, even to Abby Gibbons' children, who had become accustomed to running to her with all their little problems. A doctor told her that her retina was inflamed and that she must rest. Rest! Of all stupid prescriptions. How could she rest? Yet pinpricks of fire maddened her with each blink, her eyes streamed, her nose was stuffed, her pockets bulged with wet wads of handkerchiefs, and the pain was so bad that she wished she could die. She tried to cut down on the work by doing only what was necessary for each day, but her New England conscience pricked as hard as her eyes. To leave undone for tomorrow what she might do today was a sin. Besides, if she were not visibly busy, John popped in with offers of fruit, sweets, and pleadings for her company.

It was not much comfort to know that her eye complaint raged as an epidemic, that William Page, the artist, could not paint, and that Longfellow was unable to put a word onto paper. The doctors prescribed the same cure for all of them—to rest, and since Maria could not afford to follow his advice, she unearthed one of her old homeopathic cures. She bathed her eyes in weak, lukewarm salt water morning and night, and used a salve of sulphate of zinc. She rested when she could, and John, ever undiscouraged and kind, brought "flowers and music with unwearied love and the ever-ready sympathy of a generous heart." This, plus more sleep and the avoidance of work by lamplight, lessened the soreness and improved her health and disposition to the point that she was ready to joke about her breakdown and threaten to raise a small statue to Zinc.

Once she was really better she faced the reality that work alone had not caused her trouble but that the *Standard* bitterness was part of the fault. David, in fact, urged her to give up the job at once; and James Gibbons, who had sacrificed his personal family comfort to keep the paper going, was as disgusted as she with the political trend toward

Third Partyism among abolitionists and the ambition for power that certain of the leaders showed. Maria felt caught between the factions and said that the unpalatable position in which she was held was "just too much for one little woman."

The praise that readers heaped on her "Letters from New York" made up for much of the acidity which the Garrisons and Chapmans had hurled at her. Dr. Channing wrote to her:

> I have been delighted to see in your "Letters from New York" such sure marks of a fresh, living spirit, to see that the flow of genial, noble feeling has been in no way checked by the outward discouragement of life.

He could not have chosen a better encouragement and she set out with redoubled energy to make her "Letters" live. She covered every corner of the city, from prisons to church meetings, from phrenological experiments to valentines. Because of her outgoing sincerity, people told her anything she asked, and she in turn found them jobs, clothes, or food if they needed them. Sometimes her reports were fantasy and moonlight, but a keen eye could discern propaganda for Women's Rights, temperance, and abolition neatly inter-larded. She told James Russell Lowell:

> I *am* a reformer being constrained thereto by conscience, but please, henceforth never think of me thus. If antislavery made me take a particle less interest in the sad music of the moon, the birth and death of flowers, and above all, the rose-colored dreams of youthful love, I would abjure it tomorrow, even at the risk of the Calvinistic hell for my disobedience to conscience.

Her radicalism offended many, but as ever, when Maria wanted to make a point, she cared not whom she hit. She denounced city councilmen and the wealthy men of New York for the number of prostitutes in the city prisons.

> The men who made them such, these men live in "ceiled houses" of Broadway and sit in Council in the City Hall and pass regulations to clear the streets they have filled with sin.

She sympathized with the poor ignorant girls who were reduced to crime and debauchery because men had made them promises they did not keep. Maria's most popular story of this period was about such a girl, a foolish youngster whose head was turned by the attentions of a handsome nobleman until she stole silk to make herself a dress worthy of him and was sent to prison. It was a true story; she got her facts from the prison files and from Friend Hopper who, after making the young man pay for the girl's mistake, saw to it that she had a fresh start in life and made a successful marriage. "The Umbrella Girl," which first appeared in a "Letter," found a place in other magazines and annuals, and was read and cried over by hundreds of sentimentalists who were sure it could not be true.

The "upper ten thousand," if they had believed her work, would have disdained it, for they certainly did not want to be reminded of the disagreeable aspects of their town. Wrapped in furs, they sleighed down the margins of Broadway or danced at fantastically elaborate balls until the sun came up. The Boz Ball in honor of Charles Dickens, on which affair the committee spent thousands of dollars to prove to the writer that Americans could be civilized, was a boomerang, because Dickens remarked that the money could better have been used on the Five Points, an area so foul that "debauchery makes the very houses look old." His hosts of the ball weakly countered that Dickens' manners could stand improvement even though he was an Englishman.

Maria's heart warmed toward Dickens for his exposé of
Five Points where she had observed the filth and misery he
so condemned. When a cartoonist sketched Boz dancing at
the Points with, as the caption read, a "great, splay-footed
nigger," she and Dickens were both pleased because the satire
revealed that the Englishman's criticism had hit home. *The
Ladies' Companion,* edited by Mrs. Sigourney, carried an
editorial on Dickens' *Notes on America:*

> His indignant remarks on slavery are the effects of a lack
> of education. He had neither the time (when here) nor the
> judgement to acquire a thorough knowledge on this important
> subject and therefore may be considered as crude and
> prejudiced in the extreme.

It was at the Five Points that Dickens had seen how the
Northern free Negro had to live—furtive, filthy, and un-
wanted.

Dickens was part of the great surge of humanitarianism
of the midnineteenth century, as was Maria Child. The
public generally must have been receptive of Maria's stories,
many of which were full of loathsome detail of crime and
disease, would not have found so ready a market. Or was
it her chatty style of journalism on contemporary scenes and
events? The New York papers copied her "Letters" from
the *Courier* and the new *Tribune* used them to advance
grotesque little Horace Greeley's plans for social reform.
That pint-sized dynamo was impatient to get things done,
especially in Five Points, and used her colorful copy as
spadework to impress politicians and philanthropists.

On Christmas Day Maria and James Gibbons went to
the Points with baskets on their arms. As they walked, the
church bells at St. Marks rang out Christmas greetings and
neighbors called good cheer from house to house. During
the half-mile stroll, they caught whiffs of delicious roasts

and Christmas puddings. The air was crisp and dry, the sky was blue, and Christmas walked with them.

How different when they reached the Points—intersection of White, Bayard, Elm, Canal, and Pearl streets, where the grog shop stood and grimy little boys kicked at the drunkards that lay in the gutter. Cold though it was, the area stank and beggars lolled in their rags in the doorways. Mr. Gibbons doled out cakes from his basket to children who had never tasted sweets before, let alone had a whole piece to themselves, while Maria tried not to show how she shrank from their sore and scabby touch. Sharp blows from his contemporaries stopped any child who tried to grab for more than his share, and parents, dazed by kindness that was foreign to Points way of life, simply stared. One poor Irish father rubbed his head and exclaimed: "Did my eyes ever see the likes o' that? A gintleman givin' cakes to folks he don't know and niver askin' for a bit o' money for the same."

Gibbons and Maria, with her full basket, went into one of the tenements where the wind whistled through the walls, but the atmosphere was "morally and physically . . . like an open tomb." A mother lay on the floor with her three-day-old baby wrapped in borrowed rags, and, while the child wailed with a thin cry, a neighbor fed its mother a greasy, gray broth with the only spoon in the house. Maria shivered in her own shabby cloak, unloaded her entire basket on the spot, and hurried out with a promise to return soon with help. She thought her lungs would burst of the stench and her heart with pity, but she went back later in the day fully loaded with warm blankets, food, and baby clothes.

Her Christmas ramble resulted in an effectively sad "Letter," but she could not fall asleep that night. In the darkness she saw a procession of bony babies and haggard parents, cold, starving, and so alone in the great city. Out in the street the noise of merrymakers gradually died down and the sleighbells quieted. Maria got up to look at the falling snow, and through its dimness she saw a constable drag away a fellow who continued to bawl Christy's minstrel song, "The Belle of Baltimore." "Oh, I squashed the tender 'fections of my bloomin' Belle of Baltimore . . . hey, leggo my coat and les' find another drink," yodeled the singer. "You'll be gettin' yer drink in the city jail, me bucko," the constable gritted as he struck viciously. It was a poor ending for a Joy-to-the-World day.

The twenty-sixth of December, after the revels had ended, the Temperance Society made real headway. The Washingtonians had agents on every strategic corner to catch the shamefaced revelers, get them into a singing mood, and sign them up. "The Rum-Seller's Lament" was a fine number and familiar to most with the tune of "Dear, Dear, What Can the Matter Be?" while "Will You Sign the Pledge?" was known popularly as "Will You Come to the Bower?" Most stirring of all was the "Washingtonian Banner," sung to the melody of "The Star-Spangled Banner." There were plenty who wished they had been more temperate the day before, or who were still tipsy enough to sing out loud. All of this Maria reported faithfully to the *Courier*.

There was one event which she did not fully reveal to her *Courier* readers as being perhaps too fantastic, too mysterious, for a chatty news commentary. This was the full story of Mary Rogers, that pathetic little perfumery worker who was murdered in Weehawken. A blind girl who had been "magnetized" saw the killing in a hypnotic trance and gave the testimony to the police, who brushed it off and announced a verdict of death by "persons unknown" despite the medium's insistence that Mary's lover had first raped, then murdered her. To Maria with her Swedenborgian belief in second sight or thought transference, the police themselves were blind in their refusal to see truth wherever it was offered them. Edgar Allan Poe's version of the story, "The Mystery of Marie Roget," was not nearly as weird as the truth.

Then came the Colt case, and this one she reported entirely. She needed no second sight to know that murder had been done. John Colt had stabbed the printer, Adams, in cold blood, hacked up the body, salted the pieces and stuffed them into a trunk, which he consigned to himself under a false name, aboard a steamer bound for New Orleans. Maria, though she abhorred the crime, did not want Colt to hang, because she felt that the execution made a murderer of the hangman. The man-made law, she said, opposed God's own. She tried to intercede with Seward, the governor; she pleaded and wrote and editorialized in vain. Shades of the Spanish pirates, she was no more successful in this case than she had been in the other! Neither she nor the reporters for Bennett's New York *Herald,* who almost engineered Colt's escape, could save him from death that day.

Maria stood in the crowd outside the Tombs Prison waiting for the latest word on the execution and she saw the mob try to tear passes to the show out of one another's hands —passes which read: "You are respectfully invited to witness the execution of John C. Colt," as though it were some kind of spectacle. The blood lust in the combatants' eyes disgusted her, and she held the arm of one gray-haired woman who was about to bash her reticule over a ticket holder's head to get his bit of paper away from him. "Would you feel so if John Colt were your son?" she asked the woman. Shocked, the other shook her head as though to clear it, and color drained from her face. "Dear Lord, for-

give me," she faltered, and walked sickly away from the
scene. Yet those who remained were disappointed when the
news leaked out that Colt had killed himself by slashing his
throat with a knife that had been smuggled in. Maria wrote
to the Brook Farmers to find a place for Colt's widow and
son but there was no spot available. Nevertheless Colt's
brother Sam, later to become the revolver king, never forgot
Maria's kindness, and showed his gratitude with generous
donations toward her abolition cause.

It was an exciting time to be in the city, but even so,
Maria could not fill the void of homesickness for the New
England way of life. The Hoppers' new house on Grand
Street was larger and more comfortable than the burned one
but it still gave Maria no space of her own to entertain. Mr.
Hopper was genial enough and glad to welcome her friends,
but she craved the flights of fancy in her conversation, far too
exotic for that plainest of Friends, whose conversation, like
his furniture, was solid and unadorned. When Whittier or
the others from home came to see her, they waited bolt
upright on the black horsehair sofa in the parlor until she
put on her bonnet and then escorted her to the Tappans' or
other mutual friends. Maria's domestic leanings were
frustrated with no parlor of her own but she enjoyed
Whittier's company whenever and wherever she saw him.
The poet, with his burning eyes and helpless air, had a way
about him that women could not resist and his frail health
gave Maria an excuse to mother him. His blend of poesy
and practicality was exactly the right diet for her, for
Whittier combined reform, poetry, and politics satisfactorily.
He and Maria spent evenings with Lewis Tappan and
Charles Marriot, another Friend who had been disowned by
the Cherry Street group, mulling over antislavery problems,
encouraging Maria's *Standard* policy, and wondering at the

increasing factionalism in the antislavery partisans. They were terribly concerned over a rift that daily loomed more unavoidable. The men tried to compliment Maria for her editorial work possibly with the thought, malewise, that a few kind words were all she needed to keep her going, but they could not have been more mistaken.

Other visitors to Grand Street were the Osgoods, neighbors from Roxbury. Maria wrote to Loring: "Mr. Osgood had a delicate moustache resting on his chin like a fairy moss which a zephyr had wafted there and might blow off again . . . rather a ghost of a moustache," the only light note in her mail for weeks. Reminders of Roxbury and the old, uncomplicated days of her marriage dispirited her further, and she wondered if she had sacrificed her happiness for a misdirected purpose, if the golden-haired Mrs. Chapman, who had urged her in the beginning to "pour oil on troubled waters" of the *Standard* and now was all for controversy, was the true reason for Garrison's loss of interest in the paper. Mrs. Chapman obviously had him under her thumb. Maria had formerly considered Mrs. Chapman one of the most remarkable women of her time and had been amused when Harriet Martineau had described her as being very tall. "Miss Martineau evidently measured her by the soul," Maria commented then, but the picture was distorted now and Maria said that Mrs. Chapman was Garrison's "evil genius and acted her own plans through him and that she could magnetize the Devil himself." Whittier, though he appreciated beautiful women, no longer spoke to Garrison's "evil genius" at all.

The most welcome visitor of all should have been David, and would have been too, if he had not brought disagreeable news—the forced sale of their furniture and most of their personal belongings for bankruptcy. All the things she had

so carefullly packed away were gone except for her love
rings and a few books. The farm was there but it remained
in her father's name. David brought bad news and found a
packet of it for him on his arrival. It began to appear that
the *Standard* itself might have to suspend publication
because the accounts showed that even with the increased
circulation there was not enough backlog for salary arrears
for the printers and typesetters. Maria's argument was that
the paper could succeed with a business manager, one who
knew efficient business practice, not she with her head half
in the clouds of mysticism. She refused to go on with the job
no matter how Gibbons and the others connected with the
paper pleaded with her. "I am willing," she said, "to take
any kind of position as long as it has no connection with
the antislavery treadmill."

She finally agreed to stay on until a new editor-manager
could be found and then go back to free-lance writing. The
editorial experience had taught her to keep free of organized
reform. She lashed at Mrs. Chapman:

> In the first place I feel no vexation. I know not where you
> received the impression that I was so sensitive to the opinion
> of others. I care not the turning of a copper whether the
> Channingites or the Quakers approve my course or not—and
> I care as little whether the Chapmanites and the Garrisonites
> . . . give me a blowing up. I am glad they should do it if it is
> any relief to their minds. Every day I live, I thank God more
> and more that He gives me the power and the will to be an
> *individual*.

No Philothea, no mysticism, no moonbeams here but an
angry, determined woman.

David had never seen his wife behave so. Her illness must
have been worse than she had written to him, for her eyes
were still red-rimmed and puffy, her hair lusterless, and her

hands given to quick, nervous flexing. She flushed and paled easily, while sudden noises made her shiver. He begged her to give up the job then and there but she had given her word; and besides, thanks to the bankruptcy, she wanted more than ever to try to salvage a part of the salary due her. David's deficiency in business matters was an undeniable fact, an "incurable flaw," as she confided to Mrs. Shaw.

He, completely routed by her disappointment and disregard for his expressed wishes, went back to Massachusetts while she finished her stint on the paper. After he left she discovered that Loring had withheld four hundred dollars which the Anti-Slavery Society had finally raised to help out the Childs. He had held it back to keep David from using it for experiments. Maria demanded furiously that Loring send it on immediately and allow her in the future to make her own decisions about her money. She flared that her purpose in working in New York had been to help David, "the best and kindest of husbands," and that their immediate need for cash was to settle old accounts, not to set up new experiments. She was too fond of Loring to whip him verbally with the fact that the money might have saved some of her precious keepsakes from the auctioneer's hammer.

Loring's implications stung her to think analytically, and a few days later she wrote to him to say that she had decided to separate her earnings from David's from then on "in self-defense to pursue my own way without reference to his whereabouts or whatabouts." Henceforth her husband would have to finance his bubbles himself. Bitterly she added, "Water pumped into a sieve for fourteen years is enough to break the most energetic spirit."

John Hopper, her business adviser in New York, may have been slightly responsible for her change in attitude, for she made it clear all around that she hoped to resume her literary life to live permanently in New York in a household made up of David, John, and herself. She ignored what other people would think of this setup.

She announced her resignation from the *Standard* in June, 1843, in explanation of her efforts to keep her promise of "diligence and fidelity and respect for the freedom of others"; and though she had made mistakes, none of them had originated in personal or partisan feeling. She reiterated her lack of faith in the political trend of the antislavery movement and complained that she personally had been pulled to pieces for the moderation she had practiced in preference to intrigue and duplicity. She regretted that she had pleased no one, not even those to whom she was most sympathetic. In closing she said:

> To those friends who have urged me to remain at the post which from the beginning had been most irksome to me, I return cordial thanks for their kind and encouraging words. To all their arguments I briefly answer that the freedom of my own spirit makes it absolutely necessary for me to retire. I am too distinctly an individual to edit the organ of any association.

That was to be her valedictory. Her hurt was deep and she turned her back on the *Standard* and vowed never to write another line for it. She was done with the dreary round of the "demnition grind."

XII

Her Carriage Passes

MARIA WAITED FOR THE NEW EDITOR IN AN UNEASY STATE of mind. For one thing she still held that her methods of moderation were wiser than the fire advocated by Mrs. Chapman and she resented any intimation that a *man* would do a better job. For another, the person chosen to represent the best interests of the Anti-Slavery Society was none other than David Lee Child, her husband. Maria had fought against his acceptance of the offer, not because of hurt pride, but because she thought it had been bad enough that one of them had been caught in the *"Standard* trap." The only difference between then and now would be that the Society would owe back salaries to both of them. Moreover, she doubted that David in the long run would please the backers any better than she. He had proved himself a capable editor, writing-wise, with the *Massachusetts Whig Journal,* but how could he, of all people, save the *Standard* from financial disaster? As she had told them baldly, they needed a businessman—a business manager, not a new editor.

She was wary on another score. She and David had been apart for two years with very brief exception, and, though she had worked herself into a breakdown to bring them together again, she was frightened of the changes in both of them. Living in a house not their own, adjusting to the Hoppers' habits, getting used to their new selves, and with John thrown in for good measure. . . . It had been hard enough when they had lived with her father in Northampton. Besides, she would have to accept the fact that David was in charge in Nassau Street and that she must keep her ideas on that score to herself. She prayed for the wisdom of Athena and the sophistry of a Delphic oracle to save their marriage.

How would the Hoppers take to David? His constant classical jokes or sarcasms would puzzle her landlord, who spoke as he thought, straight out. Would these plain Quakers think David was flaunting his intellectuality? Would Friend Hopper, wise though he was, perceive David's basic insecurity? Would John and David get on? She loved all of them, and she told herself sternly that long ago she had said she could accomplish anything to which she set her will. This situation challenged tact and ingeniuity but it was vital that she succeed, and the first step must be to build up her husband's ego into believing that she fullly appreciated the value of his editorship.

The Society had given David "full freedom to speak on all subjects connected with the Anti-Slavery enterprise," a permission which they hoped would unleash a far more militant abolitionism than Maria's; yet curiously enough, with a swift return of dependence or perhaps wisdom born of tenderness, he asked Maria's help in selecting news copy for the paper. He made her feel that his "little woman" was still of use. She fell in with his plan, but he wrote the editorials independently. As to salary, the Society had voted them $1,500 a year, apparently assuming them to be co-editors in spite of all of Maria's blasts; but the Childs refused the raise, a noble if meaningless gesture, since they were not paid in full even on the old terms.

David's familiarity with current politics, economics, and the international scene enabled him to deal efficiently with the abolitionist factions in the beginning. He knew law and he was neither as cautious nor as conciliatory as Maria, which made the Chapman-Garrison group applaud its wisdom in choosing him. But Maria continued to worry. His vigor might be that of a "new broom," and though he would sweep away the cobwebs, she doubted that he could give the *Standard* the strength its underpinning needed.

Mr. Hopper meanwhile had rented a still larger house, at 20 Third Street, which gave the Childs a separate apartment of two rooms while John continued to live right downstairs. Maria wrote to Loring to tease him with his warnings and to tell him how pleasant the arrangement was. "Am I not a happy woman," she said, "to have such a good husband and such a good son, doing all they can for my comfort?"

Most of her writing now was done in her sitting room, and often as she worked over a story or a verse for her latest book, *Flowers for Children,* one of the small Gibbonses peeked around the door to see if Aunt Maria would stop long enough to tell them a story. The Gibbonses lived a few blocks to the north, on Seventh Street, and the children came every day to see their grandfather and Aunt Maria when she would have them. She made up tales out of workaday incidents anytime. Elves and friendly goblins lived in the round knobs on Grandfather's desk and in the stuffing of the horsehair sofa that sqeaked when fat people sat on it. She told them jokes about what one letter of the alphabet said to the next, bang, bang, bang, all through the twenty-six, and before they knew it, they could reel off all the letters as easy as anything. She took them to the flower stalls in

Washington Square where they learned the family history of roses, tulips, and violets as if the blossoms were personal friends, as was the lady who ran the stall. Best of all, later they could read the stories she made up for them in her books, the ones she wrote just for children.

Maria had other books in mind, though. She wanted to put her "Letters from New York" into a volume, but no publisher thought it would sell well enough to risk his money on a work with so much reform in it. Confident that it would be successful, Maria borrowed the costs from Francis Shaw and paid for the publishing, while her friend Loring proofread for her. Loring risked his friendship with the Childs on this project, for Maria could be a demon over so much as an altered comma; but now she humbly reminded Loring that she wanted his suggestions and that the "Letters" had been mentally addressed to him all along as a "safety valve for an expanding spirit, pent up like steam in a boiler."

Nevertheless she did not dedicate the volume to him. It was John Hopper she chose in thanks to his devotion to her during her husbandless years in New York and with the expressed thought that her public acknowledgment to him might help him in his law practice. Perhaps she chuckled to herself, "This will show Convers and Ellis Loring how far-fetched their concern has been. Would I so honor my 'dear adopted son' if he were in any other relationship to me?" The tribute to John read:

These pages are so deeply tinged with romance and mysticism, that they might seem unfit offering to one who has the crowning merit of the 19th century—that of being a cautious and energetic businessman. But in a city full of strangers, you have been to me as a brother; most of the scenes mentioned in these letters we have visited together; and I know that the young lawyer, busily making his way in a crowded world, has not driven from his mind a love of nature and poetry, or closed his heart against a most genial sympathy for the whole family of man. Therefore, this volume is inscribed to you, with grateful friendship, by

The Author

The "cautious and energetic businessman" looked at her testimonial with his weak eyes and scarcely knew whether to laugh or cry.

The publishers who had turned down her manuscript were furious at their poor judgment for everyone who had read the "Letters" in the *Courier* or the *Tribune* was eager to own them in book form, and the first edition quickly sold out. Booksellers pleaded for her autograph; invitations to balls, soirees, and dinners came from strangers, and Maria herself was overwhelmed by her success. She had hoped to use the *Letters* as a lever to boost herself back into the world of literature, but she had not dreamed of immediate success. C. S. Francis, her publishers, urged her to plan a second series, this time at their expense, and because they had done well for her now and long ago when they had been the New York agents for the *Juvenile Miscellany,* she adopted their suggestion with the thought that they would be useful to her to establish permanent literary connections in this city.

All in all, that first year with David back was a busy and productive one, and Maria, busy if not as ecstatic as she might have hoped, wrote to John's Philadelphia sister, "It is a great thing to find one's place in the machinery of life and be satisfied to keep it." Had she found that place through reunion with her husband, or through her withdrawal from the *Standard,* or did she mean that she had attained resignation and a substitute serenity through being able to write how, what, and when she pleased? David must have loomed large in that remark, for he seemed settled for the moment with no windmills for the tilting, and she wrote again to Miss Hopper that she had long ago given up the idea of being happy but "am contented with my lot." The truth was that Maria enjoyed misery and, like many of her contemporaries, may have thought it romantic and ladylike to appear so. Had life gone smoothly, she would have found it unendurable. With her belief in the unreal and the occult, it was as if she knocked on wood for luck when she mentioned her "contentment."

More than fifteen hundred copies of the *Letters* sold in the first four months and a hundred more were on order for a second edition, so that Mr. Shaw's loan was secure. The critics either condemned or praised her work but none were lukewarm about it. One said that her sincerity was so penetrating that it went straight to the heart of the reader while the Transcendental *Dial* called the *Letters* a "contribution to American literature, recording in a generous spirit, and with lively truth, the pulsations of one great center of national existence." Others objected to her style, to "the overrefinement of the language of the streets." Would the ragged drunk of her second letter have pleaded so nicely, "Oh, don't take me to the Police Office, please don't take me there," or would he not have talked like the tough he was? One reviewer pointed out that Mrs. Child's sentimentality weakened the force of her work while another fussed because she was not sentimental enough. Logically, the severest criticism came from anti-abolitionists, which made Maria's triumph all the sweeter.

Nevertheless she kept her head in the face of all the furore and refused most of the invitations that poured in each morning rather than again be hurt by a change in the public climate toward her. She had enough ideas for writing

to fill every possible hour of the day without wasting time
on a fickle society, and she was convinced that her ability
to write was at its peak. She dreamed one night of a road
dense with people, milling, swarming, silent, when suddenly
a voice rang out, "Make way there. Let Mrs. Child's carriage
pass."

Whether she dreamed or daydreamed her vision, there
was truth in it. The editors of *Sartain's Union Magazine,*
Poe's *Broadway Journal,* a dozen gift books and annuals
begged her to contribute to them, and Park Benjamin wanted
some of her work for his *New World,* an offer she declined
on the ground that he was "a doubtful paymaster." Her
Second Flowers for Children was off the press, a book of
verses on sights familiar to any young New Yorker, such as
"The Boy's Song to Croton." She also published her *Christ
Child and Other Stories* and sent stories to the *Liberty Bell,*
the *Anti-Slavery Almanac,* and various abolition papers; but
no matter how much she produced, she and David were still
in debt.

David too was writing, much of it outside of his *Standard*
stint. Park Godwin, at Maria's request, placed two of David's
tracts, the first on the Texas Revolution based, according to
Maria, "on historical, not poetical facts," the second, "The
Taking of Naboth's Vineyard." With husband and wife
writing simultaneously, their pens could scratch companion-
ably together, and later David read what each had written
while Maria mended. David's lean frame seemed forever
to be coming through his clothes, and Maria darned history
and children's jingles into her handsome patches. Sometimes
too they entertained, in their sitting room, friends such as
Theodore Parker, Lowell, and Bronson Alcott, who came
together to Third Street. Maria liked young Lowell and
respected Alcott's educational theories, though she con-

sidered the man downright peculiar for bragging that his wife had proposed to him. Theodore Parker she could admire without reservation for his limitless learning and curiosity and his mastery of fifteen languages. His collections of miniature bears in wood, plaster, metal, and ivory showed that the man was human as well as erudite. All in all, she spoke of him as the greatest man alive. In Parker and in Maria Child, Transcendentalism was mixed with some pretty earthy matter, for though the only collection she could afford was rainbows, she and he were aware of the value of the "boat of practical endeavor."

One evening David and John went off for a transcendental confab with Lowell, Alcott, and William Henry Channing. David, who never could abide these vague discussions that got nowhere, came home early with a headache and the comment that he did not know what they had been fussing about. "Well, what did they discuss?" she asked, wishing that she had been there. "I don't know," he answered crossly. "Can't you recall any of it?" she persisted. "Very well. I'll sum it up briefly for you and go to bed. Lowell divided man into three states, the disconscious, the conscious, and the unconscious. The disconscious is the state of the pig, the conscious is baptism by water, and the unconscious is baptism by fire. Good night."

"But David, how did the discussion affect your mind?" she asked. "I tell you, after I heard them talk for a few minutes, I'll be cursed if I knew whether I had any mind at all," and off he stormed upstairs.

John had stayed behind to hear the conversation to the finish and Maria waited to hear his report. He told her, "They put my mind in a devil of a muss and I wish they'd stayed at home." "But why, John? Why did their talking upset you? What did they talk about?" "They didn't know themselves, so how should I?" he answered, and then added, "Dr. Channing seemed to think there was some connection between mind and body but those Boston folks, as far as I could understand them, seemed to think the body was all damned sham."

John blushed and took off his thick glasses to clear them, embarrassed that he should have spoken in such terms to Maria of all people; but she, instead of being offended, thought his and David's reaction hilariously funny. John was sure she was laughing at him and stalked away. Now both of her men were annoyed with her. It was good to find David still awake and get him to laugh with her.

The next morning when Friend Hopper's cowbell called them to breakfast, Maria was gentle with John. "You know, people frequently call me a transcendentalist," she said, "but some of this talk puzzles me too. There are people, very intellectual ones too, who mystify me in the strangest fashion. After talking to them, my spirit always has to bite its finger to know whether it exists or not, and even then, the question arises whether a sensation *is* a sensation." And John, who was never quite sure when he was being teased, had to accept her transcendental explanation of transcendentalism as an apology.

The vogue for transcendentalism, deviating from John Locke's principle of understanding through observation and experience to the Emersonian perception through intuition, was too nebulous for New Yorkers. Maria wrote:

New York is in too much of a hurry scurry for all time to "lie still in the sunshine" and ripen such fruit as either transcendental philosophy or its poverty stricken limitations. It never enters the head of a Wall Street merchant that he is personally responsible for the obliquity of the earth's axis.

Gothamites were familiar with the new thinking in a

distorted form and, being culturally self-conscious, had given a commercial tinge to the term of transcendentalism, and to all the other "isms" that gullible masses will accept. Millerism, for example. An old ex-soldier named William Miller had studied his Bible and babbled of the end of the world in 1843. When that year had gone by without the predicted doom coming to pass, Miller refigured his Biblical data and announced that the Lord was due to leave His mercy seat on the thirteenth of October, 1844, and to appear in the clouds on the twenty-second. Maria did her best to calm the fears of some of the simple tradesmen she knew—the cobbler who tried to give away all his boots and slippers and thus win heavenly grace, the poor apple seller who distributed his fruit to hungry children for the same reason. Thousands went mad with that fear. They flocked to dry-goods counters in Chatham Street and the Bowery to buy muslin for their transcendental shrouds, and readers wrote to Maria herself to warn her of the day of doom. She did not lose sleep over the coming end of the world but thought her frightened correspondents deserved an answer:

> If there has been no preparation in my previous life, the effort to make ready in a few days could avail but little. Even if I thought the end of all things so very near, I could see no better way of preparing for it than by purity of life and conversation, a heart at peace with all men and diligent efforts to do all in my power to save and bless. . . . My belief in spirit is so strong that matter to me seems the illusion . . . Death never seems to me an end of life, but a beginning.

Here was Platonism, Locke, and Emersonian transcendentalism with Maria's own inimitable flavor.

Spiritualism was one of the major fads of the hectic forties and one in which Maria became more and more involved. She urged one friend who had lost a child to investigate

Swedenborg's writings for consolation and then perhaps go
to a "trustworthy medium for guidance to contact the spirit
world." She had company in this belief in spiritualism; even
among abolitionists. Garrison was a strong supporter of
Swedenborg's contention that "two persons or spirits whose
affections are in a similar state are near together the moment
they think of each other." Because of Garrison's feeling on
this point, Maria was never entirely out of sympathy with
him and would remain his friend to the end of their lives no
matter how deeply they disagreed on antislavery.

Probably partly to be a thorough reporter for her *Letters*,
she went to séances with hypnotists and mesmerists and
talked to as many of the new witch doctors with fancy titles
as she could, not without being a little convinced by some
of the bizarre demonstrations. When the phrenologists at
the Fowler and Wells' Cabinet on Nassau Street told her
that the bump of justice was highly developed on her head, it
pleased her no end and she paid the bump feeler with an
autographed copy of *Philothea*.

Cures for the body ran neck and neck with those for the
mind. There were hydropathists like Mary Gove Nichols,
who called water the panacea for any ill, and newspaper
accounts of miraculous cures for fever, jaundice; even
broken bones benefited by water, swallowed or applied.
Faith moved mountains or drowned the patients. And if
water would not do it, vegetarianism took over. Grahamites,
Mrs. Horace Greeley among them, who ate only vegetables,
cereals, and Graham flour, served food that was shockingly
bad in the name of health. Again Maria might have been
persuaded by a fad, for she tried to serve the diet to David
with the excuse that meat was not good for his liver. She
did not mention that less meat meant more money for them,
but David was too fond of his food to care for fads or this

brand of economy. He and Friend Hopper continued to invite all comers to the house for meals while Maria and Mrs. Hopper stretched their recipes with potatoes, tapioca, and cereals spread generously over the ironstone platters.

Maria paid their board and lodging, and David, perhaps to protect his pride, ignored the private agreement he had made with his wife which gave her the right to do as she pleased with her money. He would have had to make such concessions privately because the New York law stipulated that married women had no rights financially at all. So he conveniently "forgot" and whose money it really was bothered neither of them for the time being. Early in the morning they whispered poetry to one another until the brick wall opposite their window brightened with the sun. There had been a time when Maria, pining for the nearness of her David, had seen brick walls as ugly as "the shining face of a heated cook." Now, in these moments, lying relaxed and satisfied beside him, she thought even brick walls were beautiful.

Christmas filled them with an additional sense of home, for David had found a sour-smelling, filthy, ten-year-old at the Tombs where the boy had been taken because he was too old for the orphan asylum. Maria cut his hair, scrubbed him until he was "nearly white," and dressed him in clothes borrowed from the Gibbonses. They gave him brand new boots as a present. "Are them boots truly for me?" he stammered as he clutched his gift tight. When they assured him it was all his, "it seemed as if the sun shone out all over his face." Christmas dinner was the best and happiest ever, even though there was little food or variety. They had a child in the house, a child they could care for; and when, after dinner, the boy grew sleepy after drawing dozens of pictures of boots on a slate, he fell drowsily into David's own

chair where he lay warm, clean, and protected. A child of
their own. What a difference that might have made. When he
woke up, he told them he had dreamed of living in a house
with lots of other children and trees and horses and cows.
The poor little thing was lonely for other children. Maria
sighed, but within a short time she found just the home he
had described where he lived "happily ever after."

New Year's Eve came and went, fireworks, practical
jokes, and stomach-aches. She told about the holiday:

> In New York, they observe this festival after the old Dutch
> fashion, and the Dutch, you know, were famous lovers of
> good eating. No lady, that *is* a lady, will be out in the streets
> on the first of January. Every woman that is *anybody* stays at
> home, dressed in her best, and by her side is a table covered
> with cakes, preserves, wines, oysters, hot coffee and so on. And
> as every gentleman is in honor bound to call on every lady
> whose acquaintance he does not intend to cut, the amount of
> eating and drinking done by some fashionable beaux must, of
> course, be very considerable. The number of calls is a matter
> of pride and boasting among ladies and there, of course, is
> considerable rivalry in the magnificence of the eating tables.
> This custom is eminently Dutch in its character and will pass
> away before a higher civilization.

Perhaps she insinuated that the "higher civilization" of New
England's sparce eating habits could supersede the abund-
ance of this yearly gorging, but if the overstuffing bothered
her, she appreciated the other part of the day's custom, that
of bringing all feuds and quarrels to an end. There had been
too many hurts in her own family that took years to patch
up for her not to recognize the generosity of New York's
happiest thought for the New Year.

The early months of 1844 skipped away and then, exactly
a year from David's advent as *Standard* editor, he quit. She

had been right. The post was not for him nor he for it. All hands had condemned him for letting the paper slip from "its former excellence," and because his Whig partisanship "became too gross for any honest abolitionist to endure and he was compelled to resign. . . ." David's own story read just slightly differently:

> For fifteen years I have striven according to my humble means at home and abroad, in public and in private, by speech and press, to expose and defeat these frightful machinations (the annexation of Texas, the intrigues and policies of Andrew Jackson and slave-trading) . . . My position or principles are not changed. The change is in others, not in me. . . . The Whigs, in my opinion, are the only sincere and true Democrats . . . they have repeatedly and powerfully acted in defence of human rights . . . they have shown that, as a party, they can neither be moved by the violence nor seduced by the corruption of slavery.

David had had enough of the petty carping of the Anti-Slavery Society, which by now was so riddled with dissension that its most loyal supporters hardly knew which way to turn. David's enthusiasm for Whig principles was the very reason that Mrs. Chapman and some of the other abolitionists initially had doubted his fitness to carry on as editor. Now they suggested that he had only been chosen because he had been available. One theory about his resignation was that he refused to agree, as requested by the American Anti-Slavery Society, not to vote for or help a political party "which countenances continuing alliance with slave-holding states." Who dared to direct David not to vote for the Whigs? He resigned.

Tremendous forces were shaping the nation. The air buzzed with Texas! The Liberty Party! Henry Clay! David felt impelled to be in Washington to watch the pot simmer, to whisper legal turns to Charles Sumner who was glad for his advice, and to learn for himself how he might advance the cause of abolition. For once he was practical. The Massachusetts Anti-Slavery Society, apparently pleased by his resignation, paid his expenses to Washington to act as reporter for the *Standard*!

The step was the end of another phase in the Child marriage. He was through, not only with his job in New York, but with the quiet domesticity that had meant so much to his wife. His trips lasted one, two, or three weeks. Between times for a bit, he came back to the Hoppers', but she knew that she could not count on him. His awful restlessness once again had begun to gnaw.

XIII

Mrs Child and Miss Fuller

ONCE AGAIN HOME HAD LOST ITS ANCHOR AND MARIA DID NOT
know how to plan for the future. Was marriage, even a part-
time one like hers, worth all the effort and worry she put into
it, especially now when she had put all hope of a successful
career into living in New York with the strong associations
she had formed? She had friends aplenty; some of them, like
herself, were transplanted New Englanders such as good-
looking, redheaded Caroline Sturgis who kept it as a secret
that she was the author of a pleasant book, *Rainbows for
Children,* which Maria edited and was given public credit
for. *Rainbows* was only one of many books Maria helped
to launch, for young authors knew that her name as editor
and her sure touch were as good as insurance toward success.
Generous Maria never refused anyone who asked her help.

The young German, Edmund Benzon, had become one of
her closest friends and was her frequent escort to concerts
by the New York Philharmonic at the Apollo Rooms on
Broadway where the musicians as well as the audience were
expected to wear white gloves. He took her to the opera at
Palmi's, "an extremely pretty little building fitted up with
gilded ornaments and gaily colored medallions," where they

heard Borghese, the lyric soprano, soar and swoop tonally until, one night, the great star turned her talents to begging the bassoons and violins to play on for love of music without salary until poor Palmi could find the money to pay them. The impresario had overextended his advertising and his expenses by hiring special cars on the Harlem Railroad to bring patrons to his house, the charming place which he had remodeled out of a former elaborate bathing establishment, Stoppani's Arcade Baths. Now, to the regret of music lovers, opera was stilled on Chambers Street and Palmi went back to bartending.

And where was John when Benzon took Maria to a box at Niblo's "fairyland garden with brilliant lights, shell fountains and oriental shrubbery"? Oh, John was around, ready to be called, too unsophisticated for elegance but eager to take her to the Castle Garden concerts which the young German, with his more worldly taste, disdained. Maria still loved the Battery for its clean breezes and its memories of her early days in town which John could share.

The most thrilling of all musical times were the concerts of Ole Bull, the Norwegian violinist. Nothing she had ever heard exalted her like Ole's playing, which, she said, came from his soul into hers and "carried it up to worship with the angels." When someone offered to introduce her to Ole, she became skittish and snapped: "I never like lions. I am no Mrs. Leo Hunter. Moreover I am too ignorant of musical science to appreciate his skill," but when Ole drew his bow over the strings, she melted and wrote: "I had no need of knowledge to feel this subtle influence any more than I needed to study optics to perceive the beauty of a rainbow. It overcame me like a miracle . . . I was baptised in music." Bull finished his concert with an adagio of his own and the audience wept and screamed for encores, and when he obliged with "Yankee Doodle," Maria reported:

It shocked me like Harlequin tumbling on the altar of a temple. I had no idea that he would comply with what seemed to me an absurd request. But, smiling, he drew his bow across his violin, and our national tune rose on the air, transfigured, in a veil of glorious variations. It was Yankee Doodle in a state of clairvoyance.

Bull's performance could not disappoint her, for his stage presence was dramatic and as impressive as his playing, and she described his full impact on her when she said, "I would stay in hell twice as long as Eurydice if I might be led out to the strains of Ole's fiddle." His playing inspired several "Letters" for the *Courier* and numerous articles for other publications. She wrote two versions of his biography, parts of which appeared in newspapers and gift books, as well as some vignettes on his musical composition based on her so-called "ignorance." These in turn inspired an essay on what she called "Musical Correspondences," a potpourri of transcendental inference. Further research produced pieces on other musicians, the bellringers at Stuttgart and M. Guzikow, a Polish xylophonist. "Bul Bul," as she nicknamed her untamed violinist, put new zest into her writing.

Ole Bull therefore became another in the string of men Maria elected to "mother." In this case, however, she had to compete with half of the ladies in town who fluttered after Ole and deluged him with embroidered suspenders, jackets and—nightcaps. The wife and children he had left in Norway did not deter the American female susceptibles. Anne Charlotte Lynch, a minor poet but a major hostess, fell deeply in love with him while Maria remained merely "one of the more articulate ladies who took him in hand" and with whom he was consequently more at ease, since they made their designs on him less pressing. He turned to Maria at last, grateful for her quiet sympathy in a bustling world.

He gave her his portrait painted against a backdrop of Niagara Falls, bow poised over his fiddle as though he were ready to compete with the thunder of the water. Maria added the picture to the clutter of transparencies, busts, statues, bunches of dried herbs, plumes of swamp weed, the frames of pressed ferns, and flowers embedded in milkweed down—the accumulation of her friendships in New York. The portrait happily dominated the lot after she asked a painter friend to daub the horrible watery background over with a conventional velvet drapery. "Niagara" was one of Ole's greatest pieces of showmanship, but the painted model was not up to the violin virtuosity with which he played "The Falls" at each of his December concerts.

Maria, an unpretentious figure in her one good black silk and plain cap, held her breath as he began to play. Afterward she was so stimulated that she could not sleep but simply stared at his portrait and heard his glorious melodies until her eyes glazed and she collapsed exhausted. Sometimes she wished that she might go alone to the concerts without one of her devoted young men, for they intruded on her "winged fancies."

They seldom left her alone and her moods increased. When her conscience pricked her for living in New York, when David came back looking tireder than when he left, or when he neither wrote nor came, she drooped. When he was there, she was charming and entertained by drawing out the best in their visitors without dominating the conversation herself. She was a sympathetic listener and she laughed as easily as she cried. Children, immigrants, jailbirds confided in her and had a generous response. To lovers the quality of her understanding was equally precious. A new chapter in that understanding was soon to open. Maria the mother and Maria the romanticist soon would blend, in a design that neither had planned. As Emerson said, "We only row; we are steered by fate."

Late in 1844 Mrs. Horace Greeley persuaded her husband to hire Margaret Fuller to work in New York on the *Tribune*. The contract included the fact that Margaret would live at the Greeley home. Knowing how she liked to queen it, Horace fought against having Margaret for a boarder but had to give in rather than lose the prestige she would bring to his paper. Her book, *Woman in the Nineteenth Century*, was proof that she would give the *Tribune* a literary tone which his own masterful but slangy style lacked.

Why did he not engage Maria instead? She was already in New York, she certainly knew how to write for newspapers, and she had a place to live. The answer was Mrs. Greeley's doing. Horace, poor man, hagridden as he was, had to give in. Those were the days of newspaper giants in New York—Greeley, Bryant, Bennett and Poe and Willis—on different levels but giants nonetheless. Maria was a little giant who knew them all and all of them knew her. Why did he then give in to his wife—this smart *Tribune* giant? For one thing, the Child name was synonymous with abolition and that would not sell any papers to his public. For another, Greeley knew the value of dramatic effect. The truth was that Maria was bread and butter while Margaret was cake.

Cake and trimmings swept into town in the fall and descended on the *Tribune* office and the Greeley house, which she promptly called "The Castle Doleful." Mary Greeley, flattered to have Miss Fuller as a house guest, made no concessions, however, for her comfort—probably not knowing how. The place had no curtains, pictures, or comfortable chairs. The beds were made for nightmares. Mrs. Greeley, dressed as usual "in clouds of muslin and oriental coiffure composed of strands of gold and pearls," bored both her guest and her husband.

The Greeley place was out on Turtle Bay, near Fiftieth Street of the future and opposite Blackwell's Island in the East River. It took Margaret a full hour in poor weather to reach the *Tribune* office by bumping over ruts and cobbles via Murphy's four-horse stage, a ride that often brought on those headaches she dreaded, that stabbed over one eye until half of her head was an aching weight. Greeley was unsympathetic. His own energy in the face of the hemorrhoidal pains that dogged him day and night made him impatient with weaklings who gave in to theirs, and he asserted bluntly that more organization and fewer complaints would overcome her troubles. He told his wife, "Two or three bouncing babies would emancipate Margaret from a good deal of cant and nonsense."

Margaret's answer was to work at home and prove so demanding a guest that Mary Greeley wished she had never heard of her. There were calls for tea and coffee late at night, a deplorable habit. Once the guest came down to breakfast, her face drawn with pain, and Greeley informed her that her headache undoubtedly was due to her last night's tea. Furious, she stormed, "I decline being lectured on the food or beverage I see fit to take," and Greeley was so afraid of losing her, and at the same, so attracted by her, that he stopped his criticism. Mary did not stop, however, and grew less than cordial, for she suspected that her husband, who spent all of his leisure with Margaret instead of with his wife, had fallen in love with his lady reporter.

Margaret meanwhile had found relief from tension with

her old friend, Maria Child. The *Tribune* office and that of
the *Anti-Slavery Almanac,* where David had a desk when he
was in town, were only a step apart and Margaret sent
streams of messages to Third Street in the hope of an invitation for dinner or longer. The two women still shared their
interest in mysticism, in ancient political and religious
theories, in German literature and music, and now in reform,
though Margaret was not and would not be an abolitionist.
Particularly on the subject of Woman were they of one mind
and resented, for every woman, being considered less than
the equal of men.

There was that talk Margaret had with Greeley one day.
"I said to him that women should have full social and
political equality and free access to professions and employ-
ments with men and, Maria, do you know what he answered?
That until I was willing to walk alone a half a mile at night,
my theory of Women's Rights was nothing but a logically
indefensible abstraction." That sneering, shambling, un-
appetizing, smart little man, how he flicked them on the
raw. Of course they would *not* walk alone. No lady would.
It had nothing to do with inconsistency either.

In *Woman in the Nineteenth Century,* Margaret had
praised Maria's heroic support of Amelia Norman, a girl
accused of trying to stab her seducer with a dirk on the steps
of the Astor House. Maria went to the trial, saw the frail
childlike Amelia acquitted, and then not only wrote editorials
and scathing essays on the need for laws against seducers
but found a home and new identity for the disgraced girl.
Not even Margaret Fuller knew that while Amelia had been
living, actually living with Maria for a while, she admitted
being guilty of a number of minor crimes. Maria contended
that the girl's miserable associations had dragged her into
mistake after mistake and that, though she might still be

lying a little, it would take time to erase the shadows from
her mind. This whole incident was the perfect example of
the difference between Margaret the thinker and Maria the
doer. Maria was no so-called "new woman." Rather was
she all woman, kind and energetic in the most practical way
she knew.

Maria believed in equality, of course, but she maintained
that women must be educated to that place gradually and
that this education be based on a firm foundation or, like a
suddenly freed, ignorant Negro population, the irresponsible
masses would endanger society. She wrote:

> For surely as there is a God of Harmony in the universe,
> so surely will woman one day become the acknowledged
> equal and co-worker of man in every department of life, and
> yet be more gentle and affectionate than she is.

It was because Maria herself was so affectionate and
sympathetic and womanly that Margaret Fuller came to her
with her personal problems.

It did Margaret good to go to concerts with Maria, to be
with her, relaxed and natural. Heads in the clouds, middle
fingers calloused from their pens, they listened to Ole Bull
and wrote rapturous reviews and kissed when they met,
because Ole's music broke down any reserve between them.
After the concerts, they frequently stayed up half the night
discussing the reappearance of religious ideas in various
forms and ages, just as they had when they were young, but
now, when David was home, his voice interrupted their
flights with a demand that Maria give them something to
eat, or darn his hose, or come to bed. Nevertheless these
talks were valuable, for a new book was taking shape in
Maria's mind, more ambitious than any she had yet
attempted and based on the facts and theories which she and

Margaret had unearthed. She sent John Hopper back and forth for religious and philosophic books to the New York Society Library of which he was a shareholder, and the scraps of paper which held her notes piled higher and higher.

The two lady reporters often combined forces for their writing stints and looked for material together. With Margaret's cousin, the Reverend William Henry Channing, they investigated the back streets of the town. They explored Murderer's Lane and Cow Alley where even police marshals hesitated to go. These Five Points labyrinths were so foul, so vice-ridden, that the law almost preferred to let the criminal escape rather than be caught in their warrens. Yet these two ladies, in order to give accurate and vivid reports, went everywhere and told their readers how badly the city took care of its poor. Maria signed her articles with her name while Margaret signed hers with a mystic asterisk.

They found their way into the most sordid situations and their accounts of visits to the Blackwell's Island Penitentiary were revealing not only of the conditions in the prison but of the attitudes of the writers themselves. Margaret could break down the most hardened criminal by her compassion and the clever way she phrased her questions, so that they sensed another tortured soul and were able to respond to her in a kind of sisterhood. Maria did not come with questions. Instead she brought a home-baked pie or a warm shawl and the promise of honest work and a shelter once this phase was past. She had the reputation for keeping these promises and doing even more than she said. When Margaret's dramatics were long forgotten, Maria still kept in touch with the women she had helped back to self-respect.

Meanwhile, Greeley, who truly liked his lady reporter's articles, nagged at her to write more and pleaded for her to work out at Turtle Bay with him in the evenings; but she, exhausted after her slum researches, simply could not face either the trip or Mary Greeley's jealousy. Greeley's devotion to her could not compensate for that grim atmosphere, though Margaret had captured the heart of the Greeleys' son Pickie, as well as his father's. Mary Greeley could not tolerate a love in which she had no share. An unbalanced egomaniac, she made herself sick with her suspicions and she punished the child for her faults. Greeley stayed away from home for days at a time to keep his sanity and Margaret endured Mary's tantrums for the sake of the boy until her own megrims forced her to run to Maria Child for help.

It was during one of these relief visits to the Child apartment on Third Street that Margaret met the suave young European who turned her head and heart. When Edmond Benzon brought sleek James Nathan around, Margaret was ripe for attraction. Nathan seemed to embody the ideals she had written about and sought for so long, and he was, in addition, decidedly virile and polished, while music and poetry blended in the compliments he paid her. She took all he offered for truth and rejected any notion that he might simply be trying to capitalize on her literary position. Her ego would not permit her such doubts. The Greeleys had met Nathan and tried sincerely to warn Margaret against the "foreign young upstart," but she put their kindness down to bad nature and refused to listen. Greeley, the same age as Nathan, and bound to his own weird wife, had to stand by and watch the love of his life be made a fool of.

It was clear that Margaret could not entertain her young man out at Turtle Bay and, as in the old days, she turned to Maria. The plain sitting room at Third Street became the lovers' refuge, but since it was the only place the Childs had, they only too often spent the evening with their guests. David's constant harping on the Texas problem frustrated Margaret. She was as well aware as anyone how important it was not to annex Texas and she had said so in her *Woman of the Nineteenth Century,* but surely Texas, Henry Clay and abolition need not be discussed in these shining hours of her love. She tried to suppress David with her lorgnette but he was too firmly astride his hobby horse. She praised Ole Bull's new adagio in the hope of bringing Maria to her support, but Mrs. Child, amused, kept demurely still. Margaret brushed her brow with one frail hand, a piteous gesture to fend off a headache, but no one even was solicitous and the tide of Texas flowed on. Nathan knew she needed hartshorn for faintness but he continued to ask interested questions of David about the culture of the beet, on possible crops for the Southwest, on the effect of free labor in a slaveholding area. David and he examined theories and counter-theories, Maria added occasional shrewd inter-jections, and Margaret conceded defeat.

Not without countercharge, though. From then on, Margaret considered David a bore and openly disparaged Maria's choice of a husband. She told Nathan that Maria had married in haste and misspent her energy on the match. She confided anything and everything to this young opportunist who had duped her into believing herself beloved. The truth of the situation was that Nathan did not want the woman. For him the chase and the victory sufficed. Margaret, the clever, was blinded by her own ardor.

The tragicomedy continued with letters, fervent on her part, flowery on his. Occasionally, after too strong a dose of surging emotion, Nathan had to call for her at Dr. Leger's office where the hypnotist worked on the source of her headaches. The tumult threatened to swamp Nathan at last and he fled to Europe on an assignment which Greeley was glad enough to find for him as overseas reporter for the *Tribune*.

Nathan had escaped but he left behind him a newly aroused woman tortured by feelings that she could neither express nor conquer. Her physical female self overpowered her intellectuality. She went to parties, theaters, concerts in feverish succession to lift herself out of despair, but she was devoured by love. Greeley escorted Margaret in her feverish search for diversion. They went to the soirées at Miss Lynch's, at 116 Waverly Place, parties which were the nearest thing to a salon of which New York could boast. There one found the artists and writers of the town dressed in their best white gloves and brightest wit, each one bursting to outshine the other. Margaret would not have missed a "Poe Night" for anything, for she considered that frail young poet with the burning eyes one of the greatest figures of American literature and she felt that she must hear every word when he read "The Raven" or his other pieces. She scoffed at Emerson for calling Poe the "Jingle Man."

Margaret walked alone through the crowds, for there was an aura of cold about her now. Her gloves were immaculate, the folds and flounces of her iridescent silks hung rich and full around her dumpy figure and fresh flowers adorned her, but she was unapproachable and her loneliness for her lost love insulated her from warmth. Maria would have gone with her to make her feel less lost, but Margaret wanted no sympathy from those who had been closest during the days of her romance, and Maria therefore refused Miss Lynch's cordial invitations but sent a copy of the *Letters* to soften that regret. John Hopper, whom she asked to act as her messenger, was too shy to carry the book with *his* dedication in it, and she had to find another friend to tell Miss Lynch that Mrs. Child never went to large parties. Everyone, from her sisters-in-law on, had always urged Maria to be more sociable for the sake of her literary reputation at least, but she wouldn't "waste the time." And now, when she might have gone to help Margaret, her help was not wanted.

Margaret, who still kept Nathan's small dog and showered all the affection on it that its owner might have received, was finally convinced of Nathan's desertion when she heard of his coming marriage to a German girl. She moved then to Brooklyn, and when the Marcus Springs invited her to go to Europe for an extended trip, she resigned from the *Tribune* and accepted their invitation at once.

At the pier, everyone tried to avoid all reference to Nathan or the years just past and chattered about the changes on the river where square-rigged barks and brigs had lost their berths to steamships. The forest of masts in the harbor had thinned and, instead, funnels veiled the blue sky with smoke. Margaret had spent the night before sailing with the Gibbons family, and all of them, Maria included, were down to see her off. It was August, 1846, a lovely time of the year for a sea voyage and certainly time for Margaret to get away from the scene of her defeat and to turn again toward life. Pickie, the Greeley's little boy, sobbed bitterly as Margaret moved toward the gangplank, begging her not to go. Maria too was curiously moved but none of them could know for certain that this was the last time they would see "Queen Margaret." The ship pulled away and Maria sighed, half in envy of the trip, half with relief that another of her waifs' problems had been eased. She sighed again. Italy. When, oh, when would she too be lucky enough to go there?

XIV

Over the River

MARGARET'S LEAVING WAS THE FIRST OF A NUMBER OF partings. Edmond Benzon found a job in Boston. John found Rosa d'Wolf, a pretty young thing who apparently was more receptive to his charms than Maria had been; and between his position as agent for the New England Mutual Life Insurance Company and Rosa, he saw little of Maria, who commented waspishly on his neglect. Friend Hopper had become an officer of the Prison Association and spent less time on the Anti-Slavery Society. To cap it all, David decided to go back to Northampton, independence, and his minute law practice rather than act as consort to an important literary lady. He was unwilling to call the two rooms, of which she was so proud and which they had painted themselves, home; when he was gone, the little parlor breathed desertion. She wrote to Susan Hopper, "David is still at Northampton selling rocks, and a feeling of sadness very often comes over me that I cannot see my way clear for a permanent home together."

The sole advantage to her loneliness was that she could write voluminously. She quickly finished the second volume of *Flowers for Children,* which the public bought out as soon

as it hit the bookshops. Probably its great popularity
stemmed from the nostalgia which one of its poems held
for all readers, a wonderful, clopping rhythm that sounded
like the striking of hoofs on hard-packed snow. It was called
"The Boy's Thanksgiving Song," but children for endless
generations would remember it best by the first two lines:

> Over the river and through the wood
> To grandmother's house we go.

Maria managed in that poem to transplant the excitements
of her own childhood Thanksgivings when the entire Francis
brood bundled into the sleigh and were whisked over the
"white and drifting snow" to her grandparents' house in
Charlestown. She could remember the tingle in her fingers,
and the welcome of the old people as they stood in the
doorway, and the fragrance of the dinner floated out to the
hungry children. It made Maria feel good to describe those
far-off times to a generation of city-bred youngsters where
the white snow only too often was stained with the blood of
dogs that the catchers had clubbed to death rather than
bother to take to a pound.

Between her children's books, letters for the *Courier* and
her strictly nonorganized interest in reform movements, she
contributed to magazines and particularly *The Columbian
Lady's and Gentleman's Magazine.* Her dealings with these
people satisfied her completely because they paid promptly,
never cut so much as a comma, and gave her the lead spot in
their book, month after month. They seemed to prefer her
work to Poe's, perhaps because, while she did not frighten
their readers, her pieces were moral in tone with enough
moonlight to please the sentimental. She drenched the
public with tears, vapors and temperance, prison reform, or
a tender little anecdote on children, nature study, or an essay
on marriage. She could write feelingly about anything,

because she cared enough to try to make wrong right. She gave of love and hope in her writing because she was in herself the embodiment of her favorite quotation from Frederika Bremer: "The human heart is like heaven; the more angels, the more room."

She dedicated the second series of *Letters from New York* to Edmond Benzon "affectionately and gratefully" for his endless generosity to her causes and his personal devotion to her. It was through her that he had a better position in Boston, through her and Loring, but she felt that she owed him the thanks which this new dedication gave. Because of the variety of subjects and the number of toes she stepped on, critical reaction to her book was mixed. One reviewer called her "fanciful" because of her "letter" on second sight, while another said she was an "honest penciller." Poe's *Broadway Journal* claimed that "these [letters] appeal directly to the human heart because the author opens her own and thus gains admittance to others . . . stories of washerwomen, of streetsweepers and little beggar children interest us beyond the most elaborate history of merely official personages."

Her opinion was devastating on one phase of city life, the "sad and inert women" who stifled under a burden of wealth. "Genteel limitations" were the culprits here to destroy strength of character and make the ladies less than their capabilities could prove them to be. Money, she felt, should widen the scope of her sex rather than clamp it deeper into vacuity. This opinion was not only unpopular with Man the Master, but with the aimless ladies themselves, who felt their position as clinging vines threatened. Yet *The Christian Examiner and Religious Miscellany,* in 1845, carried this review of her Second Series:

. . . Mrs. Child is undoubtedly a woman of remarkable character and the finest qualities. . . .

We should not be surprised if some readers, knowing her through her books alone, should have formed a conception of her as a home-forsaking person with a weatherbeaten bonnet, double-soled shoes, a green umbrella and a huge portfolio, plunging and prying about all the corners of New York City for materials to correspond about. She is no such being but a true, genuine woman. The passion for a wider sphere, as they call it, does not unsex her, nor render her neglectful of domestic duty. It is a great comfort to speak of the productions of an individual who can be told of her few faults, is open to conviction, and loves plainness of speech.

That review struck home with her because so much of what it denied was partly true, especially the neglect of "domestic duty." It was time for some self-examination.

The tone of the *Letters* disturbed conservatives. She stopped at nothing but exhorted society to better itself through music, education, help for the poor, aged or imprisoned and, strongly, through equality for women. All of these reforms must be undertaken in a humanitarian rather than scientific effort, and when she went to report on the Eccaloebion, a machine for hatching eggs by artificial warmth, she said, "This idea of substituting machinery for mothers generates in me some resistance." Thomas Wentworth Higginson said that she was "talking radicalism in a greenhouse and becoming all the more dangerous for its perfumes." Certainly her comments on the Night Blooming Cereus which mistakenly blossomed on a Sunday at the Botanic Garden was a radical gem. To those observers who stayed away because it was the Sabbath, she said, "If there was anything wrong about coming out on Sunday, the flower would have known about it."

The *Letters* found an audience in diversified areas. Emily Dickinson, a child in her father's Amherst parsonage, hid them in a secret place in the box hedge beside the front door after one of her father's theology students had smuggled them to her. She had to hide them because that "radicalism in a greenhouse" was pretty wide reading for the daughter of the parsonage, dealing as it did with everything from mythology to prostitution.

Fact and Fiction, the next book, was well on the way. It was a collection of periodical contributions some of which went back as far as the old *Miscellany.* "Rosenglory," which used the Amelia Norton case as its "Springboard of reality," appeared first in the May issue of *The Columbian* magazine and was so popular that Maria decided to include it in her new volume. "Rosenglory" oozed triumphant virtue in every syllable. Its heroine, poor, beautiful, frail in physique as well as morality, "whose life paths were so tangled that she lost her virtue," was the perfect example of the neglected multitudes Maria sought to help. Other stories in *Fact and Fiction* ranged from Homeric legends to the quaint marriage customs among the Quakers in colonial New Jersey. The public, bored with harangues over the Mexican War, dazed by exhibitions of clairvoyance and mesmerism, welcomed the simplicity of the new book. Maria's friends actually bought the book instead of waiting for her presentation copies, a sure sign of success, for although friends may be willing to pay for an author's first work, they rarely feel obliged to contribute to the success of a fifteenth unless they are sure they really want to read or own it.

Maria also continued her reports to the *Courier* though she missed Margaret Fuller's companionship on these expeditions to New York's unending show. On the blackened ruins of the great fire of 1845, new stone buildings were rising to

erase the city's former squat look. The innovation of huge
plate-glass windows, all of six by eleven feet, at Stewart's
Department Store at Broadway and Chambers, made all of
the other merchants mutter jealously that the glass was rank
extravagance and an invitation to slingshots. The proof of
Stewart's wisdom came in the fine mansion he quickly built
from the profits of his modernized store.

One of the reporting jobs Maria liked best was to tell
about the musical benefits given in honor of notables. Every
week there were several of them but she was especially
pleased when Anthony Philip Heinrich, familiarly known as
"Vater Heinrich," was guest of honor for a successful affair.
Heinrich had presided over the founding meeting of the
New York Philharmonic in 1842 and since then had managed to keep peace among musical factions by his talent for
tender whimsy as well as by his musical taste. He was the
first noted composer to write music based on American
inspiration, and one of his weirdest essays, according to
reviews, found its source in Indian chants. His music was a
distinct facet in the surge of nationalism that expressed itself
in the arts.

"Who reads an American book?" Sidney Smith asked
with a sneer in 1820. Cooper, Irving, and Charles Brockden
Brown had answered him. *Leatherstocking, Knickerbocker,*
and *Wieland*. And Maria's *Hobomok, Mother's Book,* and
Rebels. Now Heinrich wanted to know, "Who plays an
American symphony?" but the answer came slower and
fainter. Americans had songs, to be sure, many of them of
slave origin or adaptations of sea chanties or medieval lays.
Christy's Minstrel melodies were whistled in the streets, but
for the greater part, American music was untried. Determined to make his point, "Vater Heinrich" conducted his
new compositions in the Broadway Tabernacle for audiences

of thousands, ranged row on circular row in the great dark hall, nicknamed "The Cave," because its owners kept their illuminating gas bills down. Heinrich felt that it mattered very little if the audience could not see, as long as the music was heard. He was dedicated to his native-music theory.

On the evening of his benefit, Maria, dressed in her sole remaining good black dress and bonnet, applauding wildly at the program's end, was so carried away by enthusiasm that she hurled the laurel wreath she had brought to lay at his feet, straight at the conductor's head, where it landed with a bull's-eye. For once her marksmanship had been accurate. The audience craned its collective neck to see who was playing ringtoss with the head of the guest of honor, but Heinrich himself laughed and Maria was in such a state of exaltation that she wrote to Susan Hopper that very same night to describe the evening. The letter ended, "God made music and man made dice and cards."

Her happy times were rare, for the news from home was not reassuring. Both David and her father presented problems that time seemed to aggravate. Age was creeping over Mr. Francis like a slow-moving fog, while David's depression over Texas annexation, which had come about in spite of all his Washington lobbying, deepened with every bulletin from the Capitol. John Quincy Adams and Charles Sumner insisted that it was mainly through David's efforts that Texas had been kept out of the Union to that date, but David felt himself a failure. He needed his wife to bear the hurt with him, but she weighed love against the lucrative market she found for her voluminous output and love lost. His debts had corroded the tenderness with which she had written to him so long ago that she could never "go pleasuring" without him. David struggled on alone in Northampton while her career bloomed in New York and she put conscience and love away.

Her activities boiled as the year went on. It was as if she had to prove the value of New York to a writer—to herself. She sold a story a month to *The Columbian,* plus various other magazines; she collected material by working with Friend Hopper and Abby on prison reform; she wrote for the Women's Rights movement though she told its leaders that she shunned official connection with it. She tangled and untangled the skeins of comparative religions with endless patience and research. She reported anything newsworthy to the *Courier* and she gave as little thought as possible to home problems. For the moment her "knight" was out of focus.

So were a number of other things. The house on Third Street was no longer the same haven to her, though the Hoppers were as dear as ever. The element of John's insistent courtship of pretty Rosa d'Wolf made a difference. Maria's reign there was definitely over and, womanlike, when the engagement was finally announced, she pretended to feel relieved and made elaborate references to the fact that Rosa's practical simplicity would calm John's overemotionalism. She confided to her correspondents that his moon-calf attitudes had been rather a bore and that she was grateful to have one less complication in her life. Marianne Silsbee, wife of the mayor of Salem, to whom she wrote all this and much other trivia, tried to persuade her not to withdraw from society altogether. Maria went ahead with her plans. She wanted to get away from the Hoppers and out into the quiet of the country. Her attitude was inconsistent. If quiet was what she wanted, why not Northampton? Simply, she asked for quiet without responsibility, to do her research, cull the valuable from the expendable in her notes, and add to the towering pile of her published works.

She wrote long letters to Mrs. Silsbee on fashions, books, and people. She touched on her own and others' personal problems. She confessed that she envied Margaret Fuller's European journey—the Italian part of it, at any rate—but not the French. "The French," she sniffed, "do not create. They only manufacture. Their culture is typical of the Parisian lady who prefers artificial roses to natural ones because they are so much what a rose should be."

Her letters included comments on Ole Bull too, not on his music alone, but on his lukewarm acceptance of her friendship. She could not understand why, after she had shown him his bust, crowned with immortelle, in her sitting room, he showed no eagerness to see her again. It did not occur to her that the volatile musician might be bored with her gushings and that if he ever needed her, he would come quickly enough. Meanwhile it was enough for Ole to know that when he grew tired of pursuing adoring females, he could always run home to Mrs. Child who wrote such admirable articles about him and called his tone "Ole-agenous."

Mrs. Silsbee, concerned over Maria's apparent loss of attraction for the company of gentlemen, wanted to introduce her to some new ones, but Maria kept insisting on quiet, with no strangers. Critical of Margaret Fuller who entertained Italian and American artists in Italy, she wrote, "M.F., it seems, is so much in love with Italy, that she will not return home until she has expended her last dollar." The two women had exchanged roles. Now Margaret was the gregarious one and Maria the solitary.

John and Rosa's marriage took place toward the last of the year and while they were away on their honeymoon, Maria moved out to New Rochelle to live with the Carpenters, a Quaker family with whom she had stayed years before when David was in Europe. She went to Northampton for

Christmas and returned by ship from Boston over New Year's Day. It was a tedious voyage, but fortunately Edmund was aboard and made the time pass. The fog was thick, and Benzon, with several other hardy young men, "groped their way ashore in a small boat to get their transatlantic letters on board the British steamer," while the other passengers leaned over the rail to cheer them on. "Edmund," Maria wrote to Mrs. Silsbee, "is so fond of excitement that I think it was delightful of him to have to make unparalleled exertions to transact the usual routine of business." "Delightful" perhaps, but she must have compared this energetic, successful youngster to her own dreamy David, who put his energy into one failure after another.

Therefore, when at the trip's end, Benzon invited her to the opera, *I Puritani,* she refused with the excuse that she was too tired—tired from tensions. It had been terribly hard to explain to her farmer brother in Natick, her minister brother in Cambridge, and her father at Wayland why she continued to live apart from the husband she professed to love. She was worn by their sympathy and their criticism and she hated to be torn until she doubted the wisdom of her course. They behaved almost as though she were one of the "new" women. Their attitude rankled, and in the mood of her return from New England she wrote to Mrs. Silsbee, "The more I am brought into contact with the world, the more I long for solitude . . . for my quiet den in New Rochelle."

Once there, it was as secluded and quiet as she had hoped, the monotony of her days soothed her nerves and she enjoyed the "common simple things in life." Her letters told of rest and contentment as if she did nothing but dream pleasantly at night and review her dreams all day; but the truth was that her whitewashed little room inspired her to prodigious writing activity, stimulated further by her frequent trips to the Society library in New York for deeper light on the philosophies of Luther or Confucius. She took her notes on the backs of used envelopes or scraps of wrapping paper and transcribed them later into foolscap notebooks in the box room which the Hopper family still reserved for her as her city headquarters.

On one such trip she called on the Marcus Springs, who brought an ivory breastpin for her from Italy and were bursting with news about Margaret Fuller, whose career as a revolutionary was as colorful and more shocking than her friends could envisage. Maria sighed. Margaret had broken loose for fair, but the dreams of Italy of long ago had not included the violence or blood lust in which she was now embroiled. No longer could Margaret be satisfied with art or literature; she had to be in the center of the storm that swept through Europe and churned the Italian boot into a massive kick.

After such reports, the tame atmosphere at the Hoppers' even with Rosa's inspired piano playing, grated, and Maria was eager for her country solitude. Yet her work did not satisfy her; her research lacked precision and she finally moved back to the Hoppers to be closer to the sources of information. This phase lasted for two months during which she picked up still another "waif," a Spanish girl in need of friends and English lessons. Dolores embroidered ruchings and ruffles for Maria out of gratitude. The delicate bits went off to Salem as samples for Mrs. Silsbee, who immediately ordered headdresses, scarves, and bags at a nice price, which gave Dolores independence from the dour old uncle who offered a home and beating on any occasion. The crimson velvet headdress trimmed in gold thread which she made as a gift for Maria went to Mrs. Silsbee as well, since it was hardly the proper replacement for the plain little cap that habitually sat atop the Child head.

At the end of the two months, Maria went back to New Rochelle, to writing and to reading the new novel *Jane Eyre,* about a stupid girl who deserted her lover out of moral scruples even though she had no relatives like Maria to account to. Maria considered the law which prevented Rochester's divorce from his insane wife to be "tyrannical and a mere figment." Yet a few days later, in writing about George Sand, she wrote:

. . . I do not hastily pass judgement. A woman who steps aside ever so little from the conventional path is sure to be misrepresented. . . .

Obviously what might do as a moral judgment for a novel's heroine was impractical for real life. There it was again, that penetrating everlasting cleavage in her own thinking and emotion. Her life in New Rochelle was a model of conventionality and she wrote to Parke Godwin, one of her publishers, that she "would not give a brass farthing for all the lovers between here and Oregon" and that all she wanted was "a warm blanket, a cup of tea and a warm corner to die in." She was forty-six, and on her black days she wrote as though she were eighty.

Summer past, back she went to New York to work on her religious philosophies and her reportage. The Whigs had put up Zachary Taylor for President, a man who lacked statesmanship as well as any other attribute for the country's top position, and whose party had failed to back the Wilmot Proviso which would have excluded slavery from all territory gained by the United States in the Mexican War. The Whig Party, David's party, had done this, had put forward a candidate unfit to lead America. If she had only been able to vote, her ballot would have gone for Van Buren and the new Free Soilers, and her comfort was that though "Van" did not carry a single state, the slavery issue was at last squarely before the American people.

She was so seething with political frustration that she carried her feeling over into the letters to Mrs. Silsbee, whose own interests were far more taken up with home, carriage, and bonnets, and in the all-important question as to whether one should wear the fashionable "curtain" at the back of the headgear to shield one's throat and shoulders from the sun. Marianne Silsbee cared less about "third partyism" than the compliments which her friends in Salem cooed to her about her pretty verses on seashells and babies. Her poems, bound in gold-tooled leather, were displayed on the best marble-topped tables in Salem, not entirely because they were written by the mayor's wife. If Mrs. Silsbee had wanted to be smug, her old friend Maria's heckling would have reduced her to a grit of irritation. Every letter laced protestations of friendship against anger at that friend's indifference to the evils of slavery and the machinations of the Democratic party. And Mayor Silsbee was a Democrat.

Mrs. Silsbee was generous. She ignored the attacks because she implied that a proper home, husband, and babies might have produced another Maria. Her refusal to be drawn into rebuttal scored the victory over Maria, who could only smart and try again. Perhaps it was this very generosity of Marianne Silsbee that helped Maria to see for herself that it was time for her to settle down. The two sides of her nature were still at war; she saw everything either as black or white, with no blending. Wrong or right, rich or poor, career or husband. She had no choice. Once again she quoted Emerson to herself: "We only row; we are steered by fate." The years in New York had brought new friends and an improved literary reputation, with four books and a sheaf of stories and articles; but on the debit side, her marriage had tottered, her finances were still rocky, and happiness was a mirage. How she envied the young Hoppers, whose union had settled on "deep and sure foundation." She wrote to Mrs. Silsbee: "What is there in life equal to domestic love? How blameworthy is anyone who selfishly mars it by any unhealthy influence!" She asked herself if David would have lost the incentive toward success if she had shown her need of him clearly, if her appreciation of him had outweighed her criticisms of his moneymaking.

David came to New York for a visit when she moved back to Hoppers' in March of 1849. Living in that tiny room was complicated but as good as a honeymoon, for she had thought things through and decided ultimately that being a wife mattered most. When they went downstairs, the Hopper clan welcomed them. David worked at the sturdy flip-down desk with its plain polished doors that Josiah Hopper had made, while Maria sat and sewed on the rosewood sofa and Rosa played softly to her adoring John. The tangles of Maria's marriage began to unwind and she wrote again to Salem:

> Domestic love is the best of earth's blessings and worth having even at the price of many heavy drawbacks, but my little gleam of it at the present time has not been without a tax for I have been constantly harried with making and mending to get David into repair.

Getting David into repair undoubtedly referred in part to his morale. In the early hours of the morning when he lay quiet by her side, she realized that she had denied her husband the generosity she had given so unstintingly to others. When they married, she knew him to be more of a pale knight than a practical man of business, and if he turned out to be more of a Galahad than a Lancelot, the fault was partly hers. She must make amends.

So eagerly did she try to make their reunion meaningful that David decided to stay on for the winter and her joy bubbled over in surges of affection. In that tiny room she could turn around and hug him without having to move a step and she did—frequently. She could share with him every incident in her day while it was fresh. He took her to theater as often as she liked and she was prouder of her escort than she had ever been of her string of younger men. They went to the opera to hear Julia Northall sing, and Maria was pleased when someone asked her who her distinguished companion was. Softened by David's efforts to be as she wanted, she wrote to Mrs. Silsbee: "He is the kindest soul that ever lived and though I sometimes wish he was more mercurial or I less so, I nevertheless love him with that generous sort of affection which his noble nature deserves."

By the time he left her in the spring of '50, they knew they could not stay apart. Though they had not set the exact time or place of their reunion, Maria packed her odds and ends, bits and pieces of statuary and pressed glass and stowed them in labeled boxes in the Hoppers' cellar. With Dolores' help, she sorted the accumulation of nine years' living in New York for shipment home, wherever home might be. C. S. Francis and Company arranged for any future editions of the *Letters from New York* and *Fact and Fiction*, and Mrs. Caroline Kirkland, editor of the *Union Magazine*, pressed Maria to keep sending stories as fast as she could turn them out. Life was settling into a pattern, and strangely enough, now that she had decided to go back to conventional matrimony, her career prospered as well.

The Lorings had a farm in West Newton which they offered to rent to the Childs. Maria made ready to leave at once. She rushed over to the Marcus Springs to say good-bye and to hear the latest on Margaret, who had acquired a husband and child though no one was sure in which order. She kissed the little Gibbonses and made them promise to visit her. She looked at, smelled, heard New York with intensity, to carry it along with her, but her whole being was drawn home to New England. On the eighteenth of April, she wrote to Susan Hopper: "I have been *very busy* and extremely well-contented." Time had set her relationships satisfactorily. Her New York days were over.

XV

Way Station to Home

FOR THE NEXT TWO YEARS, WEST NEWTON BECAME HER WAY station, her point of transition. She was near enough Wayland to see her father, and David came to her as often as he could leave the beet farm, which was on the point of sale. Mr. Francis, to whom the place legally belonged, had arranged for a token sale to Ellis Loring with the stipulation that any rent or income revert to Maria. This was the only method by which the old man could make her future secure, because Massachusetts law did not permit married women to hold property separately from their husbands, even as a legacy from their parents or earned wholly by themselves. The price of those rocky acres over which David had labored so long was one single dollar.

Maria's gratitude to her father, despite this latest humiliation for David, was full and warm. It was delicious, too, to be back in the circle of her old friends the Lorings, Sewalls, and Russells and pleasant to see how they took to young Dolores, who had come to New England with her. Neighbors dropped in for a cup of tea and Mrs. Lowell sent seedlings wrapped in damp moss, from her own garden. Mrs. Silsbee journeyed over from Salem with chandelier drops to hang in the window so that Maria might "have rainbows dancing over everything." The mayor's wife left a second surprise propped against the door—a little pitcher twined with a china grapevine and Bacchus peeping through the leaves. But because David and she were not yet really together, Maria was dissatisfied and admitted that she was still "bogged down by actualities," which seemed to come, as they always do, in multiples. Her namesake niece, Lydia Maria Francis, had died just before the West Newton move, and now, with their twenty-two-year-old daughter gone, the James Francises faced the loss of their son William as well. Aunt Maria's simple remedies could not cure that hacking cough no matter how gladly she would have nursed him.

Margaret Fuller's death was another dreadful actuality. At forty she died as dramatically as she had lived. She had fought for her baby's life during months of revolution and cholera in Italy, but shipwreck just off Fire Island canceled her victory. Baby Angelo's body and Margaret's lap desk rolled up to the beach—all that remained of Margaret, the Marchioness Ossoli.

The Fugitive Slave Law was another problem that pressed personally and horribly on Maria. She believed that Daniel Webster had "sold his soul to the Devil," by which devil she meant the South, in order to assure his nomination to the Presidency. She called it a "diabolical law . . . by which the citizens of Massachusetts were converted into slave-catchers." Even Emerson, no active abolitionist, raved, "This filthy enactment was made in the nineteenth century by men and women who could read and write. I will not obey it, by God." Whittier raged that no civilized man could sub-scribe to the law any more than he could be a cannibal. There were many who spoke and ranted and wrote against it, but even in Massachusetts there were others who favored it; and on the day the law became legal, Boston greeted it with a salute of a hundred guns.

New Underground Railway Stations sprang up and the "lonesomest travellers," as poets called the runaways, were sheltered in schoolhouses and cisterns, ballrooms and huts. Like Theodore Parker who wrote sermons with a pistol on the desk beside him to defend fugitives who had come to him for help, Maria risked her safety to feed, clothe, and guide the helpless to freedom. "How any man who upholds that abominable law can call himself religious!" she sputtered to David. "It is those who live their religion, not those who talk about it and buy a new bonnet for Easter services, that truly walk in the way of God." Her study of religions of the past and her hatred of bigotry deepened her convictions and made her strong on those dark nights when a tap at the back door called her to serve.

The case of Thomas Sims in April, 1851, brought abolitionist fervor to a boil. The seventeen-year-old fugitive had been caught in Boston and held at the Court House while a hundred policemen guarded him. A great chain stretched all around the building three or four feet above the ground and Chief Justice Shaw, who was to conduct the hearing, had to crawl under it to enter his chambers. To abolitionists and to an increasing number of sympathizers, that chain was a symbol of Massachusetts' enslavement to slavocracy. The judge ordered Sims to be returned to his Georgia master, and on April 13, at three in the morning, the boy, prodded by the police, stumbled aboard the brig *Acorn*. His long flight from bondage had ended in defeat and only a few onlookers in the dim dawn saw the youngster slump at the rail and heard him say, "So this is Massachusetts freedom." As the ship moved away from her Long

Wharf moorings, the watchers intoned Bishop Heber's doleful hymn:

> From many a Southern river
> And field of sugar cane,
> They call us to deliver
> Their land from slavery's chain.

Capture and hearing had cost Boston $2996.95, far more than young Sims would have brought on the slave block. Nothing that Parker, Higginson, and the rest could do had saved him, because his master was determined to make this case the crux to force the North to obey the Fugitive Slave Law. The men let Sims go and turned back to their everyday activities, but Maria was adamant. The boy, scarcely more than a child, needed help. She raged, "I swear, 'by the Eternal' as General Jackson used to say, that as Massachusetts sent him into slavery Massachusetts shall bring him back and I mean that I, as a Massachusettser will do it and what's more, with proslavery money." Her friends told her that she had finally reached beyond herself, but little Maria smiled bleakly and answered, "It shall be done; like General Jackson, I never recant." Nor did she, though it took a long, long time.

Webster died in October, 1852, after a prolonged illness that made some wiseacres sneer that his bad conscience had worn him to death. Antislavery goading had certainly not helped his insomnia, nor had the kind of remark that Emerson seared him with: "The word, liberty, in the mouth of Mr. Webster sounds like the word, love, in the mouth of a courtesan." Maria added her bit to the torrent of hate that poured over the dead man's memory. "What do you think," she wrote to Garrison, "of pasting something on Webster's statue . . . to rouse the moral sense of the people, some caustic rebuke, hung on his hollow breast every week until the abomination [the statue] is taken down?" She enclosed some rhymes for the purpose of which the third ran:

But for us and for our children, the vow which we have given
For Freedom and Humanity, is registered in Heaven.
No slave-hunt in *our* borders! No pirate on *our* strand!
No fetters in the Bay State! No slave upon *our* land!

Propaganda! That was what antislavery needed, and the pitiful dramatic recapture of Sims was a prelude to the most powerful bludgeon of all, *Uncle Tom's Cabin*. Mrs. Stowe's novel unleashed a whirlwind of sobs, fury, humanitarianism and wicked reprisals on helpless blacks by their envenomed masters. More copies of the book were sold than of any other except the Bible. Hawthorne's *Scarlet Letter* and Melville's *Moby Dick,* which were its direct contemporaries, stirred scarcely a ripple by comparison. The whiteness of Little Eva and the whiteness of the souls of Uncle Tom and even of Topsy were much easier to understand than the symbolism of the white whale or the crimson letter "A." Everybody, but everybody, read and cried over Uncle Tom, and the public's reaction made Maria chortle. She quipped to one Southern acquaintance: "Mrs. Stowe's book carried the outworks of your institution [slavery] and left the citadel open to besiegers."

One night while reading the newspaper, she laughed out loud. "Look at this fool of a man, David. Here's a quotation about Mrs. Stowe from the senator from Maryland. He says straight out, 'Here's a writer who knows how to sympathize with the South! I could fall at the feet of that woman. She knows how to feel for a man when he is obliged to sell a good honest slave.' He couldn't have read very far, or maybe he got hold of one of those pappy expurgated versions that are flooding the South." She had an author's sympathy for Mrs. Stowe, whose work had been pirated and changed just enough to propagandize the South ever more in favor of "Slave-ownia." Dozens of plays and versions of the novel would appear until Mrs. Stowe could hardly recognize her own creation.

"The vile wretch in petticoats" who had written *Uncle Tom* had done more to dramatize slavery than any man, and what was more, she had done it in the conventional, man-encouraged atmosphere for women—in the home. She had turned out her best-seller while she rocked her babies, settled her older children's quarrels, and quieted the fears of her neurotic husband. When a Southern reader sent her a black man's ear as a souvenir of the South's opinion of her, Mrs. Stowe knew that the vision which she had translated into her tale was a worthy one.

Maria's own writing of her book on religions had slowed down. Had she been a faithful, confident churchgoer, formulas and interpretations would have come easily; but since her personal doubts continued to disturb her, she sifted, analyzed and reported her findings as honestly as she could, "let Christians and Infidel, Orthodox and Unitarians, Catholics and Protestants and Swedenborgians growl as they like." Sectarianism was not the answer to faith but fitting of deed to creed, as the Hopper family lived, was truly Religion. Now that she had left their Quaker home, she was more than ever aware of the goodness that had surrounded her for nine years, and her fond little notes on foolscap, stamped in the corner with her own crested die, proved her affection for them.

The letters to Mrs. Silsbee were very different, covering every quarter inch of the paper and any subject except politics, from the sale of a horse to Harriet Hosmer's latest Italian sculpture. That conspiracy of silence about the political world frustrated Maria, and every so often her bitterness gnawed away the superficial pleasantries; for example she congratulated her friend on a new volume of verses by saying: "It is a tasteful selection from the pen of an accomplished lady but its popularity would have come in any case because of your special position." Mrs. Silsbee ignored the thrust but forgave Maria because she knew that it was truly not Marianne Silsbee the wife but the Mayor's politics being attacked.

Soon the Silsbee's little daughter, Mary, came to West Newton for a visit and bitterness fled, while all the softness that was the essence of Maria came to the fore. Mary's mind was still on flowers and fairies and Maria taught her color patterns and the arrangement of petals and how stamens sometimes resembled yellow pincushions and sometimes Maltese crosses. They listened to the *whir-clack* of the male grasshopper, a great showoff, while the female went quietly about her business, and they examined the walking stick, that grotesque insect that grows a new leg if one of its six is broken. Mary found fairies under toadstools and in the beams from the prisms in the windows. At the end of her visit, she hated to go back to the starchy Salem atmosphere, and Maria felt strong in her victory. But so lonely. A house without a child˙ . . . and David still not with her entirely.

Depression might have downed her then, but Frederika Bremer, the Scandinavian writer, came over from the Horace Manns' house with some disturbing news. She had just left New York where she had spent time with the Hoppers and disturbingly reported that Friend Hopper was ill, so ill that the doctors had forbidden him to smoke. Maria took off for New York as soon as she could and was there at the bedside of that good old man with eight of his children when he died. The family asked her to write his biography, a labor of love for which she was glad to put aside the *Progress of Religions*. By November, five months later, her tribute to a true philanthropist, the *Life of Isaac T. Hopper,* was ready to offer to his family.

The kindly Quaker in his plain coat and laced breeches lived again on her pages. His silver shoe buckles shone as brightly as they had after every Saturday night polish, and his children were pleased with her portrait though Catherine Sedgewick, a close friend of the family, complained that the book was not up to Maria's usual form because she had used the anecdotes as he had told them to her without embroidery.

She stayed in New York for several weeks to arrange for a twelfth edition of the *Letters,* and for a higher rate of pay for her stories from magazine editors who were willing by now to meet her own valuations. She shipped her boxes from the Hopper cellar to Massachusetts, impatient to get at the wealth of material for more stories. Besides, with the death of the old man, the link with the Hoppers lost much of its strength.

It was all Ole Bull's fault. He had told her a fantastic tale which her common sense rejected but her emotions could not—quite. According to the violinist, John Hopper had misused funds that Ole had given him to invest in land in western New York. It was only after Ole had put a small fortune into developing Olean that he discovered his title to it to be invalid; but when he accused John, that young man tried to kill him with poison rather than let the truth come out. Of course Maria disregarded the poison talk as being part of Ole's overheated imagination, but for a short time she almost believed that John had mulcted Ole. The truth was that John had asked Ole for a percentage fee for his work, a perfectly fair and honest demand. No one know-

ing of John's innate goodness believed slander of him; but
her momentary hesitation embarrassed Maria into wanting to
get away from John once and for all, a silly and shameful
way to end those years of affection.

Back in Massachusetts, she and David at last found a
home together and they tried not to let one another feel their
doubts. Mr. Francis, old, feeble, and alone, needed care. His
sons had places and families of their own while his daughter,
Mary Preston, had died in Maine in 1847. Everyone expected
Maria to do her duty by the old man and she, glad to be
needed and able to give, was relieved to go to Wayland,
especially since Mr. Francis told them that they would have
private quarters.

Private quarters indeed. A pretty name for the one-room
shed which the old man allowed them. A room no more
than ten by thirteen feet into which light and air came
through a small window. They had to seal the second one as
an outlet for their Franklin stove. A heavy door led into the
kitchen of the main house but no heat escaped through it to
them because Mr. Francis insisted on keeping it shut. Planks
laid over two-by-fours, turned on their sides, barely raised
the splintery wooden floor above the damp earth and the
Childs were soon in torment with rheumatism. David whitewashed the overhead timbers and stuffed the shingled leaky
roof with sphagnum moss which he found in the bogs. Yet
for all their lack of comfort, they loved their tiny shelter.
Maria had the knack somehow of making a home nest
wherever she was, and their shed soon possessed a comfort-
ing personality of its own. In winter the Franklin stove
glowed and kept them cozier than the shallow fireplaces in
the main house ever could. David set pegs into the wall for
their cooking pots and spider, and Maria's deft needle provided them with colorful, concealing curtains for their other

gear. They felt like bona fide homesteaders. The old man could be as cantankerous as he liked as long as they could get off by themselves at night and David kept out of his way at all times. And each morning, when she went to get her father his breakfast, her eyes filled with tears at the warmth in his greeting: "You're welcome home, Maria."

The Childs ate, slept, and wrote in that single room. David, who was one of the town's four lawyers, prepared his briefs there. Maria said, "We are as cosy as two squirrels in the hole of a tree." Her only ambition, she insisted, was to do no one harm. A negative state of mind for her and actually only the mood of the moment. Her ambition was not dead, but contentment had come to her in the knowledge that David at last had her full and uninterrupted love.

XVI

Without a Cloak

WAYLAND WAS A QUIET TOWN AND FEW OF ITS FIFTEEN
hundred inhabitants visited the low-eaved, leather-brown
farmhouse out on the Old Sudbury Road. Maria had no
time to waste on local gossip unless it could serve as basis
for a story, a risky undertaking if she wanted to go on living
there. And she did.

The Childs were thankful to be fifteen miles away from
the bustle and grime of Boston and a full half mile from
Wayland's center. Twice a day the Sudbury stage bumbled
around the curves, but otherwise traffic was light on the
winding road. The house and its extension hugged a rise,
shaded by two huge cherry trees which perhaps were not so
huge as that the house was small. It was a plain, undramatic,
practical place for plain, undramatic living. Fifty yards to
the right and overrun with weeds and brambles stood a
curious, triangular shed that had been built for the winter
storage of vegetables. According to old-timers, its rough
plank flooring covered a disused well which Mr. Francis had
never troubled to investigate, but Maria and David soon were
familiar with.

She always claimed that her writing prevented her from

welcoming unexpected guests, that creative work demanded no interruptions, but Maria had another reason for her plea for privacy. She and David sheltered fugitive slaves in that old shed and looked noncommittal when gossip whispered about a secret passage from the shed to their cellar, but none of the pryers could prove a thing especially since a few shriveled vegetables were strewn carelessly over the giveaway seams in the boarding over the old cistern.

Yet even without those interruptions, Maria would have had enough to do. She and David divided the garden work, flowers her province, vegetables and fruit trees his. Early in the spring he lifted a handful of dirt, squeezed it to see if it would hold together, and the first day it was dry enough to crumble he began to dig. Maria's dooryard garden had priority, so that she could transplant wood and meadow spring beauties; the odd yellow, red, and brown wood betony; rare ferns and moccasin flowers; and a clump of bee balm to attract the hummingbirds. Like her mother sixty years before in Medford, Maria's flowers were her friends.

Tired of digging or cramped with writing or bored with the pressures of father, house, and David, she wandered up the hill behind the house, through the sweet-scented apple orchard and the glen where the mayflowers were loveliest. Baldwin Pond reflected its lacy margins of honeysuckle and pickerel weed, and birds rose lazily from the sedge. Her restlessness subsided as the sunset discovered itself in the quiet water. She called her retreat "Flora's Mirror."

As age made more insistent demands on her father, David's impatience with the situation increased. Perhaps subconsciously he resented the care she so willingly gave the old man, and though she tried desperately to enlist David's compassion it did not make up for the time she spent nursing her father. She was grateful for the law cases and the speaking tours that took David away occasionally so that she could give full attention to the whims and needs of her older charge. Often his gifts of money had pricked her conscience, but his way of giving had dampened any expression of affection on her part. Sometimes she had thought that the money was merely a sop to his own conscience for his neglect of her as a girl, but she had always known he loved her in his way and now that he was old, sick, and dependent, he clung to her. Her mother instinct was aroused by him, her pathetic father.

When David saw that tenderness, he sulked just as the first child does when a mother gives her new baby attention. Maria told him over and over again how lonely she was when he left, and she wrote:

> I have thought enough about my dear absent mate but have found it nearly impossible to get an hour to tell him so. Oh dear! how I have missed you . . . I have nobody to plague, nobody to scold at, nobody to talk loving nonsense to. I do long to have you back.

It was worse for him when they moved into the main house to be close to the old man in case of emergency, or it could have been but for the clever way the house itself was divided, with a steep staircase ending in a tiny landing and two bedrooms on either side. Maria had only to slip from their room across the landing if Mr. Francis called, and back again when David whistled for her. She felt as though she were torn in half at times and her mouth twisted as she remembered that she had told Mrs. Silsbee that she was "mercurial." When she was depressed, no one knew it now. At last Maria had learned to mind her tongue.

Nor did she complain to her friends in Wayland who spoke of her as "that wonderful little center of energy on the Sudbury Road." There was Miss Louisa Parmenter with whom she discussed Goethe, as in Margaret Fuller's time; and the Cuttings in the salt box next door, and the Damons who lived closer to town by the Burying Ground. She visited with them over the fence or walking to the post office. Susan Francis, James's daughter, came to the brown house often, however, and Maria welcomed the young bride who, during Maria's years in New York, had written her aunt reams of family news and kindness. Susan was not one of those relatives about whom Maria had written to Parke Godwin that she felt closer to her friends than to those "tied to me by blood."

But there were others—the in-laws. When people complained to Mrs. Convers Francis that Mrs. Child rarely appeared in public, Mrs. Francis retorted that it was wrong of Maria, famous as she was, to seclude herself—a remark that did not endear her to Maria, who merely said that she did not belong to the world but to herself.

That independence was more than a family byword, however. Once, Harriet Beecher Stowe asked to meet Maria at an antislavery bazaar. Maria drew down her mouth when Wendell Phillips told her of Mrs. Stowe's disappointment at missing her. "I don't want to see a lion," she said. "But," countered the diplomat, Phillips, "one lion may look at another, I suppose." The ladies did meet shortly and Maria, who had admired Harriet all along, now spoke of her as her favorite author, mainly because, despite fame and fortune, Mrs. Stowe retained her humility. One of the pet stories told about the author of *Uncle Tom's Cabin* was that in England someone asked her, "How do you feel when earls and dukes solicit the honor of touching your hand?" to which Mrs. Stowe bluntly answered, "As if I were a great humbug!" A typical Maria answer, that.

Meanwhile national politics darkened the future. The

Kansas-Nebraska Act of 1854, by which a new western area would have the right to choose whether or no slavery could exist within its boundaries, seemed to Maria to be a straight compromise with evil, a kowtowing to the slave interests of the South. After Stephen Douglas, that "little steam engine in britches," had pushed the bill through Congress, John Brown went out to Kansas with the emigrants, the free-state settlers of the territory, and became the hero of Pottawatomie. He was backed by the Massachusetts State–Kansas Committee, a group of influential abolitionists and, all of them, Maria's friends. This proclaimed the end of the North's "servile submission."

Soon Boston was rocked by the capture of Anthony Burns, the first such slave-catching since the Sims affair. Parker, Higginson, and Phillips joined a Vigilance Committee to try to rescue Burns, but in spite of some bloodshed the slave went back to his owner, and Maria stormed that her very soul cursed "law and order seeing them both arrayed on the wrong side." Burns's capture put iron into her determination to liberate Sims according to her promise three years before. The devastation caused by the two acts, the Fugitive Slave and the Kansas-Nebraska, were personal affronts which she would not let pass.

However, in order to afford the "luxury" of reform, she had to make money and, many a night, her lamp burned long after her two men were asleep while she scratched out the stories that appeared in the *Dewdrop,* the *Gem,* the *Moss Rose,* the *Ladies' Casket,* the *Philopena,* and others. Some of the tales were new, others overhauled from her old collections. New editions still came out of the *Housewife,* the *Mother's Book,* and the *Letters from New York.* Between times she struggled on with the *Progress of Religions,* and it was while they worked together after Mr. Francis was settled of other men's opinions. As if a man could not be good, unless he believed in the Trinity, or the Atonement! Perhaps I have not so much patience with such assumptions, as I ought to have. But I know, by experience, that we can not choose our belief. It is literally impossible for me to believe now what I believed thirty years ago. It is neither a fault nor a merit in me.

The simple fact is, I have outgrown my old spiritual garments, and now they will not go on. And not only difference of years, but diversity of temperaments necessarily modifies belief. A doctrine that is essential to one person is non-essential to another, and to a third may prove a positive hindrance to religion. God intended this diversity in spiritual structure and growth, as He intended diversity in natural structure and growth. Henry Ward Beecher accepts

Letter to Theodore Tiebon

for the night that she and David rejoiced in their companionship. David's aptitude with language constantly astonished
her. He could translate intricate, archaic passages as easily
as she took down the words, and with his fluency in seven
tongues she had little need for dictionaries nor for the tiny
Wayland library which had opened only in 1848. David's
erudition and compassion (except where his father-in-law was
concerned), put a fresh emphasis on the ancient formulas for
identifying God and made a ponderous work tremendously
exciting.

At last, after eight years of effort, she finished the book
and the publishers accepted it without changes. Maria was
in a fighting mood and said she did not care whether critics
praised or banned it. She wrote to Lucy Osgood:

> This is the second time I have walked out in stormy weather
> without a cloak. My *Appeal,* in favor of antislavery and attack-
> ing colonization, marched into the enemy's camp alone. . . .
> Charles Sumner writes me that the influence of my antislavery
> writings years ago has had an important effect on his course
> in Congress. . . . Who can tell how many young minds may
> be so influenced by the *Progress of Religious Ideas* as to
> materially change their career? I trust I have never impelled
> anyone in the wrong direction. In the simplest things I write,
> whether for children or for grown people, I try to sow some
> seeds for freedom, truth and humanity.

Maria in all humility knew the value and the hazards of her
three-volume labors and she knew that her thesis, "Theology
is not religion," would find faint welcome in certain quarters.
The "baptized hatreds of the human race" limited broad
thinking and she suggested that such bigots were better off
without her book. None of which helped sales.

Her emergence from the *Religions* gave her so strong a
sense of release that she said, "I feel like an inhabitant of

the second or third century and everything seems foreign
as it did when I came out of Athens into Boston after
writing *Philothea.*" Her amazing concentration in the face
of interruption was the secret, plus one other factor, that
old Puritan response to self-flagellation; for she admitted,
"This *Progress of Religious Ideas* was a real pilgrimage of
penance with peas in my shoes walking over rubble-stones
all the way." The penance somehow made up for her
defection from sympathy with the church of her fathers and
gave her the answer she had sought since her childhood. She
put it thus:

> Most devoutly do I believe in the pervasive and ever-guiding
> spirit of God but I do not believe that it was ever shut up
> within the covers of any book or that it ever can be. Portions
> of it or rather breathings of it are in many books. The words
> of Christ seem to me full of it as no other words are. But if we
> want the truth, we must listen to the voice of God in the silence
> of our own souls as He did.

Maria had found her home in Wayland in more ways than
one.

All summer she had worked with such intensity that if
David had not weeded her flowers, the poor things would
have choked; and by October, when she picked the last
nasturtium, the fall closed in rapidly. As the days darkened,
her father grew weaker and kept more to his bed. David was
at home most of the time but whenever he was writing or
working on his terraces and dry walls, she stayed by her
father's bed and stroked his hand. It seemed to soothe him
and it gave her time to think. In that dark, chilly chamber,
she realized fully how she had confused her "nearest duty,"
when she had used that phrase to explain her preference for
a career to the hurdles and obstacles of marriage. Because
she knew, as she heard the clink of shovel upon rock for the

fountain he was building for her, that life without David was no life at all and that the years in New York had been an irreparable loss.

XVII

Hiatus

THE "PROGRESS OF RELIGIOUS IDEAS" BARELY PAID FOR THE paper and ink with which it was written. Had it been identified with a purely historical point of view, it would have been more successful, for history was popular with the public that gobbled up long works by Prescott, Motley, and Parkman. But Maria's dispassionate judgments on controversial religious themes bored and irritated her handful of readers who demanded that she take one side or another. She was too "all-sided," just as Convers was known to be. Her straddling was dull and out of character, not like her usual straightforward opinions on any subject. Normally, things appeared either black or white to her with no in-betweens. This new view of her made her friends wonder if, by forfeiting independence to preserve her marriage, she had become one of those heavy, humorless intellectuals lacking all spark or zest.

Such superficial criticism by careless and uncaring readers overlooked Maria's intention, which she clearly stated in her preface. Out with the theological underbrush and expose the entire panorama of religious thinking of Christians, Hindus, or Jews! Then let the free man discover for himself where his serenity, where his personal conception of God might be found. This was a contemplative, intense, and embracive study, overpacked with fact, understated with emotion. Glancing neither left nor right, Maria put Christianity on an intellectual par, no higher, no lower than the other religions and thereby lost her audience. She fussed and fretted over sending Whittier a copy for fear of offending his Quaker orthodoxy, and she was tremendously relieved when he told her that he had read with care every word of the three volumes.

What the *Progress* really came to was a writing out of her spiritual growing pains, and, once this was out of the way, her next book was a *New Flower for Children,* which included the favorite of all of her stories, "The Royal Rosebud." It was a child's version of the death of the two little princes in the Tower of London and of their mournful little sister. Rosebud's foibles gave a new dimension to the familiar story, inspired by history but colored by the alabaster transparency of the princes which hung in Maria's sitting room. The Cutting children, on their daily visit from next door, begged to see "up close" how the poor little boys slept peacefully while the wicked uncles menaced them. Allie Cutting sighed with relief when "Mitty Chile" hooked the transparency back on the window to let the sun shine through the red and purple glass frame again. Allie hated to be near the ugly uncles but neither could he stay away. Maria loved the piece and said it added a touch of romance to her Spartan surroundings.

She rather liked to picture herself as a Spartan wife, a self-sacrificing one, working hard day after day to keep her family comfortable. It pleased her to amaze her friends by accomplishing so much with so little, and it made her feel noble. She ran from one job to the next—gardening, writing, caring for the old father, sewing for the Kansas emigrants, rummaging through her chests and boxes for old clothes to make over for fugitives. She dreamed about excitements for the future and called the present drab but necessary.

Autumnal Leaves, the next effusion to pour from her pen, like the season for which it was named, was tinged with sadness. Some of the rhymes were gay, but often she cried out from the depths of her own anxieties:

> God help us all to kindly view
> The world that we are passing through.

The world lost its rosy light when she read of the dreadful massacres in Kansas and fretted over how little she could do for the Kansas emigrants. Nor could she be less than sad as vitality ebbed from her father, who frequently crooned quietly to himself like a lonesome child.

When the cloud lifted, when Mr. Francis was more of his old self, he surprised her with gifts that he had hidden away for her long before in a locked cabinet beside his bed. One day he burrowed and brought out Hillard's *Six Months in Italy* to comfort her for having to stay so close to Wayland. What irony. As she kissed him, she thought, How little does he know what constituted the charm of Italy, the freedom from actualities. But he did understand, poor old man, and he commiserated silently with her because she was chained to her "nearest duties."

On cold, damp days while her father drowsed, she sat on the floor beside her own chest of particular treasures, souvenirs from her friends. She fondled them one by one— the Italian orange- and olivewood box sent by Mrs. Shaw, the Florentine inkstand from the Benzons, Mrs. Lowell's bracelet of Venetian pearl shells. The iridescence of the pearls added miniature rainbows to the prismatic ones in the window. She poured the shells from one hand to the other, amused that she held both ends of the rainbow at the same time. The winter sun shone palely into the room and in its faint warmth she dreamed of Italy. Then the tap of her father's cane roused her and she took him his bowl of gruel.

In the spring David repaired the picket fence, redug the dooryard garden, and cleared away the old bricks he had used to protect her tender plants. Maria opened her tins of seeds and broadcast them over the waiting earth, which pushed them into a carpet of soft green. She traded her surplus seedlings, which she dug out with an old pewter spoon, with the Damons down the road. The Damons' garden was the pride of Wayland and many a serious conference did they have with the Childs on how to keep phlox and petunias true to color. One of the small Damons often came with a new plant for Maria, with a trail of other children close behind. They hung on the fence while Maria told them stories. The children paid no attention to Mitty Chile's famous insistence on privacy, for they realized that they were always welcome with either of the Childs. Often when David expounded on the reasons for a five-petaled honeysuckle and a six-stamened lily, Maria popped a berry into a child's mouth. Then David saw that the discussion had become too serious and brayed like a donkey or cock-a-doodled to send the visitors scampering away half scared, half charmed.

By fall Mr. Francis needed help simply to stand up, and David devoted himself to the old man's comfort. Her father's decline brought the realization to Maria that she herself was no longer young; not that she feared death, the river "spanned by a rainbow bridge," but that she wanted to do many things before she crossed that bridge. She took the first step toward action by writing to Loring:

David has signed my will and I have sealed it up and put it away. It excited my towering indignation to think that it was necessary for him to sign it, and if you had been by, you would have made the matter worse by repeating your old manly "fling and twit" about married women being dead in the law. I was not indignant on my own account for David respects the freedom of all women on principle and mine in particular by reason of affection super-added. But I was indignant for womankind made chattels personal from the beginning of time, perpetually insulted by literature, law and custom. The very phrases used with regard to us are abominable. "Dead in the law." "Femme Couverte." How I detest such language! I must come out with a broadside on that subject before I die. If I don't, I shall walk and rap afterward.

Loring of course knew that she had managed the family finances for years and that it was ironical that David should have any say in the matter of money; nor did he, for he never opened his mouth when she sent twelve copies of *Autumnal Leaves* to friends—twelve copies for which she had to pay. He only praised her when she gave contributions to the Kansas sufferers, for he too was wholly sympathetic to their struggles and would have done the same if he had held the purse strings.

Kansas became a personal issue with them when Charles Sumner, their idol, was caned by a Southerner at his Senate desk for his tactless and vitriolic speech on the evils perpetrated by Southerners in Kansas. David had probably given him many of the facts, quotations, and legal precedents for the speech, "The Crime Against Kansas," in which accusations were strong against Senator Butler. The Senator's cousin, Preston Brooks of South Carolina, strode toward Sumner, who tried to rise from his desk to ward off the attack. His long legs jammed in the kneehole, he wrenched his back trying to free himself, and fell to the floor where Brooks beat him unconscious.

A few conservative Northerners conceded that the speech had fallen short of good taste, but no one believed that it warranted a vicious beating and Sumner was hailed as a martyr. The South, however, welcomed Brooks as its hero and souvenir replicas of his cane still rest as family heirlooms in dusty attics.

Maria could not put the attack out of her mind and made herself sick over it with headaches and palpitations. She wrote frenzied articles and letters for the papers, whirled new volunteers into activity for the Kansas emigrants, and alone sewed sixty yards of cotton into clothes—an eight-night orgy of self-punishment that exhausted her. She had begged the material from a Mr. Hovey, who told her that her money and energy might better be expended on the immediate abolition of slavery and the dissolution of the Union, to which she snapped: "I don't consider it wise to wait for either of these before I make up the cloth, as winter is coming on and fever and ague won't wait on politics."

The election of 1856 was not far off, and while she sewed or waited on her father, she schemed ways to help John Frémont become the next President. Dashing Frémont, the Free-Soiler, was the only possible candidate who might swing the former Whigs, the abolitionists, and all the undecided voters squarely behind the Republicans. Frémont had saved California for the United States in 1845; now he might well preserve the states—united for themselves. She wished as she had never wished before that women had the right to vote, and she wrote to David who was away for a few days, "I do long to have you back. Voting day will bring you of course. If you don't come, I shall put on your old hat and coat and vote for you."

In a letter to Mrs. Shaw she said:

What a shame that women can't vote! We'd carry our Jessie (Mrs. Frémont) into the White House on our shoulders, wouldn't we? Never mind. Wait a while! Woman stock is rising in the market. I shall not live to see women vote but I'll come and rap at the ballot box. I was never bitten by politics before but such mighty results are depending on this election that I cannot be indifferent.

Frémont, the Pathfinder, and his "Jessie" had captured all imaginations, even Nathaniel Willis'; and Maria was disgusted that he, a fop, a flibbergibbet, who edited the proslavery *Mirror* in New York, had serious rights which she, being a woman, did not. She wrote again to Mrs. Shaw:

N.P.W. announced his intention to deposit his "virgin" vote for Frémont. It was pleasant to learn that he had anything "virgin" left to swear by. What a Rip! to lie sleeping for fifty years, dreaming of kid gloves, embroidered vests, and perfumed handkerchiefs, taking it for granted that his country was all the while going forward in a righteous and glorious career. Isn't it too bad that such parasol holders should have the right to vote while earnest souls like you and me must await the results of agonizing inaction?

Her personal grudges against Willis for his quips about her stale gingerbread recipes in the *Frugal Housewife* and even more for that other long-buried secret that everyone but she had forgotten—these were the basis for her fury.

But she really cared about women's right to vote. "Why should women be politically mute?" she argued in a letter to Sumner. "I reduce it to very simple elements. I pay taxes for property of my own earning and I do not believe in 'taxation without representation.'" It made no sense whatever.

On Election Day David put on his greatcoat to go to the polls. Mr. Francis, feeble as he was, cried as he insisted on his right as a male citizen to vote. He quavered, "I cast my first ballot for George Washington and I'll give my last to Frémont." Maria doubted that he would come home alive but she bundled him up and David carried him out to the buggy and put a warm soapstone at his feet.

Frémont, the Pathfinder, could not find the new Republican road and lost the election. "Free Soil, free speech and Frémont" were not enough. It was "Safe and Sane" Buchanan who won. Mr. Francis' tired old brain and body refused to rally from the disappointment. He retreated into a far-off land where Maria could not reach him. Only his frail hands, the hands that had been so gentle with her as a little girl, and now picking endlessly at the quilt, showed that he was conscious. He was too weak even to sing in his forlorn little way.

In early December, less than a month after the election, he died. Maria was torn by grief and leaned on David for comfort. For three years she had cared for her father night and day with a love born of his dependence on her. Now she felt emptied, lost, with only the memory of his pride in her, his youngest and dearest child. A week after his death she wrote to Mrs. Shaw:

> Yes, the old man has gone home and unless you had such a charge, you could not imagine how lonely and desolate I feel. . . . The occupation of my life seems gone. I went to Boston and spent four days but the dreariness was with me. The old man loved me and you know when I came back from Boston, there was a bright firelight in his room for me and his hand eagerly stretched out and the old face lighted up as he said, "You're welcome back, Maria." This time when I came home, it was dark and silent. I almost cried myself blind and thought I would willingly be fettered to his bedside for years if I could only hear that voice again. This is weakness, I know. My spirits will doubtless rebound from the pressure as soon as

I get fairly to work. Work! Work! that is my unfailing cure for all troubles.

Hers was a healthy prescription, for there was work enough to be done and her life was by no means over. David still needed her, and to be so loved, so needed, gave her strength for the years and trials ahead.

XVIII

Moral Arithmetic

AND NOW THE LITTLE BROWN HOUSE, THE GARDEN, AND THE
tiny orchards were all Maria's, for she inherited them from
her father. She was secure at last behind her own picket
fence and with money enough to modernize the run-down
pre-Revolutionary property, money from a legacy which
Abby Francis, Convers' daughter, had inherited and then
passed over to her aunt Maria.

There was freedom, too, to spend all the time she liked in
Boston with the friends she had missed during her
father's long illness, friends like Charles Sumner, who
brought her his latest photograph as a remembrance. He
intended to reassure her of his recovery from his caning,
though his poor color and the lines of pain in his face made
her doubt his brave words. He stayed for two hours to
discuss the rights of slaves and of women while Maria
admired him for not saying one unkind word against his
political enemies, who continued to threaten him against
returning to his Senate post. But return he would, though she
and everyone else tried to persuade him to convalesce a
bit longer. The Union's desperate state was of more importance than his broken bones he said. He was quite ready to
face the Cavaliers again. Sensitive to his pride, Maria did

not help him out of his chair, though perspiration beaded his forehead in his efforts to get up alone.

Sumner did not exaggerate the temper of Southern congressmen. Senator Henry Wilson of Massachusetts told Maria that he never left his office to enter the Senate Chamber with having arranged his desk as though he would not return alive. He added: "Members of Congress go armed in the streets and sit with loaded revolvers at their desks." Sumner's beating had alerted all the Northerners, but caution could not halt their determination to hold back the extension of slavery.

Maria at home refused to be outdone by the men. She begged money from friends and strangers and cheered when Edmund Benzon sent one hundred dollars as a Christmas gift for the Kansas settlers. Kansas must be free to grow in peace. She wrote articles, stories, and letters to any newspaper that would publish them, to encourage help for the emigrants and discourage attacks from the pro-slavery Missourians across the border. She did a series for the *Tribune* called "The Kansas Immigrants." Sumner, whom she called "the chief architect of the wall," worked superhumanly while her own efforts poured forth in a steady stream.

Her admiration for Sumner impelled her to ask Josiah Quincy his opinion of erecting a statue to the "architect," and Quincy answered, "All men should wait for such permanent memories until death has opened the door of fame and shut the door of envy." Alive, Sumner's reward was the support of his constituents. Theodore Parker's answer to her suggestion was that he preferred to use any available money for corn and gunpowder to protect and feed the Kansans for whom Sumner fought so hard. A practical man, that Parker.

With feeling at so high a pitch, Maria did not hide her contempt for Mrs. Silsbee's ostrich indifference to the "impending crisis." Mrs. Silsbee ventured one day that she suspected that the brutality of slaveholders was provoked by abolitionist interference and that the outrages in Kansas were probably the fault of the Kansas Emigrant Aid Society. Marianne Silsbee knew perfectly well that the Society was composed of Maria's dearest friends and she should have expected the answer that flamed back at her. Maria, goaded beyond tact or silence, splattered blots as her pen raced over the paper:

> The different points of view from which we habitually look at things is manifested by the fact that I have seldom been with you for more than an hour without hearing some hit at my especial favorites. I dare say that I, without thinking of it, run against your predilections in the same way. Theodore Parker, T. W. Higginson . . . are the chosen sons and brothers of my soul.

The more she wrote, the hotter she steamed. She flung out old grievances. Sims—how Marianne had ridiculed her promise to effect his release from slavery. Webster—how the Silsbees had praised that black-hearted "Ichabod." She lashed out:

> And when my soul was boiling over with shame and indignation that my native commonwealth should, by tyrants and their base tools (such as Webster) be converted into a slave huntingground, you called it "making a ridiculous fuss about one nigger." How hard I tried not to enter into a pitched battle then and there, you will never know or imagine because you have never realized how strongly I feel on all subjects connected with human freedom and equality.

The interchange cleared the air between them, for a few months afterward Maria's tone was less vitriolic:

You have never realized the depth and strength of my feelings on the points whereon we differ. You are simply amused by the zeal of reformers while I have staked social and literary success on the issue of these questions and hold myself ready to stake my life. I love you and shall always love you.

The sophisticated Mrs. Silsbee may have thought these to be typical Maria-like dramatics. How wrong she was the next few years would prove, for Maria, though dramatic, spoke the absolute truth.

Abolitionists were still in danger of life and property and guards stood watch over the homes of Garrison and Phillips. But though friends suggested to Phillips that his house on Essex Street in Boston was vulnerable to mob attack, neither he nor his invalid wife would consider moving. Higginson noted: "I spent one night on guard at Phillips' house with his young henchmen and was struck then as before with his high-bred bearing. It was hard to make him adopt ordinary precautions." Perhaps Higginson did not know that Phillips carried a loaded revolver in his pocket; confident of his marksmanship, he was not afraid of being attacked from the rear. When someone cautioned him on that possibility, he answered with a drawl, "I can see over my shoulder and before a man can touch me, I will shoot."

Dark nights often brought broken windows and mud-spattered paint to antislavery homes, yet Maria had no fear for her own trim little place. Why should anyone come so far in a busy world to trample her flowerbeds or smash the bubbled glass that framed her front door? Had they come while she was there, she would probably have disarmed them with a cup of tea and a bunch of herbs for their wives. Face to face, Maria was a simple little wren of a woman, motherly,

feminine, and serene. She was not afraid for her home, and
the blue jays and swallows were her only watchmen when
she was away.

On her Boston trips she often went to art galleries, and
it was there that she saw William Page's "Venus." He was
horrified when, instead of the splendid, quotable compliments he expected, she called his masterpiece "simpering
Victorianism and immodest," not because the figure was
undraped but because it was self-conscious. Her long study
of the art of Greece convinced her that Page's approach was
slightly obscene.

Harriet Hosmer's "Beatrice Cenci" was more to her taste.
The young Hosmer with her flyaway curls, smocks and flowing ties, and gamin expression appealed to Maria because
the sculptress was unpretentious despite her success, unpretentious and self-reliant too in her plans to travel down
the coast of Italy alone and to deal with horses, pistols, and
banditti if necessary. Maria wrote to Mrs. Silsbee that the
work of Hosmer, the poems of Elizabeth Barrett Browning,
and Rosa Bonheur's "Horse Fair" bolstered her faith in
women's progress. Pridefully she crowed, "We women are
getting up in the world. Certainly in every department,
woman stock is rising in the market."

Lucy Stone, who though she had married Henry Blackwell
in 1855, still used her maiden name with her husband's
consent and thus set a personal example for feminists. Miss
Stone met Maria one day at Marston's restaurant. As usual
Maria's arms were full of packages, and one small one
dangled from a string around her little finger. "Why don't
you let them be carried by someone else or send them by
post?" asked Miss Lucy.

"I want to show my respect for the people who have to
carry burdens. There is so much work the world needs that

I want to do all I can," answered Maria. This was a hard example for other spoiled women to follow.

Undoubtedly there were many who were bored and irritated by the exacting standards she set. Mrs. Stone said that the dress Maria wore that day could not have cost more than seven or eight cents a yard, that her calico cape was unfringed and her bonnet had not "perhaps been altered in twenty years." Lucy's own clothes, her velvet-collared coats and "breeches of black silk with gaiters beneath," were a far cry from the crinolined fashion of the day. She too was "as independent in mind as in dress" but she was not shabby and she was in the right about that bonnet. The antiques Maria wore on her head exasperated her own nieces who tried just about any subterfuge to make her spruce up, with no success. She still did her hair in the unflattering arrangement, parted spaniel-like in the middle and coiled flat over the ears, on which she and Margaret Fuller had decided years before; and her bonnets, large, green with age, were "plenty good enough." When the girls continued to nag, she turned on them with the comment, "I'd rather go to State Prison than be a fashionable woman."

By comparison with Maria, Elizabeth Peabody was a fashion plate, or so their friends said. No one looked less like a Godey print than Miss Peabody. Maria's own view was that the world was too full of visible wonders to bother with looking at her reflection in a glass. Life itself was the mirror, for life gave back only in the measure one put into it. It pleased her vanity, though, to hear that someone asked a stagecoach driver about her, saying: "Who is that woman who dresses like a peasant and speaks like a scholar?" Lucy Stone was proud to know her and called her one of the greatest women of the age.

Home from her Boston jaunts, Maria found David waiting. The light shone its welcome through the kitchen window and he met her at the foot of the rise, arms outstretched. It was sweet of David to remember how her father had always greeted her. The cracked old voice was still, but she still had someone to say, "You're welcome home, Maria." David's tenderness made her ashamed of her occasional discontent as she wrote to Mrs. Silsbee: "Constant affection is such a rare blessing in this world that it is wise to make the most of what one has." Her life would have been full and happy with children and grandchildren to bless it, for, as she admitted to Mrs. Shaw, she was one of those who find it more necessary to love than to be loved, though she wanted both. "Bad, isn't it, for a childless woman of nearly sixty years. But then my good David serves me for my husband and baby and all."

Another cause of her frequent depression was that she still had found no church affiliation that satisfied her. She had even tried Spiritualism, as did many of her contemporaries, but there was no cure for the bleakness that descended on her with the death of Susan Francis Bigelow, her favorite niece, who was buried in the family plot in October, 1857. Susan was the third of James Francis' children to go in seven years. Shortly after, Ellis Gray Loring, Maria's friend and counselor, her "chief reliance for over thirty years," died. Loring's death brought grief to Whittier as well, and the bond of sympathy he and Maria shared brought them close.

On the first anniversary of Loring's death, she published a poem in his memory which Whittier answered with one of his own called, "Lines to L. M. Child in Response to her Verses on the Death of Ellis Gray Loring." His second stanza read:

> O woman greatly loved! I join thee
> In tender memories of our friend:
> With thee across the awful spaces
> The greeting of a soul I send.

And so she was, a woman loved, by people of high and low degree, people she helped, people she amused and entertained with her writing, people to whom she gave the unending gift of her own great heart. As she often said, "To make people happy without violating the truth or compromising my own sincerity is the moral arithmetic of my life."

That moral arithmetic was put to a severe test when the Benzons invited her on a three-year trip to Europe. Italy at last! The golden pot at the end of the rainbow. But they did not invite David; and when it came down to facts, in David and the little home he had made so snug for her, was romance enough. She had only to look toward the pool and fountain he had built in remembrance of her love for the fountains in New York and his promise of long ago. The Benzons were welcome to the canals and aqueducts of Leonardo; she would stay at home with her own master builder. All summer when David rested from his labors of love for her, they sat hand in hand watching the rainbows arch into his fountain. And David became the wonder of the neighborhood, for while he set pipes and poured cement, he discoursed on the ancient waterworks of Minos and Caesar.

Outside of making money, the one and only thing he could not manage was to take care of himself. With a job to do, he worked in the dampness until he stiffened with rheumatism and caught cold with every turn in the weather. Maria soaked his feet in hot water, poulticed them in sliced, hot onions and popped him into a warm bed. She dosed him with infusions of prickly ash or horse radish laced with red pepper and wrapped his swollen legs in flannel sprinkled with cayenne. He drank pennyroyal and catnip tea to please her; and when she, exhausted, took to her own bed, he tried, in his man's way, to do as much for her. Her kitchen after a day of his nursing was a shambles; it was not worth her while to be sick.

Worried, busy, sick or well, it was good to be alone at last with David. Often he sang to her:

> There's nothing half so sweet in life
> As love's old dream.

She knew now that he loved her as he had when they were young and that the nonessentials no longer interfered with them. When he went away on a law case, he tucked little notes in her sewing basket and under the tea cosy. He asked the neighbors to keep a weather eye on her and piled kindling beside the stove. Mrs. Silsbee and Mrs. Shaw told her she was a lucky woman to have so thoughtful a husband. Times had changed since the days when her choice of a mate had been looked upon quizzically. Not that the in-laws were convinced of David's worth. Never the in-laws.

Once, with David away, a northeaster flattened her beloved flowers. Her little house stood sturdily against the storm which wrenched a sparrow's nest out of a rosebush and tossed two eggs to the ground. The nest dangled from a thorn while the mother darted back and forth cheeping her agitation. Maria found the eggs, still warm and unbroken, and put them and the nest safely back. The mother bird went straight back to the business of incubation as though nothing had happened. Even birds trusted Maria.

If David had to be away, she preferred to be alone, a preference for which family and friends criticized her. Her own company pleased her, she told them. "I'd rather be forever alone than have an indiscriminate inrush of the world into my sanctum." Her sisters-in-law knew very well what she meant. Convers' wife, hurt by Maria's withdrawal even from Convers, who still adored his baby sister, told Sallie Holley who asked for her company to Wayland, "I'll be glad to go along with you to see my famous sister-in-law but I suspect you'll have more success with her on your own." Mrs. Convers was quite right, for Maria demanded company that either stimulated her intellectually or with whom she could work on a Cause, and Mrs. Convers did neither. But Miss Holley, who combined the two attributes, became a firm friend.

Again church membership might have provided social activity but Maria was not one of those to whom church meant box suppers. She wrote to Lucy Osgood, who still lived in Medford and knew her longer than anyone but her brothers:

> I assure you that if I could only find a church, I would nestle into it as gladly as a bird nestled into her covert in a storm. . . . I have an unfortunate sincerity which demands living realities and will not be put off with respectable shams. I sometimes wish it were otherwise; there is such a plenty of respectable shams to be had without the seeking.

The Wayland Unitarian Church had, however, a remarkable minister; and again as with John Dwight in Northampton, Maria found a friend in Mr. Sears. The Reverend Edmund Sears lived two miles away on an out-of-the-way boggy road and difficult to reach, but when they met, their conversation was music- and mystic-filled. A kind of "lunar halo of Swedenborgianism" in his preaching drew her to an occasional Sunday service, and if anyone could have persuaded her to accept organized religion, Mr. Sears was that man.

He and she discussed literature—European and American, old and new—and he listed the sources for his sermons to see what pattern she could evolve from the same material. He read her his own verses, among them the Christmas carols, "Calm on the Listening Ear of Night" and "It Came Upon a Midnight Clear." They agreed on the immortality of the soul and the theme that old age is merely the gateway from one life into the next. He joined her on the transcendental path which David would not, and other Waylanders could not, follow.

But though she told friends that she and David lived like dormice in the winter and that she talked to herself or the pictures on the wall for company, people actually did come to visit. Five ladies arrived one day just as she was opening the latest gift from Mrs. Silsbee, a moss agate set into a dull gold brooch. Just because she knew how curious her guests were about the present, she took her time in opening it, smoothed away and folded the wrapping paper and the string before they got a glimpse. They pursed their lips and agreed that she could be the most exasperating of women, and Mrs. Silsbee probably thought the same when she had Maria's note of thanks. "The brooch is lovely but a cheap little vase bought at the Anti-Slavery Fair for fifty cents would have pleased my reformer's heart as well."

Why did Marianne Silsbee always forgive her boorishness? The Wayland "recluse" wrote a bit shamefacedly to the Mayor's lady:

> Very few people in the relative social position which you bear to me would have done anything to pick up the dropped stitches of our friendship. It shows a large nature and a kind heart.

In August, Abby Hopper Gibbons came for a visit with her daughter Lucy and while the girl played with the Childs' fat old bulldog, the ladies gossiped. Abby said that John and Rosa Hopper were delighted with their little son William Gibbons Hopper, named for Abby's Willie who had recently died. Abby and Maria shook their heads over the way Rosa spoiled the baby and were sure she would have trouble with him later on, wait and see. If either of them had been gifted with the "second sight" in which Maria was so interested, they would have been amazed at the emergence of this same spoiled baby as the matinee idol, DeWolf Hopper.

Abby told of changes in New York. It was now fashionable to be informed about and generous to the poor, so that the Isaac T. Hopper Home had been taken up by the bluebloods and was well endowed. St. Patrick's Cathedral way out at Fiftieth Street was under construction, though one could hardly envisage the city actually spreading so far uptown. There had been frightful bread riots with ten thousand starving people in line for something to eat as a result of the '57 panic and the riot quieted only when the Seventh Regiment soldiers put it down. Abby said that New York's political tension had been heightened by the Dred Scott decision whereby the bringing of a slave into free territory did not render him a free man. Horace Greeley had stated in his *Tribune,* "[The decision] was entitled to just so much moral weight as would be the judgment of the majority of those congregated in a Washington barroom."

That decision impelled Maria to new writing efforts, and she was soon deep in three pamphlets, each a hundred pages or more, each a plea for emancipation from a different point of view. David's hand was plainly visible in the parts on economics, whether his name appeared on the cover or no.

But money must be earned and the *Atlantic Monthly* was one of Maria's most active markets for articles and stories, and a well-paying one too. James T. Fields was her editor, a hearty, good-tempered man who allowed his authors to be as temperamental as they liked provided they kept up the standards of his magazine. Yet even his good nature was too hard pressed by Maria's stipulation that a piece of hers must appear no later than the following month with not a line changed or she would expect the work to be returned forthwith. He did!

Maria's nerves nearly went to pieces with the political news. Lincoln, on June 16, 1858, while campaigning for an Illinois Senate seat, flayed the conscience of the nation. "This government cannot endure permanently half slave and half free." From south and west came rumblings of war. Then in October, 1859, came John Brown's raid on Harper's Ferry and with it, the climax to Maria Child's life.

XIX

High Noon

JOHN BROWN TOOK HIS FAMILY TO KANSAS IN 1854 WITH HIS
rifles and his printing press. They believed fervently that the
abolition of slavery was a sacred cause and now he taught
them to shoot to kill to protect those beliefs. When his anti-
slavery press was destroyed by a Missouri mob that sacked
the town of Lawrence and burned most of its buildings,
Brown and six followers retaliated by murdering five proslavery men at the Pottawatomie Massacre. The South struck
back in revenge and two hundred others died in Bleeding
Kansas, one of them Brown's own son. Mrs. Brown, tall,
handsome and hardy, fought side by side with her husband
and, when he rested for a moment, shielded his body from
the hail of bullets with her own great frame. Courage and
religious fanaticism made John Brown a leader, a man with
a mission, a self-appointed emissary of a wrathful God.

After Pottawatomie, he looked around for another
abolitionist plan. In May, 1857, George Luther Stearns of
Medford wrote to Abby Gibbons in New York to tell her of
Brown's latest scheme, of which the second part read:

> To organize a secret force, well-armed, and under the
> control of the farmer, John Brown, to repel border ruffian

outrage and defend Free State men from all illegal impositions.
This organization is to be a strictly defensive one. . . . I am
personally acquainted with Capt. Brown and have great
confidence in his courage, prudence and good judgment. He
has control of the whole affair including contributions of
arms, clothing, etc. to the amount of $13,000.

Nephew George, married to Maria's niece, Mary Preston,
was too much of a gentleman to say that his contribution of
$7,000 was the largest private one the Brown fund had
received.

"Prudent" Brown with control of arms and money conveniently forgot that his was to be a "strictly defensive
organization" and simply went ahead with his plans. He
confided in few sympathizers: Stearns, Gerrit Smith,
Thomas Wentworth Higginson, Frank Sanborn, Dr. Howe,
Theodore Parker; but these he mesmerized into backing
him. They knew about his Harper's Ferry proposal. They
further encouraged him by raising another $3,800 and then,
primed for action, they advised delay. Those men, some of
them mighty thinkers, shoved a rifle into a madman's grasp
and told him not to fire. Brown had not confided in either
Garrison or Phillips, knowing that the nonresistance policy
of one and the common sense of the other would force
them to oppose him.

Toward the end of September in 1859, Brown went to see
Mrs. Gibbons in New York on a day when everyone was
out of the house but herself. He told her every detail of
his plan, and Abby, fearless and practical as ever, pointed
out the flaws to him. Couldn't he see that he would harm
the cause they all had worked so long for by his recklessness?
Brown's eyes glowed wildly. Suddenly she asked, "And
what will you do with the women and children who come in

your way?" He gentled immediately. "Not touch a hair on their heads," he replied.

He asked that she keep his confidence and she, believing that his harebrained scheme could never go through, agreed, just because the authorities too would not have believed that such madness was in the wind. No one thought Brown would proceed with Harper's Ferry, certainly not the statesmen and public servants who had contributed to his "secret service" without inquiring the use he intended for their money. Salmon P. Chase was one of those who later disclaimed knowledge of his intentions.

Brown was sentenced to hang on December 2, after his attack on the Harper's Ferry Arsenal. Maria knew nothing about the event until it became history, so well had the secret been kept, but she was in Medford on a visit to Lucy Osgood when the news broke, and her heart went out to the ill-advised, impulsive old captain lying wounded in Charles Town jail. Once again her heart at flood tide swamped her head. Brown needed a woman to nurse him; his own wife in upstate New York, apparently was out of touch with him and the news, and Maria felt impelled to do something. She wrote to Garrison:

> My thoughts are so much with Capt. John Brown that I can scarcely take comfort in anything. I would expend all I have to save his life. Brave old man! Brave and generous though sadly mistaken in his mode of operation. Whether they put him to death or he escapes from their hands, I think this will prove the "Concord Fight" of an impending revolution and that the "Bunker Hill Battle" will surely follow. May God make us strong for freedom.

Maria talked over the situation with Mary Stearns, who was hysterical with worry over her husband since he and the others who were implicated in the Brown plot had fled to

Canada. Mary refused flatly to go off to nurse Madman Brown while her own George was heaven knew where. Maria took over. First she wrote to Governor Wise of Virginia:

> I and all my large circle of abolition acquaintances were taken with surprise when news came of Capt. Brown's recent attempt nor do I know a single person who would have approved of it had they been apprised of his intention. But I and thousands of others feel a natural impulse of sympathy for a brave and suffering man. . . . He needs a mother or a sister to dress his wounds and speak soothingly to him. Will you allow me to perform that mission of humanity? . . . I give you my word of honor which was never broken that I would use that permission solely and singly for the purpose of nursing your prisoner and for no other purpose whatever.

She enclosed a note to Brown for his permission for her to come to him.

Governor Wise answered her in three days by saying that Brown was accused of murder, robbery, and treason but that if she wanted to tend him, Virginia's "chivalrous and Christian spirit" would not stop her even though some Virginians might think less of her for wanting to care for a man who "whetted knives of butchery for our mothers, sisters, daughters and babes." The letter fortified her determination to go to Brown as soon as the old man gave his consent, and while she waited, she scraped lint for his wounds, begged for donations, and packed supplies. And— she wrote a sixteen-page rebuttal to Wise to answer his charge that abolition prodding had driven Brown to Harper's Ferry.

> You may believe it or not, Governor Wise, but it is certainly the truth that because slaveholders so recklessly sowed the wind in Kansas, they reaped the whirlwind at Harper's Ferry.

Brown's answer, though, was not expected. He wrote that while he appreciated her kindness and would have been proud to meet her under other circumstances, he preferred her not to come to Charles Town. "I am in charge of a most humane gentleman . . . and I am so recovered of my wounds as no longer to require nursing," he said, and pleaded that instead she find help for his family on their isolated farm in Albion, New York. Tactfully he did not tell her that his lawyers had warned him that Maria's presence would hurt more than help his chances of avoiding hanging. One lawyer wrote to Boston:

> Do not allow Mrs. Child to visit Brown . . . he don't want women to unman his heroic determination to maintain a firm and consistent composure. Keep Mrs. Child away at all hazards. Brown and associates will certainly be lynched if she goes there.

Stymied, Maria unpacked her trunk and settled down for a quiet visit with Lucy Osgood. Quiet! Anything but, for the Child-Wise correspondence got into Greeley's hands who printed it complete in his *Tribune,* and Maria found herself once more a "lion." She was furious with Greeley for turning her sincere, friendly gesture into a political hullaballoo.

Praise and condemnation bombarded her and at last a Mrs. Mason, wife of the author of the Fugitive Slave Act, added her blast:

> Do you read your Bible, Mrs. Child? If you do, read there, "Woe unto you, hypocrites," and take to yourself with two-fold damnation that terrible sentence; for rest assured, in the day of judgment it shall be more tolerable for those thus scathed by the awful denunciation of the Son of God, than for you. *You* would soothe with sisterly and motherly care the hoary-headed murderer of Harper's Ferry! A man whose

aim and intention was to incite the horrors of a servile war—
to condemn women of your own race, ere death closed their
eyes on their sufferings from violence and outrage, to see their
husbands and fathers murdered, their children butchered, the
ground strewn with the brains of their babes. . . . What
would have been our fate had they [Brown's band] found as
many sympathizers in Virginia as they seem to have found in
Massachusetts?

Accustomed as she was to denunciation as an abolitionist,
no one had ever questioned Maria's acquaintance with the
Bible. Mrs. Mason fell into a web, spun tighter and tighter
by the author of the *Progress of Religions*.

I have no disposition [she began] to retort upon you "the
twofold damnation" to which you consign me. On the con-
trary I wish you well both in this world and the next. If the
anathema proved a safety valve to your own boiling spirit, it
did some good to you while it fell harmless upon me.

She taunted, with verse after verse from the Holy Writ, on
the sins of slaveholding. She flung Proverbs, Isaiah,
Jeremiah, Job, James, and Hebrews at Mrs. Mason, after
which she became more insulting. So many advertisements
for runaways described the "merchandise" as having straight
blond hair and blue eyes. How could that be unless some-
where along the line Southern gentlemen had turned from
their ladylike wives for sex?

Mrs. Mason had asked if New England women nursed
sick servants and helped them in childbirth, and to this
Maria answered:

To all the personal questions you ask me, I will try to reply
in the name of all the women of New England. It would be
extremely difficult to find any woman in our villages who does
not sew for the poor and watch with the sick whenever the
occasion requires. We pay our domestics generous wages . . .

a process better for their characters, as well as our own, than to receive their clothing for charity after being deprived of just payment for their labor. I have never known an instance where the "pangs of maternity" did not meet with requisite assistance and here at the North, after we have helped the mothers, *we do not sell the children.*

This explosion released something in Maria and she agreed happily to let Greeley publish all of the Mason-Child letters for propaganda purposes. "I would even use the Irish privilege of voting in thirteen wards in one day if it would do any good," she said, and it turned out to be profitable to be sharp, because three hundred thousand copies of the Child-Wise-Mason letters, bound in a hard cover, sold overnight and the name of Lydia Maria Child was forever inscribed in the record of John Brown.

At tea with Whittier and his sister in Amesbury one day, there came a knock on the door. A delegation of Republicans had left their own political meeting to greet and cheer the "woman who had poured hot shot into Governor Wise." The Whittiers joined in the applause. A few days later Maria had a letter from Emerson thanking her for the courage of her offer to nurse Brown. The philosopher added his hope that Brown's sentence might still be commuted and that the captain might be "one of those on whom miracles wait."

No miracle intervened and Brown was hanged on December 2, after (some said) stopping on his way to the gallows to kiss a Negro child. All over the North that day bells tolled and voices hushed as they prayed for the new martyr. Maria prayed at an all-day Negro meeting.

Someone asked her to explain Brown's behavior. "I can't explain it," she said. "The more I cogitate upon it, the more unaccountable it seems that anyone in his senses could have undertaken such an enterprise." But she realized that his fanaticism had shaped history when she wrote:

> Others may spend their time debating whether John Brown did wrong or not, whether he was sane or not; all I know is that his example has stirred me to concentrate myself with renewed earnestness on the righteous cause for which he died.

Brown's death fused Northern feelings. A month after the hanging, Garrison addressed the Massachusetts Anti-Slavery Society, and never had the hall been so jammed, the atmosphere so tense. Maria, with heart bursting to do, do, do, heard him flame:

> Whereas ten years since, there were thousands who could not endure my slightest word of rebuke to the South, they now can swallow John Brown whole and his rifle into the bargain. In firing his gun he has merely told us what time of the day it is. It is high noon, *thank God*.

XX

Yankees Brave and Dandy

WHEN THE BROWN DRAMA FINALLY PLAYED ITSELF OUT, Maria felt as drained and weary as if her bones had lost their marrow. She longed to be back at Wayland with David, free to forget the world and its worries. But once again duty won over love and they stayed on with Miss Lucy Osgood, whose sister had just died. Maria tried to comfort her old friend with Swedenborgian faith in immortality. Miss Lucy, daughter of a Unitarian minister, had need of such comfort and warmth of belief.

Maria bustled about, setting the physical as well as the spiritual Osgood house in order and cooking up the spicy hashes for which she was famous. Scraps of this and scraps of that, chopped fine in a huge wooden bowl, homemade catsup doused on to hold the meat together and the whole dumped into an iron spider and allowed to rest far back on the wood range until a crust formed on the bottom and then served like pie with an extra dash of catsup—ambrosia. And while the fragrance and Maria's tuneless humming rose from the kitchen, David charmed Miss Lucy with quotations from Horace and Aristophanes.

As long as the Childs had remained in Medford, they were

bound to be immersed in any antislavery activity the town provided. A Ladies' Antislavery Meeting had been scheduled at the Medford Town Hall for that month of December, 1859, with Sallie Holley as guest speaker. People streamed over from the surrounding towns, Woburn, Melrose, and Lexington to hear the well-known lecturer discuss her trials as an abolitionist. Early arrivals found the door of the hall placarded with the announcement that the town fathers had rescinded permission to hold the meeting there. Even in liberal Medford, feeling against abolition still ran high but what infuriated the partisans was that the authorities had waited until the last minute to cancel their given word. Knots of bewildered, angry people stood there in the street, waiting for something to happen, for someone to lead them. A small boy pelted down the street and swerved toward the nearest group. His words tumbled out between gasps. "Miz Child says all who want to, come on up to Osgoods."

The crowd began to move and the boy raced back up the hill before it. "They're a-comin', Miz Child. Right now, they're a-comin'."

"Thank you, Seth," answered that efficient lady as she directed her husband to set out all the chairs he and the boy could find and, at the same time, got Miss Lucy to work on the parlor. Stools came down from the attic, the center parlor table was cleared of its brass-hasped family albums and shoved between the two front windows for a speaker's stand, and in a twinkling, the Osgood parlor had become a snug meeting hall from which no town authority dared to eject an audience.

By the time the ladies had puffed their way up the hill, Miss Lucy was as excited as could be. Even with Sister gone, she could be of some use after all. And she gave Maria a quick hug for her inspiration, while the guests found

perches on chairs, hassocks, and the stools or stood out in
the hallway to crane their necks not only to see Miss Holley
but their own local celebrity, Maria Child. They strained,
too, to see David, the charming, elusive husband, whom
many of them had never glimpsed before. Town gossip still
whispered that Maria should have done better, but strangers,
seeing his handsome, fine-drawn face, smirked, " 'Pears to
me that man'd be worth the keeping." Perhaps he heard
them or sensed their warmth for he smiled at them in his
very special way with eyes crinkled at the corners and mouth
turned just a bit to one side as though he and the sharer of
that smile had an understanding, privately. Then he turned
toward his wife and across the room; what she saw in his
eyes made her blush. For a moment she was lost in the
glow; then she busied herself by asking her neighbors how
they did and the progress of their grandchildren.

What a thrill to see so many of the families she had known
all her life loyal to the cause for which she had been willing
to give up her own. Her eye rested on Mary Preston Stearns,
plump, married for sixteen years to George, still a fugitive in
Canada. Mary too had sacrificed; there were rumors that
George would have to face Congressional investigation if he
were returned. Maria looked fondly toward David. His days
of wandering seemed to be over at last though his correspondence with the Republican leaders in Washington was as
voluminous as ever. She gave herself a little shake. She had
no right to go woolgathering in this earnest and overheated
crowd.

The meeting was a success, for Miss Holley was a
persuasive character and new committees for sewing, tract
distribution, and vigilance against slave catching were
formed. Lucy Osgood found plenty to do and when everyone
had left, she again squeezed Maria's round little waist and

thanked her for making life worth living. Guest and hostess
straightened the dried flowers on the mantel, repinned the
antimacassers, and commented on the sincerity of those who
had volunteered to work. With Miss Lucy's energies so
restored, she would probably take on whatever the
delinquents left.

A few days later, the Childs went home to Wayland for
Christmas. Both of them had jobs of writing to finish—
David his article on John Quincy Adams for the *Homes of
American Statesmen* series, and Maria the final revision on
her "The Right Way, the Safe Way" pamphlet by which she
expected to convince Southern planters and Northern
business interests that slavery was uneconomic. All she
needed was the right argument. She cited the facts that
proved that West Indian emancipation had given the islands
more efficient and willing labor. She asked why the United
States, which prided itself on being progressive, should lag
behind the British West Indies? She refrained from con-
demning the sluggishness of the Republicans, though her
own fervor nearly choked her. David had told Sumner flatly
that the withdrawal of Southerners from the Union would
come "not as a loss but as a relief" and that there was
"nothing valuable or lovable in the Union (as it now stands)
except the inherent facility of falling to pieces." She agreed
fully with David.

She sent the pamphlet to Sumner with a diatribe against
the "timidity" of his Party, and added:

> I hope this package will not be inspected before it reaches
> your hands, for what I have written above would be proof
> positive that Mrs. John Brown and I, with twenty Amazons,
> were coming to take the Old Dominion and were backed by
> the Republican Party.

Poor Sumner, heckled constantly by both of the Childs, yet

aware better than most of the service they gave by the information which somehow came their way and which they unfailingly passed on to Washington. Their quiet Wayland life was the perfect screen for the help they gave their country during these stressful years.

Some of this information undoubtedly filtered through by reason of the visitors to the little brown house. Those who called Maria unsociable would have been amazed at the trouble she took to make her guests comfortable and if everyone had not known that she was a housekeeping perfectionist, they would have ridiculed the lengths to which she went. Yet she told Mrs. Shaw and Mrs. Silsbee that she would rather live in a tree than go without seeing them; and when they came, they could see that she had scrubbed the wide floor boards, aired the mattresses, and put up fresh muslin curtains all over the house. She apologized for the grimy greasiness of the banister rope threaded through iron rings. It was worn smooth; few would dare to climb those steep stairs without holding onto it. She apologized further for the guest room, which was sketchily furnished because the stairwell was too narrow to pass any but small pieces up.

As it was, the guests did not realize that Maria had given her own room to them and that she and David had had to move across the landing to one of those unheated cells while the company was snug with a well-stocked fireplace. David did not like the arrangement at all and not only because of the discomfort involved. That fireplace could be a menace unless one understood its crochets, for it, like the one in the kitchen, was too shallow to be safe. He warned the guests to be careful of flying sparks.

Mrs. Silsbee brought Maria a knitted hug-me-tight as a New Year's gift and Maria gave her a new bust of Ole Bull which she thought would be more suitable for the Silsbee drawing room than her own little parlor. There was a new element in the ladies' stormy friendship, the fact that Mayor Silsbee was an active Bell-Everett, a member of that remnant of conservative Democrats so thoroughly opposed to abolition, secession, and constitutional change that they were prepared to go to violent lengths to back up their principles. Mrs. Silsbee knew very little of what they planned but she knew enough for Maria to report to Sumner. It hurt to use an old friendship for such a purpose but the national crisis allowed her no choice. The Bell-Everetts, unless they were checked, might well wreck the nation.

Throughout the summer of 1860 she and David watched the presidential campaign. Maria doubted that Lincoln was much of a leader but was thoroughly relieved that New York Boss Thurlow Weed had been unable to force Seward as presidential timber down the throat of the Republicans. Seward was unpalatable to both of the Childs and Maria warned Whittier: "Beware how you endorse William H. Seward. He is no more to be trusted than Daniel Webster was. He is thoroughly unprincipled and selfish. I do not speak rashly. I know whereof I affirm." This to Whittier who had written a sonnet in praise of the incoming Secretary of State, who only too soon made it clear that his chief interest was his personal political future. He had wanted to be President and he still wanted it. Maria sighed, "How I wish the Presidency were a disease a man could catch only once."

Her own conscience was called to account that summer. Long ago she had vowed to liberate Thomas Sims, the young mechanic who had been sent back to slavery in 1851. Now the boy's sister brought Maria a letter pleading for help and for freedom. Only Sims, of the three fugitives recaptured in Massachusetts since the passage of the Fugitive Slave Act, was still a slave. It would cost $1,800 to liberate him. Maria concentrated on the problem. "I've got to do it. I will do it," she told David. "If necessary I'll stand on the steps of the State House and besiege passers-by but I'll get that money somehow."

Get it she did. She wrote eighteen letters that very day, and her letters were long and detailed. One of those eighteen influential citizens, Major-General Devens, offered the whole amount on condition that his gift be kept confidential. Maria agreed, of course, jubilant that this former henchman of Webster's had suffered so beautiful a change of heart, had been in fact the identical marshal who had ordered Sims' recapture in 1851. How lovely was the hand of God. How she wished she could shout out, "No fetters in the Bay State."

Yet business was feeling the pinch of abolition tactics, just as Mayor Silsbee and others had predicted. "Look at this," chuckled Maria one morning as she read the *Traveller's* editorial. "David, do you know why the cotton mills are really overstocked? It's because ladies only need three yards of lace to wear under their hoops nowadays instead of the ten and a half that used to be the fashion. You see, you see, the ladies will win out one way or another!"

The smaller use of cotton was definitely causing a trade slump, and as business declined, so did work. Riots broke out. On December 3, 1860, a mob exploded into the Tremont Temple during a memorial meeting for John Brown. Wendell Phillips, the speaker, had just finished a superb peroration on "How Can Slavery Be Abolished in America" and Maria snapped her wedding band with the passion of her applause. The audience hissed at Charles Francis Adams' suggestion that New Mexico be a new Southern state since that land was not fit for the growing of slave crops in any case. This was politically stupid since, slave crop or no, it would give the South more voting power. The small business-men booed at Phillips while a group of hired bullies started trouble by pushing, and shoving, and curses that condemned antislavery skullduggery for the business slowdown. Clerks, storekeepers, cotton superintendents took fire and, in their best black suits, turned into a vicious mob. Someone called them the "Broadcloth Mob" and the name stuck.

Maria knew only too well who had pulled the strings behind the scenes, for she heard one rowdy ask another how much he had been paid for his troublemaking and the second one answered, "Five dollars." Even the police seemed to be in the pay of the Bell-Everetts, for they broke up the excitement half-heartedly and Maria said that their efforts were about as effective as "extinguishing fire with alcohol."

From then on riots were a part of any abolitionist meeting and the police hardly knew whom to protect, since strong influences pressed from both sides. Eventually the Mayor refused to send police at all. Six weeks later, on January 24, 1861, Phillips was again the speaker and it was at this meeting that Maria Child and Maria Chapman stepped in to save his life. It was nearly twenty years since the editor of the *Anti-Slavery Standard* had told Mrs. Chapman straight out that she would not work with her. Now in a moment of crisis, they moved together as protectors of a great man.

By contrast to the excitement of Boston were the quiet days in Wayland. To be sure, Maria again caused a furor with her book *Incidents in the Life of a Slave Girl,* because she had actually edited the work for a former slave, Linda Brent, though she lost money by it. Linda had been the property of Nathaniel Willis, who had refused to bring the poor woman's children out of the South. Maria unearthed an old poem of Willis' proving that he too had once, in his youth, been vehemently against slavery. At last she had settled the score with him for his spiteful remarks about stale gingerbread. What a long, long memory.

When spring came David dug her garden and the gauzy shimmer of the willows brought its annual lift to her heart. When the lilies of the valley and the peonies poked their rosy tips through the black earth, she cleared them of leaves in the morning and covered them again at night against a late frost. And the smell of the loam, and the sun on her neck, made her feel young and strong again. By May the ground was light enough to sow her seeds and those that Sumner sent her from wherever he happened to travel. Out of the tin tea caddy, carefully labeled, came sweet williams, violas, four o'clocks, marigolds, clove pinks, and poppies. She seed-sprinkled the ground generously. No thrift here. She wanted flowers in every corner and she wanted more to give away, for flowers were like love, the exact gift for anyone who needed them. To a child who asked for an autograph she wrote:

> To love one's family is good.
> To love one's country is better.
> To love one's fellow man is best.

This was the spirit that spurred her into writing for the *Atlantic* in order to earn more money to give away. She leaned on her memories of Norridgewock and Medford for the little tales that sold so profitably. The money came easily and went the same way, not for a bonnet or fashionable frippery for herself but for someone's need. A friend once mentioned that he had no dictionary but that the cheapest one at ten dollars was more than he could afford. The very next day he received a twenty-dollar one—this from Maria who did all her own washing, cooking, and even house painting.

The thunder of guns against Fort Sumter shook the lethargy from the North, to act as a catalyst and change many of the Cotton Whigs and much of the conservative element into men of action. Susan B. Anthony and her cohorts put aside the crusade for Women's Rights to hammer night and day for emancipation. Boston suddenly filled with regiments of soldiers. Maria stormed: "Only look at the sort of men who are now talking real, fanatical abolitionism, men who, only a few months ago, were the hardiest hunkers, the most proslavery demagogues!" She swept books, papers, maps to the floor, her whole being in revolt, and sobbed. "Why could they not think sooner? It is such a waste, David, such a miserable waste." "Dear heart," he pleaded, "it does no good to cry. Take it more quietly." Quietly indeed. Not she, and off she went with the tears still wet, to find wool to knit for the "Contrabands," slaves who escaped behind the Union lines.

Lincoln, whose first few months as President did very little to endear him to abolitionists, now committed a further blunder. When the Contrabands asked for protection at Fort Pickens, he ordered them returned to their owners. How reminiscent of Webster! Legally, of course, he was right, but Maria said that the order made her ill every time she looked at the flag. She wrote to Mrs. Shaw:

> When the United States treats colored people with justice and humanity, I will thank you to present me with a flag for a breast pin but, until then, I would as soon wear the rattlesnake upon my bosom, as the eagle. . . . Every instance of sending back a poor fugitive slave has cut into my heart like the stab of a bowie knife . . . the enthusiasm of soldiers and people must be diminished by it. A soldier needs a great idea to fight

for and how can the idea of freedom be otherwise than obscured by witnessing the wicked, mean, unmanly surrendering of poor, trembling fugitives?

One fugitive at least had good luck behind the Union lines. Sims, for whom negotiations had stopped with the opening of war, somehow or other escaped on his own, to Boston where General Devens, true to the promise he had made Maria, set the young man up in business. This success encouraged Maria to propagandize further. She sent out two thousand copies of the "Right Way, the Safe Way," to Southerners at her own expense. She sent more to Gerrit Smith and other influential friends in the hope that they too would distribute them. She asked Sumner to use his franking privilege to send another copy to the Emperor of Brazil in whose country slavery still flourished. David laughed at her for this last attack. He said she reminded him of the old Revolutionary soldier who climbed a hill and shouted, "Attention! The Universe! Kingdoms, wheel to the right!" She answered that she did not care and that if she had embarrassed Charles Sumner, it was because she knew nothing of red tape. "All I ask is to have things done in a natural way for I am a natural fool," she said.

The Childs' frugality became austere during the war. Maria scraped up eighteen or twenty dollars each month to send to the Contrabands with the clothing she begged and knitted for them. She knitted fifteen pairs of socks and mittens for the Kansas troops, and while her needles clicked, she hummed "Yankee Doodle" off key; and when, all at once, new words popped into her mind, she got them down on paper and sent them off to be published. This was the first stanza:

> I hearkened to the thundering noise
> And wondered what t'was for, sir;

But when I heard them tell our boys,
I started up and swore, sir.

Yankee boys will fight it out,
Yankees brave and dandy—
Freedom be our battle shout!
Yankee doodle dandy.

The troops marched off alternating that song with James Gibbons' "We are coming, Father Abraham, Three Hundred Thousand Strong."

In the midst of war work, Maria did not forget her beloved friends. She made a crib quilt for the first Shaw grandchild, tiny pink calico stars against a white ground and a wreath of roses as a border. She sewed and quilted without a frame and wondered how many thousands of stitches she had taken for other people's babies. She sighed long, long sighs.

The baby's father, George William Curtis, thanked her personally for the quilt and the "thought" she had worked into it. She answered him:

I don't think I worked many thoughts into the little quilt. Visions I had of baby's being like her blessed grandmother and her frank, sincere mother and hopes that her womanhood would dawn upon peaceful and prosperous times; and once I smiled to think that my little quilt might be prophetic of the *future* flag of the Union, all stars and *no stripes*.

The weak-kneed administration and the Secretary of State who "hung about Lincoln's neck and dragged him down, down into the mire of political compromise" discouraged the Childs, and when David asked Sumner to intercede for him as a possible minister to Portugal, Maria prayed that her husband would get the appointment. How marvelous to get away from slimy politics into a warm, lovely land. Only

Lydia Maria Child at the Age of 63

recently she had reported another Bell-Everett plot to
Sumner whereby these old-time Democrats, who now called

themselves the Constitutional Union Party, would seize Washington and replace Lincoln with John Breckinridge of Kentucky. They sent coded bundles of small sticks through the mails, tied in various knots, to communicate their plans.

The spring of 1861 dragged by as the Childs waited to hear about Portugal, but when three months passed with no word, David again wrote to Sumner for news. He refused to go to the Capitol to plead his own cause. He felt that he was entitled to consideration by reason of his services. His letter to Sumner was bitter:

> I should suppose if, in any other civilized country and under enlightened and upright government, that some sort of official favor might flow spontaneously toward a veteran laborer, who, for thirty-two years, has been digging and cementing and filling with pure water, the great reservoir.

David with all of his own lobbying experience still assumed that "official favor flowed spontaneously."

He and Maria waited in vain for their castles in Portugal.

XXI

The Sunset Crusader

THEY WAITED JULY, AUGUST, SEPTEMBER WITH NO WORD from Washington. In October David read in the newspaper that the appointment to Portugal had gone to someone else. That was that, another dream past. Both of them were deeply hurt, not only because they had lost the opportunity but because they had found it out so casually. "Evidently," commented David with some bitterness, "the time has not yet come in America when offices will go after good men instead of bad men going after offices."

There was nothing to do but to settle back in Wayland. The news from the front varied. The defeat at Bull Run, the *Trent* affair with Mason and Slidell, bounty jumping, taxes, greenbacks, General McClellan who would not fight and Burnside who fought too soon, Frémont who "emancipated" the slaves in Missouri and was slapped down by Lincoln for his pains, Shiloh, Fort Donelson, the *Monitor* and the *Merrimac,* and the first rumblings from Unconditional Surrender Grant. News! Some good, some bad, but all exciting. And the Childs kept wondering if a slipshod administration was doing its best.

269

Maria wrote to Whittier:

> My courage flags a little and hope grows faint in these latter days. The *people* head in the right direction but we are unfortunate in the men we have placed in power. Lincoln is narrow-minded, short-sighted and obstinate. . . . Charles Sumner, how erect *he* stands in his moral majesty! I always rely on *him,* as securely as I do upon the rising sun; he never disappoints me.
>
> What a moral constitution he must have had to keep such robust health amid the malaria of Washington.

Apparently it was not Sumner whom she held responsible for the Portuguese fiasco but the administration first and foremost. How much it was at fault—and how often. How blind the President was not to see that unless he freed the slaves, the South would—in order to win the support of England in the war. Frémont's emancipation order had been impulsive but Lincoln made a bad situation worse by canceling it. Yet much as Maria deplored the delays, she knew that the day of freedom had to come and she comforted other abolitionists with the story of the old Negro mammy who told the mother of a sick child that the medicine would work in time. "It will work, ma'am. Trust in God, ma'am; He's tedious but He's sure."

In October, 1862, Sumner sent Maria a copy of the Emancipation Proclamation which was to come out on the following January first. "Why, why, why does he wait for another three months? Doesn't that dunderhead [Lincoln] realize that Seward's playing for time again for his own sticky purposes?" she wept. But when the new year put the law into effect, her heart soared and she began to soften toward Lincoln. And she wrote:

> Our cause is going to mount the throne of popular favor. Then I shall bid goodbye to it and take hold of something that is unpopular. I never work on the winning side, because I

know there will always be aplenty to do such work.

David, whose rheumatics sometimes made him irritable, sighed and wished she would stop singing her favorite doggerel:

> But for me I shall never pause to ask
> Which dog may be in the right;
> For my heart will beat, while it beats at all
> For the under-dog in the fight.

Yet not even Maria realized how long the "under-dog," whether slave or free, would be kept down.

Whenever private feuds or public conniving threatened her control it was David who steadied her. He was not the oak nor she the vine, yet now it was he upon whom she relied. Her highest praise for friends was that David thought well of their accomplishments. When Whittier published his "Negro Boat Song," she congratulated him by quoting her husband's couplet:

> One bugle note from Whittier's pen
> Is worth at least ten thousand men.

Unresigned to being a stay-at-home lady during these hectic years, she would have liked to serve with the Educational Commission for the Freedmen or in the Contraband camps, but her "nearest duty" kept her in Wayland. David's health was up and down and she did not want him to feel that he was a burden to her or that she had sacrificed herself for him. She saved his pride and her own by constant activity. He complained that he got tired just watching her go through a day, scrubbing, polishing, running to her table to write a few lines, mending a neighbor child's mitten, ready to discuss anything with him from Plato to Lincoln. Once he chuckled: "You rush around so much to save time that you should really eat your breakfast the night before."

She never minded his teasing. Her movements were

always swift, for she could no more putter over a job than
abide slovenly housekeeping. It was simply her way to work
as hard and fast as she could with no corners skimped, and
she took extra pains with her care of David; this was the
"nearest duty," the most important job. Mary Todd Lincoln
was Maria's illustration in those days of a miserable sort of
mate. As she told Whittier:

> I will whisper in your *private* ear that Lincoln is unfortunate
> in having a fool for a wife. All she cares for is flattery and
> dress and parties. This is not becoming when the people are
> suffering and sacrificing so much. . . . Seward is at the
> President's ear constantly, and knows pretty well how to twist
> him round his finger, but if there is any point he doubts of
> carrying directly, he can carry it indirectly by flattering Mrs.
> L. It is the old story of Adam and Eve and the Serpent. I
> believe that Seward is really President, Lincoln only nominally
> so. . . . I confess I never disliked any man except Daniel
> Webster so much as I dislike Seward.

Maria did not doubt that the President's wife would scuttle
the good of the country for the sake of a new dress and that
"Eve" and the "Serpent" between them made a shambles
of American government. In a further letter, she added:

> If we are saved, it will be better than we *deserve*. I would
> sacrifice everything in life, and life itself, to preserve our free
> institutions, but if we must have the noble structure pulled
> about our ears by the blind giant, Slavery, I hope the poor
> Negroes will have a rollicking good time dancing on the ruins.

Yet, being fair, or trying to be, she wrote Sumner again:

> I suppose, taking all things into consideration, we can have
> no better President than "Honest Abe" with his slow mind
> and legal conscience forever pottering about details and
> calculating chances.

She conceded that he was honest but she suspected that "his fear of God is secondary to his fear of the Democratic party." Politics first, then duty.

Meanwhile her personal griefs multiplied. In April, 1863, after she had nursed him through eight hard weeks, her beloved brother Convers died. He had been her teacher, her guide, her ideal through the years of growing up. How poignant was the memory of his teasing and kindness to her, his little sister, in the old bakehouse; his letters to Norridgewock; his welcome to Watertown; his unfailing pride in her achievements despite her marriage; his warnings against her affection for John Hopper during those first years in New York. Convers had been her balance wheel for so long. There had been times when his caution had annoyed her, but now that he was dead, she could only remember that she had lost her big brother and that she would miss him for the rest of her life. Abby Francis, Convers' daughter, generously sent most of her father's library to Aunt Maria and in those books, many of them dating back to those early years, Maria found a measure of comfort. And in David, her strength.

Shortly after this, she sat one day in her east room, absorbed in working out another story for the *Atlantic*. The house was damp and chilly, the very fringes of her shawl seemed wet, and her nose was stopped up with still another cold. Deep in the problem of getting her blond hero out of the clutches of unfriendly Indians and back to the tribe which had adopted him, her tears fell to the paper in sympathy. Suddenly David's shout penetrated the fog: "Maria, quick, the house is on fire!"

She never remembered details of the next hour. The neighbors charged in with a bucket brigade and saved the place. The old extension, the kitchen, and the two rooms above it were badly damaged but most of her books and keepsakes were safe. Everything was streaked with soot and smoke. The tears really flowed then. They stood there, two elderly children, staring at the ruins. No one ever could say how the blaze began but David publicly blamed the shallow kitchen fireplace. If he suspected that the sun, shining through one of her window prisms, could have ignited a scrap of paper, he would not have told her. He could not destroy her faith in rainbows.

Mrs. Shaw, ever sympathetic and practical, sent two hundred dollars toward rebuilding, but Maria returned the money with the explanation that their insurance would cover most of the expense and Abby Francis would make up the rest. Abby, bless her, had found a memorandum in her father's handwriting setting aside a fund of $150 a year for Maria. Furthermore, one of Maria's booksellers discovered a fifty dollar credit in her favor. It was miraculous how everything worked for them. David went straight out to buy building materials.

They had a fine time papering, painting, and hammering. Up and down the ladders they went, flat on the floor or crouched near the ceiling, oblivious of the fact that years have a way of making themselves felt. Before long both of them were lame and sore but unshaken in the pride with which they pointed out the improvements they had made. They had a spick-and-span world to prove that they were young.

But after the fire Maria no longer slept soundly. She struggled through dreams of holocaust and often, half-awake, stumbled down the steep stairs to assure herself that she had been dreaming, that only imagination was responsible for the smoke. She and David decided at last reluctantly that their privacy on the Old Sudbury Road was a mixed blessing and that they would have to rent out a part of their house.

The fire had forced them to realize that they were too isolated.

The new tenants, father, mother and children, settled into the two new rooms on the other side of the landing and stayed out of the way so that David hardly felt their presence. Maria, however, took a long while to accustom herself to strangers in her house. She begged David to lower his voice when he called her "Carissima" and "Dear Heart." "Don't you want me to tell you that I love you?" he would ask with an injured, boyish look. "Of course I do," she answered helplessly. "I just want to keep it to ourselves." He shouted, "Let them hear. Let the whole world hear. You are my queen and I your willing knight." Then he dropped to one knee and looked up at her with such ardor that she forgot that they had been married more than thirty years.

The tenants stayed with them for some years, and in time, when both families were used to one another, Maria and the children became fast friends. She rarely took the rickety yellow stage to Boston without bringing home books or sweets for them. Even though their pet rabbits were mysteriously released from their cages, Charlotte and her brother wanted to hear Mitty Chile's stories. She told them that day about a caged bird owned by the daughter of Pétion, hero-patriot of Haiti. The little bird, kept behind gilt bars, drooped and lost his feathers because, as Maria insisted, birds, like children—and animals— want to be free. Charlotte cried for pity and from that day on the only pet was David's ancient bulldog who waddled where he would with no one and nothing to stop him.

Chickadees and robins flew in and out of the bushes and ruined the cherry crop. Maria refused to keep a cat, for thrushes and nuthatches meant more to her than fruit. The Cutting children, to "fuss" her, trundled their kitten over in a wheelbarrow. Maria's head popped through the window indignantly. "Your children know," she began—and then saw that the kitten was safely tied in the barrow. She rushed out, dropped a contrite kiss on each head and an apple in each hand and said, "Now you young mischiefs, get along home with that monster and don't come back until puss is safe down cellar."

The children's nonsense distracted her from her concern over her friends in New York where riots were rampant. The Gibbons' house had been burned out during one of these and one family had escaped over adjoining roofs. Why should such attacks come about? David had got hold of a circular, privately printed, which ordered the dissatisfied Irish element to set fire to New York, Boston, and Philadelphia and to sabotage the water supply. It was supposed to be masterminded by Jefferson Davis to scare the North into ending the war. Maria read that five hundred armed "banditti" were prowling around Staten Island where the Shaws now lived and she begged Mrs. Shaw to come to Wayland for safety. David called her "Madame Croaker" for her fears, but she brushed his flippancy aside with the remark, "I wonder if that viper, Seward, might have something to do with these outbreaks." Even if she had seen proof that Seward had nothing to do with it, she would have hated him.

The death of Robert Gould Shaw gave her further reason to worry about her friends. The young colonel was killed in the battle at Fort Wagner at the head of his regiment of colored troops. Maria's prayers and those of his parents had not been enough to protect that fair-haired boy who had ridden off to war singing "John Brown's Body." He and twenty-five of his Negro soldiers were cut down together and their bodies hurled pellmell into a pit near the bank of the Georgia River. Cut to pieces, he was thrown in first and his men piled on top. The attacking Southern officer supposedly had sneered, "If he liked niggers so well, let him rot with them."

Maria shivered in the summer heat as she read of young Shaw's death and supported the move to place a memorial to him on Boston Common, though she was furious that his statue would stand facing that of Daniel Webster on a slightly lower level.

John Hopper's death struck at her in a very different way. He too died a hero, but a quiet, unsung one. Because of his weak eyes, he had not been a soldier but he paid life insurance for many others and the expenses of his sister Abby and her daughter during their three years of hospital service and sent cargoes of food and supplies free to wherever they were needed. Only his family knew the extent of his generosity. Maria could not share her grief over John with David. It was twenty years since she and Hopper had walked in Battery Park by moonlight, twenty years since those awkward gifts and emotional bursts had made the Hopper house an adventure in living. She cried now over his tenderness for her and was ashamed that she had ever even slightly doubted him during that ridiculous episode with Ole Bull. She regretted her impatience with him, after he had confided his love for Rosa; she went far, far back in her musings and forgot that David was by her side. Suddenly conscious of her husband, she saw his quizzical smile. It was as though he said, "I am here, darling, as I have always been, and I love you." There was no need for shouting that day. His compassion undid her and she cried, not for John, but for love itself.

On a July day when news of Gettysburg reached Wayland, all grief was forgotten. David raced over to the Cuttings to borrow their huge flag. He ran home again, the flag strapped to his shoulders and the Cutting children pelting behind him. He climbed sixty feet to the top of the big elm in front of the house where he unfurled and fastened the flag. Maria, breathless with fright over his impetuosity, watched, tears coursing down her cheeks, a Cutting child holding tightly to each of her hands. High in the air, his white hair tossed by the wind, David sang "The Star Spangled Banner." Far below, his wife and the children took up the song; and all over the Union that day, voices strong and quavering, weak or full, sang in thankfulness.

It was not every day that David could climb that tree or that Maria would feel well enough to stand on the damp grass to watch him. She told Mrs. Silsbee, "I try to resist growing old but I cannot." Rheumatism plagued both of the Childs. Only pencilings of sun came through the tiny bedroom windows to ease the mildew damp. David made poultices of stewed white beans in thin muslin bags which he put on his wife's swollen joints. She was working against difficulties to finish another book, *Looking Toward Sunset,* and the pain in her hands often made her think that her own sunset was long past and night in full flower.

Ironically, this book was intended to help other elderly people toward a more cheerful view of life. The author, in explaining her plan to Ticknor, said she read only "chipper" books herself, a recipe for relaxed thinking. But fine purpose is no assurance of success and the new work had bad luck. None of the German illustrations which she had cut out and saved in her scrapbooks were exactly suitable. The panes of glass in one were out of proportion, the grandmother's cap was of the wrong shape in another. When the publishers did find better pictures, these were lost in the mail; and when at last the manuscript was ready, the printers went on strike so that by the time the book was ready to market, six of the old friends to whom Maria wanted to dedicate it had already died.

She felt better when it sold well, four thousand copies in the first few days, and better than ever when Whittier wrote his praises to her:

> Thy beautiful book and kind letter reached me a few days ago and my heart has been thanking thee ever since. It was an exceedingly happy thought of thine to send out these words of cheer to those of us who are beginning to pass down life's sunset declivities. I do not like, however, to have thee call thyself old. I never think of thee as such. Where the heart and fancy are still young, why should we recur to family registers?

The Quaker poet still knew how to charm the ladies.

Wendell Phillips and his wife appreciated the *Sunset* as much probably, though Mr. Phillips' supposition that she must nearly have worn out her spectacles in looking for material was not nearly as flattering. The most touching tribute of all came from William Cullen Bryant, who said:
My dear Mrs. Child:

> You are like some artists who excel in "sunset views." You give the closing stage of human life an atmosphere of the richest lights and warmest views, and make even its clouds add to its glory.

The war dragged on and the success of the new book could not lift Maria's spirits, while the young men of Wayland went away singing, "When Johnny Comes Marching Home." People were saying that Lincoln was prolonging the war for political reasons, an assertion which both of the Childs did not believe. Just before the election of 1864 when General McClellan was the nominee of the Democrats, Maria wrote to Whittier:

"Old Abe," I believe, deserves his reputation for honesty and I have no doubt that he has a hearty abhorrence of slavery . . . he is a man of details, I think, by nature and habit, incapable of taking comprehensive views. Who is there that would be better [as President] except Charles Sumner and he would not be available as a candidate.

On the eighth of November, Election Day, she wrote again:

I have never cared to vote, but today makes me sad I cannot. To think that a drunken Irishman [McClellan] may decide the destiny of this great nation while I, who have so long and carefully watched all the springs in the machinery of state, would be contemptuously thrust from the polls! What a burlesque on human institutions!

Even without the woman vote, Lincoln won overwhelmingly. After the count, Maria told Parke Godwin:

I became more and more radical. I rejoice in having a railsplitter for President and a tailor [Andrew Johnson] for Vice-President. I wish a shoe-black could be found worthy to be appointed Secretary of State, and I should be all the more pleased if he were a *black* shoe-black.

The beginnings of Lincoln's second term seemed propitious. David as a lawyer made his wife aware that the President had acted according to, and with, the full intent of the law while showing enormous skill in handling his Cabinet and the people. Maria herself recognized his humanity. To Eliza Scudder, an old friend and Women's Rights advocate, she wrote:

I am a happy woman since the election. It makes me feel that our republican form of government rests on more secure foundations. There was no enthusiasm for honest old Abe. There is no beauty in him, that men should desire him; there is no insinuating, polished manner to beguile the senses of

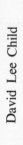

David Lee Child   Lydia Maria Child

the people; there is no dazzling military renown, no silver flow of rhetoric; in fact no glittering prestige of any kind surrounds him; yet the people triumphantly elected him, in spite of all manner of machinations, and notwithstanding the long, long drag upon their patience and their resources which this war has produced. I call this the triumph of the free schools for it was the intelligence and reason of the people that reelected Abraham Lincoln.

On April 4, 1865, six days after the end of the war, Lincoln was shot. A stunned nation mourned the loss of its leader. The Great Emancipator was dead and Andrew Johnson, the tailor, became President. How would he deal with the problems of Reconstruction? Would he stand by the Freedmen or kowtow to their former owners? Lincoln was dead. Were the principles for which he and so many soldiers died, dead too?

The ponderous machinery of government hesitated, procrastinated, while conscientious citizens lay rigid in their beds at night and wondered what the next gray dawn would bring. But not Maria. Those freedmen, now more than before needed to be educated for the difficult days ahead. Pen in hand, Maria Child set forth on her next crusade.

XXII

The Rainbow Fades

HER CONTRIBUTION TO THE EDUCATION OF THE FREEDMEN
was a simple textbook, a collection of poems, hymns, and
stories, most of which she wrote herself to extol the accom-
plishment of Negroes since the nation's start. Even though
Harriet Beecher Stowe, Whittier, and Mrs. Sigourney did
write some small items for *Freedman's Book,* publishers
refused to take it on unless Mrs. Child paid a large share of
the costs. She campaigned to raise the money among her
antislavery friends but no one would give it to her, even
on her promise to send any profits to the libraries of freedmen's schools. Gerrit Smith, always quick to open his purse
to her projects, sent only thirty dollars, and she thanked him
by writing, "I shall accomplish my project in *some* way; I am
determined to do it, and when I determine on doing a thing,
I generally carry it through." Very reminiscent of the pirates,
of Sims, and of Norridgewock.

Carry it through she did, with Ticknor and Company as
publishers, and she paying six hundred dollars of the bill,
scraped up from goodness knows where. She sent off two
hundred pages of manuscript to them, her sole copy, and
all the time it was being processed she had nightmares about

loss or fire. She would have lost two years of work if—but she was terribly impatient to see it in print. Ticknor cooperated. Her proofs arrived afternoons, she worked over them evenings, and back they went to Boston the following morning. Understandably the stepped-up tempo was hard on David but she felt she could not dare to slow down. With a job to be done, she was still that small, plump locomotive of his teasing.

If she missed the daily walk to the post office, and she rarely did, one of the Damons or the Cuttings picked up the proofs for her and sent them over by the children, who were willing to run errands for the handful of flowers or grapes or, even better, the chance that David would come out into the woods and talk to them. "Mitty Chile" was not exactly impolite to the children, but she was busy and she often got rid of them by saying, "When you are ready to leave, there is a piece of cake for you on the mantel." "Is there one for me too?" David might ask, and she blushed contritely at the possibility that she had neglected him. A moment later she would hear him telling the children that the sparrows pecking at the cherries made them sweeter, and prove his point by popping pecked and unpecked samples into their open mouths.

The small Cuttings looked forward each year to David's Annual Fruit Festival. Not even production of the *Freedman's Book* this year could prevent the gala day when David drew the big kitchen table into the sitting room in front of the east windows and heaped his finest watermelons; muskmelons; peaches; red, white, and purple grapes; red and brown pears; yellow and scarlet apples; and nosegays of pink, white, and yellow chrysanthemums tucked in between. Everyone had to wait outside until he called, "Ready." Then in they all trooped, first to admire and then to eat. Wayland children never could decide which they preferred, Mr. Child's Fruit Festival or neighbor Abel Glezen's Pancake Supper; their mothers never bothered to analyze but dosed their broods with castor oil and rhubarb tea after either party.

The tenants were no longer in the other part of the house and it was a relief to keep the kitchen as Maria pleased, with no one to share the cramped pie safe, to use up the kindling; it was pleasant to scrub the iron spider and ladles with scouring rush and know they would stay clean. With her tight schedule, if anything went awry by a quarter hour, her day was ruined and it was therefore simpler to be alone again. David invented various labor-saving devices, some that worked and some that failed, but he was so whimsical while trying them out that it was diversion enough. He held theories on everything. When the upstairs stove, on which he had "improved" the draft, blew smoke downward and smudged fresh paint and curtains, he merely remarked: "Although the experiment has failed, the principle remains." He cleaned away the soot, read Plato to her while she washed the curtains, and readjusted the damper. The second attempt turned out the same, and this time he washed the curtains as well.

One day the Cutting children came over to Baldwin's Pond to test out another of his ideas, that a child swims by instinct. Allie Cutting, with complete faith, put his hand in David's and they walked into the water. The marsh wrens, nesting in the sedge, rose in a flurry. Only when he heard screams from the shore did David realize that Allie was under water and still hanging on to his hand. Happily he also had a theory—and a successful one—for resuscitating small boys, especially a small boy who thought him the wisest of men. And Allie was not alone in that hero worship.

All the farmers roundabout relied on his weather forecasts, made by study of the sheep fluff or cumulus clouds in the sky or by holding up a red silk handkerchief to determine wind direction and velocity. His male neighbors respected his farming lore and familiarity with seven languages while the ladies still found him charming. Even Maria had to admit that a man who cemented a cistern while discussing German philosophy was versatile.

A meticulous workman himself, he expected the same of others. Once, when the village drunkard, whom Maria had tried to reform, came to repair the chimney, David inspected the job, He called down from the roof, "Yes, Tom, it looks very well but I see you have left an orifice between the bricks near the top."

"Yes sir, you're right, sir," answered Tom. "I'll be up to fetch it this instant."

As a rest from work pressures, Maria found it delightful to sit quietly in the garden with David watching giant monarch and swallowtail butterflies hover, orange, yellow, and black, over the flowers; the birds held conventions in the cherry trees; sometimes the watchers caught a flash of a red-winged blackbird or an egret moving on the margin of the pond. Often in the summer when the children's voices carried on the breeze, Maria complained that the neighbors were too close; but when the snow piled high above the windows, she wished she were within hailing distance of at least one friend who shared her interests. The Philothean side, of course. For when the great elm out front sparkled with ice in the winter sun, she shouted for joy and promised to run two miles to catch a poet to share it with her. David showed his appreciation by estimating possible ice damage.

She knew he, like Lincoln, like any good lawyer, was a man of detail. He liked to study the derivation of words and to share his finding with her, but she answered, "You do it if you like. I prefer to learn by intuition." And then she reminded him of the story of the German philologist who spent his days in the study of the Greek grammatical article and on his deathbed told his son, "Boy, take warning by my example; do not undertake too much. I ought to have confined myself to the dative case."

Why had her gifted husband made so little of himself? He knew so much, he was respected in so many fields beyond this limited life in which they now lived, and yet the best he could do was to earn four hundred dollars or less for translations of foreign documents. With so much talent could he not amount to more than being a mere translator and small-town lawyer?

What worried her particularly was his skepticism about the reality of the afterlife. Swedenborg had taught her to count on the welding of husband and wife into one perfect whole in the next world, but her Puritan ancestry darkened her concern for David's immortal soul. Though Unitarianism had not satisfied her, and though she was a most sporadic churchgoer, she did believe in God; but David seemed to lack any religious belief. And they were getting older and closer to the immortal gate.

The course of the government was a further worry. There were so few problems which the war had solved and so many new ones it had raised. Johnson's administration, instead of being merely generous to plantation owners, was downright easy on them. The new President was morally and physically weak, and she wrote to James T. Fields that the "tipsy tailor" in the White House appalled her. It was catastrophic "to have for a captain in a storm a man not fit for cabin boy!" To George Julian, editor of the *Indiana Free Soil Radical,* she wrote:

His [Johnson's] proceedings since he came to the Presidency make me fear he is one of that very common class of spurious democrats who hate aristocracy because *they* were not born to it. *Such* democrats are always ready to kiss the feet of aristocrats as soon as they doff their caps to them, though it be obviously for the mere purpose of accomplishing their own designs. Some say he will bring it all out right at last. If he does, I believe it will be because Congress compels him to do it.

She wrote to newspapers, to Congressmen, to periodical editors, pleas and diatribes to protect the rights of freedmen. She sent copies of the *Freedman's Book* to strangers whose names she got out of city directories. The newsmen printed her pieces and her articles appeared in magazines. Her name still counted.

Her postage bills were enormous, so large that she could not afford one of those new Empress Eugénie bonnets which gave her the happy excuse for refusing invitations on the grounds that she had nothing to wear. Truthfully, she loathed parties; she was too tired, and words no longer flowed easily for her when she outlined first drafts of her stories on the backs of old envelopes. She admitted to Fields:

When one gets to be between sixty and seventy imagination will not always come when it is called for, and my Pegasus is somewhat stiff in the joints from having a heavy cartload of stones to drag these many years.

Were the stones her conscience, the weight of reform, or the burden of effort to support her household? Or was the habit of complaint a superstition to ward off evil? Or impatience with David the habit itself?

When she heard him tell the Cuttings of a new idea for making substitute tobacco out of dandelion shoots, she raged at him, "Didn't you strain your back enough over beet sugar?" He countered gently that his had been the pioneer work and that others had used his identical methods successfully ever since. Which made her more furious, for she thought he deserved the credit and he did not even care. Yet he was glad she stopped him because his inflammatory rheumatism had crippled his hands too badly for a thorough job of sorting the shoots. Maria softened at his capitulation; she liked to think, secretly, that his novel ideas were a sign of youth. He was a wonderful companion, her David, and she really wanted him as he was.

One summer morning while she fumed over an *Atlantic* story that just would not come right, he called her to come into the garden. Already irritated, she resented his laughter as he called again: "Maria, come. We have a new kind of fruit."

In a burst of temper she snapped, "What? More experiments?"

"Yes, but not of my making," answered her patient spouse.

She came to see, and he showed her an oriole's nest lined with familiar lacy wisps. "My best cap! I've looked for it high and low. That little thief. I hung it out here on the bush to dry."

"Well try it on now. I'm sure it is quite as fashionable, nest and all, as the ones the ladies wear in Boston." She looked at David and he twinkled back at her and they walked arm in arm into the house. Somehow her story wrote itself without effort after that.

She had been writing another romance, a sentimental novel, valentines and lavender on the surface but founded on the old theme, fair treatment of the Negro. The *Romance of the Republic,* 442 pages of exchanged identities, flirtatious

belles and mawkish morbidity, was a symptom of the
literary taste of the time. The stupid story was her con-
cession to potboiling with which she was willing to compromise as long as she could embody in it the cry for equality
for black and white. Yet even a public which clamored for
tales of foundlings, seductions, and insanity could not
stomach the *Romance*. Only her name saved it from complete failure.

The year 1867 brought a winter of storms. Waylanders
would talk of those blizzards for years and Maria compared
them to the ones she remembered in Norridgewock when
snow had covered the second story windows. David had to
tunnel to the road to send off the *Romance* chapters as she
finished them—hard work and not worth the trouble,
according to the reviews. Luckily the kitchen still connected
with the woodshed and its supply of logs or the two old
people might have perished of the cold. Their silent Eden
was always frigid, for David still could not get the upstairs
flues to draw properly. At night he and Maria warmed their
bed gowns on the fender in the sitting room, hopped into
them, and scampered up the narrow stairs as fast as they
could. Two shivering gnomes, done up in flannel robes,
raced to see which could get under the covers first.

During the cold daytimes, after the reviews appeared,
Maria had plenty of time to blame herself for having refused
an offer of $1,000 Fields had made her to have the
Romance appear in installments in the *Atlantic*. She had
been so sure that the story was in step with the times, so sure
that her royalties would be profitable. Readers found the
adventures of the New Orleans belles not hair-raising, but
dull and dated.

It was about this time that the family persuaded Maria to
have her picture taken, a likeness that pleased none of them

I thank you, in the name of the crippled class to which I belong, for trying to enable us to walk without crutches. My disabilities as a woman have annoyed me more than I have told of. When my friend Ellis Gray Loring wanted to entertain himself with seeing my face flush and my eyes kindle, he used to repeat, "a married woman is dead in the law." To _me_, who felt so very much alive

Note to George Curtis

Mrs. Child at the Age of 65

since it so plainly showed the deep lines on either side of her compressed lips. She said the lines came from the efforts she had made for thirty-five years "for my brother, Sambo" but other burdens had forged those channels. One thing was the position of women, particularly women who had proved that they were the equal of men in business, thought, and creative work. She thanked George Curtis, the Shaws' son-in-law, for his Women's Rights speeches:

> I thank you, in the name of the crippled class to which I belong, for trying to ennable us to walk without crutches. My disabilities as a woman have annoyed me more than I have told of. When my friend Ellis Gray Loring wanted to entertain himself with seeing my face flush and my eyes kindle, he used to repeat, "A married woman's dead in the eyes of the law." To *me* who felt so very much alive. . . .

She herself was not a part of the Women's Rights or any other movement, for more and more she valued privacy. She found, like Whittier, that curiosity seekers after celebrities could upset an author's schedule beyond patience. Whittier told her, "It is hard enough to get away from intruding men but I can never lose a *her,* for the women are more pertinacious than the men." Maria commented dryly that the only answer was to live far from the railroad and to keep a pitchfork and bulldog on hand. To which he agreed.

New England. This was where she belonged. "I am so glad I was born here instead of under balmy skies," she exulted as she threw her arms to the sky one sunny day.

"But you have always longed for Italy," retorted her husband.

"Oh, only for a tour. Not for good. Those warm climates put quicksilver instead of iron into your blood and I need my strength."

The iron in her blood deepened the lines around her

mouth and drove her to extremes. With the same zest as
she put into spring cleaning, she excoriated Greeley and
Henry Ward Beecher for their "sickly sentimentality"
toward Southerners. She reminded them that the war had
been "no tournament for show, but a death-grapple between
Freedom and Despotism, and unhorsed despotism is all un-
worthy to receive his sword and spurs as if he were an
honorable knight instead of a murderous, thieving caitiff."
Strange that her thinking now was far more reminiscent of
Calvinism and the Old Testament than of the Swedenborgian
understanding she professed to follow. All she would see was
the freedmen's loss; she was blind to the fact that harsh
Reconstruction measures made for economic blunders which
would hurt the entire nation.

In June of 1867 her schedule was thoroughly interrupted.
Ole Bull, her former musical idol, had played his fiddle at
the Peace Festival at the Boston Coliseum. She heard that
he was ill and tired; so, instead of attending the concert, she
urged him to come to Wayland as soon as the recital was
over. He came without even going back to his hotel. When
the stage finally lumbered to a stop in front of the Wayland
Town Hall, the Childs were waiting for him. He did not
notice that Maria looked smaller and plumper than when
he had known her in New York, or that David, though
erect, was frail. They took the famous musician home, put
him to bed in one of the clean little cells upstairs, and left
him. Twenty-four hours later, Ole awakened to find Maria
placidly knitting by his bedside. He sat up, revitalized, and
told her that she had saved his reason.

After he left, no visitors came for a long while, but the
quiet was routed by Grant's election in 1869. The Childs
were jubilant and Maria wrote to Mrs. Shaw:

We had quite a glorification here over Grant's election.

We had a really handsome procession of five hundred men bearing flags and gay-colored lanterns, and attended by a band of music from Boston. I had no idea they would come up so far as our house, but as we had subscribed, as they thought, liberally, they concluded to pay us that compliment. When we heard the sounds coming nearer and nearer, and I saw the first torches pass our nearest neighbor's, I tore open the curtains and scrambled to place fourteen lights in the front windows, being all I could get up at such short notice. Then I went to the front door and waved a great white cloth, and joined in the hurrahs of the procession like a "strong-minded" woman as I am. The fact is, I forget half the time whether I belong to the stronger or the weaker sex. While I was demonstrating at one door, David was exercising his lungs at another. A crowd of foreigners were following the procession in a discomfited state of mind, and, seeing us so jubilant, they called out, "Three cheers for the nigger President!" a curious title to bestow on Grant who has never manifested the slightest interest in the colored people. But I don't want him to be a "nigger President." I simply want him to see that equal justice is administered to all classes of people, and I have great hopes that he will do that. So unpretending a man must be substantially good and honest, I think.

Since Maria was not gifted with the second sight she so admired in others, she could not know how far afield her guess about that "good and honest" man was. In any case, Grant or anyone else would prove more sympathetic to her views than Johnson, whose weakness was blamed by many for the bitter failure of the Reconstruction Era.

Maria did not care who heard her views on public matters but she reared up on her dignity when Tom Pry in the form of Higginson asked permission to write her biography. She resented any intrusion on privacy. As she wrote Mrs. Shaw:

I don't think anybody has a *right* to make a biography of a person who does not wish to have it done. It puts me into a

real fret. I detest notoriety. There are plenty of people who
like it. Let him [Higginson] blow the trumpet for *them*. This
mousing around after my private sentiments seems to me like
surgeons politely asking me to be dissected before I am dead.

In spite of her wishes, Higginson "blew the trumpet" in
his long sketch of her which was included in *Eminent
Women of the Age* in 1868. The company in that compilation
was notable, listing the names of Florence Nightingale, Mrs.
Sigourney, Fanny Kemble, the Empress Eugénie, Margaret
Fuller, Elizabeth Barrett Browning, Jenny Lind, Queen
Victoria, and many others. And still Mrs. Child resented it.
Then, as later, she asked only to be left alone and would not
even allow her name to be used for the game of "Authors."

In 1870 Maria received several pleading invitations to
become a member of the Radical Club which met the first
Monday of each month at the home of the Reverend and
Mrs. John T. Sargent. An intellectual landmark in Boston,
the club's purpose was "to meet a demand for the finest
investigation of all forms of religious thought and inquiry."
Maria might have enjoyed these sessions, for many of her
friends attended them—Sumner, Whittier, Elizabeth Peabody, Higginson, among others. She blessed "those who
strive in any way to strike off the shackles of human thought"
even as she admitted that her own chances of coming were
slight. She would probably have spiked some of the discussions with acid common sense, for they smacked of the
old transcendental aura and combed the edges of thought
with mystic clouds of intuition and inference.

She wanted especially to go to the meeting when Anna
Leonowens would read her paper on Oriental religions. Mrs.
Leonowens was author of a fascinating book on her experiences as a governess at the court of Siam and Maria longed
to exchange ideas with the former governess, who now was

a neighbor of the Shaws on Staten Island as well as an authority in the field of comparative religion. David, however, was miserable again and Maria could not leave him, but the prod of the book on Siam inspired her to write an important article for the *Atlantic* on the "Intermingling of Religions." It was twenty years since she had published her great dull work on religion, but now she turned out a leading piece for that fine magazine and had praise on it from all sides.

By late fall David was well again, well enough indeed to take ax and dinner pail out into the woods, where each day he chopped four cartloads for their winter fuel. It was brave going for a man well over seventy-five. Maria bragged about him the way her friends did about their grandchildren.

There came a time when causes, clubs, and writing were laid aside and her energies turned entirely to him at last. Throughout the spring of 1874, his pains increased and his gaunt frame became emaciated. Maria tried desperately to outthink him, to forestall any strain on his failing strength. It was agony to see him struggle to fasten the hasp on the shed door or tie his cravat, but he refused to be helped. He had always been proud of his manual dexterity, and the fact that his fingers refused to obey him irritated him past bearing. Maria tried by diversion, by reading, by asking his aid on research, to keep his mind from his helplessness.

Charles Sumner's death that year broke their spirits further. Ill as David was, he and Maria went to the Sumner memorial meeting with tickets sent them by Phillips. It was so long since they had appeared anywhere that Phillips said that he was as surprised to see them as if Mt. Monadnock had come to the hall. Afterwards he sent them Sumner's breakfast cup and saucer as a remembrance.

That, however, was David's last outing. By August his

AND LEE CHILD WAS BORN IN WEST BOYLSTON 8 JULY 1794 IN THE JACOB HINDS HOUSE NOW OCCUPIED BY ELWIN J CHASE GRADUATED FROM HARVARD COLLEGE 1817 SUBMASTER OF THE BOSTON LATIN SCHOOL IN 1819 APPOINTED BY PRESIDENT MONROE SECRETARY OF THE UNITED STATES LEGATION AT LISBON PORTUGAL RETURNED TO THE UNITED STATES 1824 STUDIED LAW AND WAS ADMITTED TO THE BAR IN 1828 MARRIED LYDIA MARIA FRANCIS WHO BECAME ONE OF THE MOST DISTINGUISHED AMERICAN WOMEN OF HER DAY INTRODUCED THE MANUFACTURE OF BEET SUGAR INTO THE UNITED STATES VISITING BELGIUM IN 1836 TO LEARN THE PROCESS WAS A MEMBER OF THE GENERAL COURT OF MASSACHUSETTS PRESIDED IN BOSTON AT THE FIRST ANTI-SLAVERY MEETING EVER HELD IN THIS COUNTRY IN 1844 MOVED TO NEW YORK AND WITH HIS WIFE BECAME JOINT EDITOR OF THE NATIONAL ANTI-SLAVERY STANDARD WROTE VOLUMINOUSLY ON THE SUBJECTS OF SLAVERY AND THE SLAVE TRADE AUTHOR OF A WORK ON BEET CULTURE SPENT HIS LATER YEARS IN WAYLAND MASSACHUSETTS DIED THERE 18 SEPTEMBER 1874 BEQUEATHED ONE HUNDRED DOLLARS TO THE TOWN OF WEST BOYLSTON FOR THE PURPOSE OF STARTING THE FOUNDATION OF A PUBLIC LIBRARY AS A RESULT OF HIS BEQUEST THE WEST BOYLSTON PUBLIC LIBRARY WAS FOUNDED 1878 FROM HER OWN LIBRARY HIS WIDOW LYDIA MARIA CHILD DONATED IN 1878 ONE HUNDRED SEVENTY VOLUMES TO THE WEST BOYLSTON PUBLIC LIBRARY

Placque in the Beaman Memorial Library, West Boylston, Massachusetts

growing weakness made him viciously impatient with being
a burden. Maria tried to tempt his appetite with apple butter
from his own trees and with Mrs. Damon's crusty bread,
and to cover his rejection of food, he sang to her, "There's
nothing half so sweet as love's old dream." She smiled at
him and through her tears; she saw her shining knight who
had taken counsel with his tethered steed before he asked
her to become his wife.

They assembled Maria's scrapbooks, pasting German
pictures on one side while David meticulously translated the
verses on the other. He was in the midst of one of these one
morning when his voice stopped. . . .

It was as simple as that. He broke off in mid-thought and
was gone—quiet, relaxed, without pain.

The neighbors who came to help said at the time that
Maria was wonderfully calm, but the fact was that she
simply could not realize what had happened. Then she
noticed the open book, the page where he had stopped, and
the truth engulfed her. She wept because she was grateful
to have been spared to take care of him; she wept for the
gallant gentleman he had been, for the love he had given
her and for the love she had so long withheld from him. She
walked behind the coffin to the Burying Ground. The
cortège passed the family plot of her brother James, and
wound far back from the road. David's casket came to rest
in a glade of bridal wreath, ringed and guarded by barberry
bushes. A great oak spread its protection far overhead. They
covered David with the raw earth.

Outside, the sun shone hot but there was no color anywhere. No bird sang. Only the shuffling of mourners' feet
broke the silence. Maria turned toward the brown house,
no longer home. There was nothing for her, no one anywhere. Her light had faded. The rainbows were gone.

XXIII

We Are the Living

SHE DISSOLVED INTO A FUMBLING OLD WOMAN. AS SHOCK
wore off she could not control her grief. David's death came
within a few weeks of their forty-eighth wedding anniversary
and she tottered from one room to another, touching the bits
of home that he had liked to touch, patting the pillow
against which his head had used to rest, straightening the
carpet slippers beneath his favorite chair. She had lost her
child and her husband in one blow; all at once life held no
savor and the future yawned black without meaning. She
relived the twenty-six years of their life together in Wayland,
years filled with the richness of his scholarship, love, and
understanding. Her steel-rimmed spectacles fogged as she
groped aimlessly back and forth across the uneven boards
of the old house.

Friends and relatives offered love and shelter, but their
sympathy could not penetrate the raw wound of her grief.
They urged her to leave Wayland, but she clung to her
haunting memories, and she looked at her well-wishers as
though they spoke in an incomprehensible foreign tongue.
She wanted only the familiar routines in the idiom of David's
love.

I have passed through a very severe ordeal, in parting from the loving and beloved companion of nearly half a century, and in breaking up the cozy little nest where we lived so many years, mutually depend- -ent upon each other. The deep wound will probably never heal entirely; but I trust it will heal sufficiently for me not to cast a shadow over the happiness of others. I think nothing in the world can have such a con- -soling influence as the presence of dear Frank & Sarah, who have been to me the best and most loyal of friends, through all the changes of my life.

The future seems closed to me; but I am willing, just now, simply to _wait_. I greatly desire to be of some use in the world, during what remains to me of this existence, and I trust it will prove so.

The Sewalls, with deeper perception, found the certain way to reclaim her from the past by demanding her help in trouble of their own. Mrs. Sewall was ill and needed nursing, a plea which Maria could never refuse. She rose to the bait and, as soon as she could leave David's affairs, for which she was sole executrix, she promised to come over to Melrose for her new nursing duty.

David's bequests included one for one hundred dollars to the town of his birth, West Boylston, toward the formation of a free library; and Maria, to accept his legacy, donated 170 books from her own shelves. She sorted his things and distributed many of them for souvenirs to his friends. Garrison in his thanks for her thoughtfulness wrote that he loved and honored David and added:

> I cannot refrain from renewing the expression of my earliest appreciation of your character, genius, literary productions, and self-denying and untiring efforts in the cause of universal emancipation, of suffering humanity in its varied aspects, or religious freedom of inquiry and dissent as against all sacerdotal assumptions, of equal rights and immunities without regard to sex, of reform and progress in their widest scope . . . I honor you . . . among the very first of your sex in any age or country.

Such a letter could not help but warm her even in the days of despair.

She nursed Mrs. Sewall as long as she was needed, then returned to Wayland, fortified by a sense of usefulness, to answer the letters that continued to fill the basket by the door. To Whittier she poured out her loneliness:

> I thank you from my heart for your kind, sympathizing words in my hour of great affliction. It has been a very severe ordeal, this parting from the loving and beloved companion of nearly half a century. . . . I am thankful that he did not

suffer for a very long time; I am thankful that his richly-stored mind was not overclouded for a single hour; I am thankful that my strength and faculties were preserved to take care of him to the last; and Oh, *how* thankful I am that the heavy burden of loneliness has fallen upon *me* rather than upon *him*!

But that burden was too much to bear and soon she went to Staten Island to stay with the Shaws, who gave her a cheerful, sunshiny room with a soapstone stove, a bright carpet, and a view of New York Bay, the exact reverse of the way she had viewed it in the old days when she had stood on the shore at the Battery with John Hopper. The Shaws' comfortable rockers, warm quilts, and loving solicitude almost made her at home but—their seven servants deprived her of any useful activity. She said that she felt like a "cat in a strange garret" and wished that she might "run hundreds of miles to get to my humble little home." When influenza struck the household, they called in professional nurses, and Maria, who had nursed people all of her life, withdrew further into uselessness. She was a shriveled apple of a woman whose eyes were often wet.

Always meaning to be kind, her hosts opposed her daily walks in the icy winter weather and their protectiveness for her brittle old bones froze more ice around her heart. She was not even allowed to hear George Curtis preach his weekly sermon in the pretty Gothic chapel nearby. Yet one pleasure she insisted on. She visited Rosa Hopper and her son Will, who was as spoiled and theatrical as ever. Maria wrote to Mrs. Silsbee that Will's acting was as stiff as a ramrod and that he would have to unbend before anyone would pay to watch him, a comment which Mr. DeWolf Hopper disproved for the next twenty or more years.

In the spring, on Maria's return to Wayland, she hired a

companion, Lucy Pickering, to satisfy the friends and relatives who worried over her living alone. Aware that homecoming was harder, the longer she delayed it, she went
straight to the house, unlocked the door, flung open the
windows and lighted a fire with the last of the wood David
had cut. The mourning doves cooed their welcome as she
uncovered the furniture, polished the tables, and brought
in a few flowers from the neglected garden. Her tears flowed
but it did her good to give way to the sorrow that she had
bottled up all winter, and by the time Mrs. Pickering arrived,
the house and its mistress were ready to receive her. She put
on a show of cheerfulness for her new housemate but at
dawn she heard the whippoorwill, "the watchman of the
night," with his dreary, lonely note and she wrote to Mrs.
Shaw:

> Here in my native Massachusetts, I feel like a hungry child
> lost in a dark wood. People are very kind to me, but I cannot
> banish the desolate feeling that I belong to nobody and
> nobody belongs to me.

Whittier's calls helped more than anyone's, for he assured
her that soon she and David would meet again, fuse, and
be one conjoined soul. The Quaker and Swedenborgianism
gave her answers that evaded her elsewhere and she told
Whittier tiredly one day, "I'm a little anxious to be gone for
I have so many things to tell David. I believe it [heaven]
would be of small value to me if I were not united with him."

Mrs. Pickering now did the cooking and cleaning, and
for the first time Maria was mistress of the mansion. Outside,
Tom Moulton did his best to keep the orchard and garden
neat, and his wife, grateful for his sobriety, admitted freely
that her Tom would not be half the man he was without the
old lady on the Sudbury Road. With no house chores, Maria
had time for writing and reading but the inspiration failed

and she often sat motionless, adrift in the past. She slept in the same upstairs chamber she had shared with David, but the volumes of German poetry lay dusty under the eaves.

Each fall before moving into winter quarters in a Boston boardinghouse, she dismantled her house and put it to bed with her precious plants, checked to see that Moulton shuttered doors and windows, and went with him as he fastened the hasp on the old well house now head-high in weeds. Satisfied that all was shipshape, she left the key with the Damons and then packed herself, Mrs. Pickering, and their assorted boxes and bundles aboard the Boston stage-coach.

Maria hated the boardinghouse meals and the brick wall on which their one window faced, a view which reminded her of her miserable New York winters without David. The city was unenticing. Lucy Pickering enjoyed the Christmas crowds but even the "fairylike windows" of Jordan Marsh could not lure Maria into the maelstrom of shoppers. Yet she managed Swedenborgian lectures, held seven flights up, though she confessed that the climb was "rather wearing for an old back." Weekly she went to the Free Religious Meetings "where thought is as wide as the universe and, whether I always agree with it or not, I find it mentally stimulating."

At one such meeting she encountered Bronson Alcott, who persuaded her to visit a day or two in Concord. Mrs. Alcott, Maria's girlhood friend, welcomed her warmly as did their daughters. Their house reflected their personalities, for May was always puttering about, sketching, and Louisa was always ready to discuss the books that overflowed tables and shelves. Maria thoroughly appreciated that short participation in family life.

For six years Maria went back to Wayland each spring. Annually she spent a night or two at Damons' while she put her house in order. Mornings she walked up the half-mile stretch to do her work. Mrs. Pickering stayed in Maynard with her sister while Mrs. Child opened the kitchen door with the big black iron key, and the sour smell of dust mingled with mice and mildew struck her nose. She inspected all the tiny leaks which might optimistically have mended themselves, all the boxes which had been camphored but perhaps not wrapped tightly enough, all the dishes with their thin film of greasy dust. Suds, fresh air, and energy did the trick. While she scoured and scrubbed, Moulton "aired" the well to rid it of stagnant water and cleaned the chimney. When she had it all bright-burnished to her satisfaction, back went her lace cap, home came Mrs. Pickering, and routines went on as before.

Maria was a little afraid of tramps now, but independence was preferable to living with others and Mrs. Pickering did the best she knew how. She cooked beans and chowder in the most approved New England tradition and was ever eager to spare her employer an unnecessary trip up the ladderlike stairs but—she refused to stay at home when Maria entertained, and if visitors did show up, off she went without a by-your-leave. She left instructions with the Irish washwoman to "boil the teakettle and serve the bread and butter." Life with Mrs. Pickering had its drawbacks undoubtedly, but visitors were few. The Cutting children were grown and only thought of their old friend "Mitty Chile" when they received birthday cards which had grown from postage-stamp size to poster length as they aged. Other friends came less and less frequently. As she said herself, no one really needed her.

At seventy-six she wrote her final book, *Aspirations of the World, A Chain of Opals,* a book more aspiration than inspiration despite Whittier's comment that her style showed a "wise, philosophic tone and felicity of diction." She tried to show the universal trend of religious thought but she over-simplified her purpose by tracing too grand a design on a limited canvas. In other areas her reputation survived. The newspapers nicknamed her "grandmother of American feminine literature" although she told her friend Lucy Larcom, "I understand the world only half as well as I did a half century ago."

Reporters tried to get interviews with her and she retorted that they annoyed her with "this impertinent curiosity which, after all, is only a fashionable way of earning a penny without work." The invaders tried to get her to speak at Women's Rights gatherings; they offered to send carriages for her, and when she refused they pleaded for an hour, a moment, a sight of her. To Ann Whitney, a popular poet who threatened to come to her, willy-nilly, she wrote:

> Society has never yet got me into harness and there is still enough of the colt in me to run at the sight of a halter. So you may hang up your lasso, young lady.

Interviews and speechmaking were taboo, but she was glad to write on almost any subject—politics, public education, suffrage for women. The truth was that she was afraid to speak publicly, though she laughed at others for timidity and wrote to Miss May:

> Some of the communications of women are very amusing. They seem to flutter together like a set of hens, terribly frightened lest you and I, and other strong-minded hawks, should pounce down and carry them off from their chickies.

During the summer of 1880, celebrity Maria wrote out her own six-page will. She had plenty of money to leave, for four of her friends had left her sizable legacies, including the one of $7,500 in 1873 from Edmund Benzon. Among the larger bequests she listed $1,000 for "the elevation of the character of women and the enlargement of their sphere of action." The Wayland Library was to receive a permanent book fund in her name. In addition to many other institutional bequests, she listed nephews and nieces, David's as well as her own. She encouraged Moulton's fight for temperance with a $50 yearly annuity as long as he stayed sober and she reserved the interest on $8,000 for Mrs. Pickering as long as that unsociable lady lived. The considerable balance would go to Sarah Parsons of Brooklyn, daughter of Mary Francis Preston. Maria had not been a lawyer's wife for close to a half-century without knowing legalities fairly well and she appointed Wendell Phillips her executor, a post for which she designated him to take $2,000.

She distributed her personal treasures to those who might enjoy them. The Damons chose several scrapbooks and the transparency of the little princes in the tower, while the Wayland Library proudly accepted her books for its brand new building.

In September rheumatism began its fall plague and Mrs. Pickering, skilled at nursing, followed the instructions of the doctor from Weston, who was supposed to be a wizard at curing the trouble. For a time the pain lessened and, by the twenty-third of September, Maria wrote high-heartedly of plans for the future. "I try not to be quixotic but I want to rain down blessings on all the world in token of thankfulness for the blessings that have been rained down on me."

On the twentieth of October, she awoke full of energy. The doctor had promised that she would be better by that date, and she sat up grateful for a sunny day and work to do. She put one foot gingerly over the side of the bed. There was no stiffness; all was well. As she bent to draw on her slippers, she gasped. Mrs. Pickering heard the sound and came running. One look at Maria's contorted face confirmed her fears and she rushed for help. Maria fell back across the bed. She whimpered once and was still. Her round little form lay relaxed, and a smile softened the lines in her face.

We Are the Living

They brought her over the hill to David and laid her by his side. Whittier, Phillips, the Shaws, friends, townspeople who had loved her, young geniuses who had sought her advice—all came to say farewell. The sky was overcast but it did not rain. As the coffin sank into the ground, the sun broke through and a rainbow spanned the eastern sky. "She was the kind of woman," said Phillips in his funeral oration, "one would choose to represent woman's entrance into broader life."

At her head they placed a simple stone. The two markers, hers and David's, are aloof from other graves, a little lonely under the bridal wreath but close to each other. On hers stand the words:

Lydia Maria Child

1802–1880

You Call Us Dead

We Are Not Dead

We Are Truly Living Now

The Last Will and Testament of Lydia Maria Child

Last Will and Testament of L. Maria Child.

I, Lydia Maria Child, of Wayland, Middlesex County, Massachusetts, hereby declare this to be my last Will and Testament.

I hereby appoint, Wendell Phillips of Boston, Massachusetts, sole Executor of this Will, and no sureties are to be required for the fulfilment of his bond. Should he become, in any way, unable to fulfil the duties of an Executor, I wish that William Ingersoll Bowditch should consent to fulfil that office in his stead.

All necessary expenses, and customary fees, growing out of my sickness and burial, and the settlement of my affairs; are to take precedence of all other payments.

To Wendell Phillips, of Boston, Mass — 'ts, in token of personal friendship, and of gratitude for the faithful and gratuitous care he has taken of my financial affairs, during many years, I bequeath two thousand dollars. — — — — $ 2000.

To my niece Abby B. Francis, of Cambridge, Mass — 'ts, who generously relinquished to me her portion of my father's estate, I bequeath two thousand dollars. . . . . $ 2000.

To my nephew Convers Francis of Worcester, Mass — 'ts, I bequeath five hundred dollars. $ 500.

To my niece, Mary P. Conant, of Worcester, Mass.
I bequeath five hundred dollars. $500

To my niece Abigail Pingree, of Newton, Mass—
I bequeath five hundred dollars $500

To the daughters of my deceased nephew
George W. Francis, of Waltham, Mass — to,
I bequeath six hundred dollars, to be equally
divided between the unmarried daughters;
but if all are married, to be equally divided
among them all. $600
To William W. Cleland, son of my deceased niece
Ellen Cleland, of Natick, Mass—to, I bequeath
two hundred dollars. $200

For the education of the children of William
G. Haskins, of West Boylston, Mass — to, nephew
of my dear husband, I bequeath five hundred
dollars. $500

To Lydia Marie Ross, niece of my dear
husband, and sister of the said Wm G. Haskins,
I bequeath five hundred dollars. $500
To the Town Library, of Wayland, Mass — to,
I bequeath one hundred dollars. $100

To the Home for Old Colored Women, which
is now in 27 Myrtle St. Boston, Mass. I bequeath
one thousand dollars. $1000
Should that institution not be in existence, the said
sum is to be appropriated, in the most judicious way,
for the relief of indigent old colored women, in said city.

To Hampton Agricultural College, for colored people, in Hampton, Virginia, now under the superintendence of General Armstrong, I bequeath two thousand dollars. . . . . . $ 2000.
The said sum is never to be used for any species of theological teaching.

For the elevation of the character of Women, and the enlargement of their sphere of action, I bequeath one thousand dollars. . . . . $1000.
The said sum is to be used in the manner deemed most judicious by Thomas W. Higginson and Mrs. Mary A. Livermore, the well-known friends of Suffrage for Women.

To the Free Religious Association, in Boston, Mass—'ts, of which Felix Adler is now President, I bequeath one thousand dollars . . . . $ 1000
I do this to express my cordial sympathy with those who are trying to melt away the sectarian barriers, which so balefully divide the human family, whether they exist between the different sects of Christians, or between the different religions of the world. In case the said Free Religious Association has ceased to exist, the said sum is to be expended for the propagation of ideas similar to those it has taught, according to the judgment of Thomas W. Higginson and William J. Potter, both belonging to the Free Religious Association.

I wish to have eight thousand dollars, in such stock as will be most sure to bring in not less than six per cent, reserved as a fund for my kind and faithful friend Mrs. Lucy Ann Pickering, who has long resided with me. . . . . $ 8000.

The interest of the aforesaid sum is to be paid to Mrs. Pickering, in quarterly installments, during her life-time. After her decease, I wish the said sum to be distributed as follows: viz;

For the relief of Destitute Protestant Children, one thousand dollars. . . . . . . $ 1000.

The said sum is to be used in the way deemed most judicious by Abby W. May, of Boston, Mass⁻to.

For the Consumptives Home, in Boston, Mass. one thousand dollars. $ 1000.

For the Prevention of Cruelty to Animals, to be given to the Society for that purpose in Boston, Mass. one thousand dollars, $ 1000

For schools for the Education of Indian Children, with Protestant teachers, and, if possible, entirely under the influence of the Society of Friends called Quakers, one thousand dollars. . . . $ 1000

To the Homeopathic Hospital, in East Concord St. Boston, Massachusetts, two thousand dollars. . . . . $ 2000

The sum that remains of the fund for Mrs. Pickering, after said legacies are paid, is to go to my residuary Legatee; viz Mrs. Sarah M. Parsons.

In the later years of my life I have received three successive legacies; and the use I have made this unexpected good fortune is to obey the injunction, "Freely ye have received, freely give".

The property I have inherited, or earned, I have left to those who would have been the legal heirs.

I borrowed five hundred dollars Quincy A. Shaw, of Jamaica Plain, Mass—'ts, for the use of William Powell Wilson, Botanical teacher, in Cambridge, Mass—'ts. If the said William P. Wilson, by death, or otherwise, fails repay the said five hundred dollars, I wish the said sum to be paid to Quincy A. Shaw out of my estate.

Whatever remains of my property, after the above—mentioned sums are paid, I bequeath to my niece Mrs. Sarah M. Parsons, of Brooklyn, New York.

My personal property, such as books, furniture, clothing, &c. is not included in this Will; concerning those articles I have expressed my wishes in another Memorandum, wherein I have also expressed my earnest wish for a very quiet and unexpensive funeral, a wish which I trust will be scrupulously observed.

6

If Charles Moulton, of Wayland, Mass—ts, survives me, I wish my niece, Mrs. Sarah M. Parson's to send $50 annually, for his use, to Mr. Henry Wight, of Wayland, Mass—ts; to be paid, in monthly instalments, to the said Charles Moulton, provided he abstains from intoxicating drinks, but if he does not so abstain, he is to forfeit the annuity.

I hereby declare this to be my Last Will and Testament. In witness whereof I, Lydia Maria Child, the Testator, do hereunto set my hand and seal. January 27th, 1880

Lydia Maria Child.

Signed, sealed, and published, as my Last Will and Testament, in presence of the witnesses whose names are hereunto subscribed, and in presence of the Testator, each and all being present and witnessing the signature of each.

Sarah Shaw Russell.

Maria Russell

Sarah Russell

Bibliography

Adams, James Truslow. *Album of American History 1783-1853.* New York: Charles Scribner's Sons, 1945.

Baer, Helene G. "The Bell of Father Râle," *Magnificat* (September, 1955), pp. 47-49.

————. "Boston's Last Pirate," *Yankee* (September, 1955), pp. 40-43.

————. "Mrs. Child and Miss Fuller," *The New England Quarterly*, XXVI (June, 1953), pp. 249-253.

Barnes, James A. (ed.). "Letters of a Massachusetts Woman Reformer to an Indiana Radical," *Indiana Magazine of History* (March, 1930).

Battis, Edward C. "The Brig Mexican of Salem, Captured by Pirates and her Escape," Essex Institute Historical Collections, XXXIV. 41-63.

Beach, Seth Curtis. *Daughters of the Puritans.* Boston: American Unitarian Association, 1905.

Beers, Henry A. *Nathaniel Parker Willis.* Boston: Houghton Mifflin, 1885.

Bell, Margaret. *Margaret Fuller.* New York: Charles Boni, 1930.

Bliss, W. D. P. (ed.). *The Encyclopedia of Social Reforms.* New York: Funk, 1898.

Blumenthal, Walter Hart. *American Panorama.* Worcester: Achilles J. St. Onge, 1962.

Bonham, Martha E. *A Critical and Biographical Study of Lydia Maria Child.* Unpublished Master's thesis, Columbia University, 1926.

Bonner, William T. *New York, the World's Metropolis.* New York: R. L. Polk, 1924.

Boston Almanac for 1838. Boston: Thomas Groom, 1838.

Boston Almanac for 1839. Boston: Thomas Groom, 1839.

Bowen, Abel. *Picture of Boston* (2nd edition). Boston: Lilly Wait & Co., 1883.

Bremer, Frederika. *America of the Fifties.* New York: American-Scandinavian Foundation, 1924.

———. *Homes of the New World.* New York: Harper & Bros., 1853.

Brooks, Charles. *History of Medford.* Boston: Rand, Avery & Co., 1886.

Brooks, Van Wyck. *The Flowering of New England.* New York: E. P. Dutton & Co., 1936.

Carman, Harry J., and Syrett, Harold C. *History of the American People.* New York: Alfred A. Knopf, 1952.

Chadwick, John White. *A Life for Liberty* (Salley Holley). New York: G. P. Putnam's Sons, 1899.

———. *Theodore Parker.* Boston: Houghton Mifflin & Co., 1900.

Child, David Lee. *The Culture of the Beet and the Manufacture of Beet Sugar.* Boston: Weeks, Jordan & Co., 1840.

———. *The Despotism of Freedom.* Boston: Young Men's Anti-Slavery Association for the Diffusion of Truth, 1833.

———. *Rights and duties of the U.S. relative to Slavery under the laws of War.* Boston: Anti-Slavery Press, 1861.

Child, Lydia Maria. *The Adventures of Jamie and Jeannie.* Boston: D. Lothrop & Co., undated.

———. *An Anti-Slavery Catechism.* Newburyport: Charles Whipple, 1836.

———. *An Appeal in Favor of That Class of Americans Called Africans.* Boston: Allen & Ticknor, 1833.

———. *Aspirations of the World.* Boston: Roberts Bros., 1878.

———. *Autumnal Leaves.* New York: C. S. Francis, 1856.

———. *The Boy's Heaven and Other Stories.* Boston: D. Lothrop & Co., undated.

———. *Children of Mt. Ida.* New York: C. S. Francis, 1871.

————. *The Christ Child and Other Stories.* Boston: D. Lothrop & Co., undated.

————. *Correspondence between Lydia Maria Child, Governor Wise and Mrs. Mason.* Boston: Anti-Slavery Society, 1860.

————. *The Duty of Disobedience to the Fugitive Slave Act.* Boston: Anti-Slavery Society, 1860.

————. *Emily Parker or Impulse, not Principle.* Boston: Bowles & Dearborn, 1827.

————. *The Evils of Slavery and the Cure of Slavery.* Newburyport: Charles Whipple, 1839.

————. *Fact and Fiction.* New York: C. S. Francis, 1846.

————. *The Family Nurse.* Boston: Charles J. Hendee, 1837.

————. *The First Settlers of New England.* Boston: Munro & Francis, 1829.

————. *Flowers for Children* (Series I and II), New York: C. S. Francis & Co., 1844.

————. *Flowers for Children* (Series III), New York: C. S. Francis & Co., 1846.

————. *The Freedmen's Book.* Boston: Ticknor and Fields, 1865.

————. *The Frugal Housewife.* Boston: Carter & Hendee, 1830.

————. *The Girls' Own Book.* Boston: Russell, Shattuck, 1831.

————. *Good Little Mitty.* Boston: D. Lothrop & Co., undated.

————. *Hobomok.* Boston: Cummings, Hilliard & Co., 1824.

———— (ed.). *Incidents in the Life of a Slave Girl.* Boston: published for the author, 1861.

————. *Isaac T. Hopper, A True Life.* Boston: John P. Jewett & Co., 1853.

———— (ed.). *The Juvenile Miscellany,* 1826-1834. Boston.

————. *The Juvenile Souvenir.* Boston: Marsh & Capen, 1828.

————. *The Ladies Library: Biographies of Lady Russell and Mme. Guion.* Boston: Carter & Hendee, 1832. *Biographies of Mme. de Staël and Mme. Roland.* Boston: Carter & Hendee, 1832. *Biographies of Good Wives.* New York: Francis, 1833. *History of the Condition of Women.* 2 vols. New York: Allen, 1835.

————. *Letters of L. Maria Child, with a Biographical Introduction by John G. Whittier*. Boston: Houghton, Mifflin & Co., 1882.

————. *Letters from New York*. New York: C. S. Francis, 1843.

————. *Letters from New York*, 2nd series. New York: C. S. Francis, 1845.

————. *Looking Toward Sunset*. Boston: Ticknor & Fields, 1864.

———— (ed.). *Magician's Showbox*. Boston: Ticknor & Fields, 1856.

————. *Making Something and Other Stories*. Boston: D. Lothrop, undated.

————. *The Mother's Book*. Boston: Francis, 1831.

———— (ed.). *The Oasis*. Boston: Ticknor, 1834.

————. *The Patriarchal Institution*. New York: American Anti-Slavery Society, 1860.

————. *Philothea*. Boston: Otis, Broaders, 1836.

————. *Progress of Religious Ideas Through Successive Ages*. New York: C. S. Francis & Co., 1855.

———— (ed.). *Rainbows for Children*. New York: C. S. Francis & Co., 1848.

————. *The Rebels*. Boston: Cummings & Hilliard, 1825.

————. *The Right Way, The Safe Way*. New York: 5 Beekman Street, 1860.

————. *Romance of the Republic*. Boston: Ticknor & Fields, 1867.

————. *Rose Marian and the Flower Fairies*. Boston: Crosby & Ainsworth, 1839.

Christy's. *Panorama Songster*. New York: William B. Murphy, undated.

Commager, Henry Steele. *Theodore Parker, Yankee Crusader*. New York: Henry Holt, 1939.

Cone, Helen G. "Women in Literature," *Women's Work in America*, ed. Amie Nathan Myer. New York: Henry Holt & Co., 1891.

Coolidge, Susan. "Lydia M. Child," *Famous Women,* Hartford: A. D. Worthington, 1885.

Crosby, Ernest. *Garrison, the Non-Resistant.* Chicago: The Public Publishing Co., 1905.

Curti, Merle. *The Growth of American Thought.* New York: Harper & Bros., 1943.

Curtis, George T. "Reminiscences of Nathaniel P. Willis and Lydia Maria Child," *Harper's Magazine,* LXXXI, 717-720.

Cutting, Alfred Wayland. *Old Time Wayland.* Wayland, Mass.: Privately printed, 1926.

Dictionary of American Biography. New York: Charles Scribner's Sons, 1931.

Emerson, Ralph Waldo. *Letters,* ed. Ralph L. Rusk. New York: Columbia University Press, 1939.

Emerson, Sarah Hopper. *Life of Abby Hopper Gibbons.* New York: G. P. Putnam's Sons, 1896.

Finley, Ruth E. *The Lady of Godey's.* Philadelphia: J. B. Lippincott Co., 1931.

Forten, Charlotte. *Journal.* New York: The Dryden Press, 1953.

Frothingham, O. B. "Theodore Parker" a sermon preached in New York, June 10, 1860, Boston, 1860.

————. *Transcendentalism in New England.* Boston, American Unitarian Association, 1903.

Fuller, Margaret (see also Ossoli). *Love Letters,* with an introduction by Julia Ward Howe. New York: D. Appleton & Co., 1903.

Garrison, Wendell Phillips. *William Lloyd Garrison.* New York: The Century Co., 1885-1889.

Gilder, Rodman. *The Battery.* Boston. Houghton, Mifflin & Co., 1936.

Gohdes, Clarence L. F. *The Periodicals of American Transcendentalism.* Durham: Duke University Press, 1931.

Graham, Abbie. *Ladies in Revolt.* New York: Woman's Press, 1934.

Grimke, Archibald. *William Lloyd Garrison.* New York: Funk & Wagnalls, 1891.

Griswold, Rufus W. *The Female Poets of America.* Philadelphia: Henry C. Baird, 1854.

———. *The Prose Writers of America.* Philadelphia: Parry & McMillan, 1854.

Hale, Edward Everett. *James Russell Lowell and His Friends.* Boston: Houghton, Mifflin & Co., 1899.

———. *Memories of a Hundred Years.* New York: MacMillan, 1902.

Hale, Sarah Josepha. *Woman's Record or Sketches of all Distinguished Women.* New York: Harper & Bros., 1860.

Hale, William H. *Horace Greeley, Voice of the People.* New York: Harper & Bros., 1950.

Hallowell, Anna D. "Lydia Maria Child," *Medford Historical Register,* III (July, 1900).

Harlow, Ralph Volney. *Gerrit Smith.* New York: Henry Holt & Co., 1939.

Harper, Ida Husted. *Life and Work of Susan B. Anthony,* Vol. III. Indianapolis: The Hollenbeck Press, 1908.

Hemstreet, Charles. *Literary New York.* G. P. Putnam's Sons, 1903.

Higginson, Thomas Wentworth. "Cheerful Yesterdays," *The Atlantic Monthly,* Vol. L.

———. *Letters and Journals,* ed. Mary Thacher. Higginson, Boston: Houghton, Mifflin & Co., 1921.

———. *Contemporaries.* Cambridge: The Riverside Press, 1899.

———. *Margaret Fuller Ossoli.* Cambridge, The Riverside Press, 1884.

Hone, Philip. *Diary,* ed. Bayard Tucker. New York: Dodd, Mead, 1889.

Howe, Julia Ward. *Reminiscences.* Cambridge: The Riverside Press, 1899.

Hudson, Reverend Alfred Sereno. "The Home of Lydia Maria Child," *The New England Magazine,* II (new series, 1890).

Influence and History of the Boston Athenaeum. Boston: The Athenaeum, 1907.

Irwin, Inez Haynes. *Angels and Amazons.* New York: Doubleday, Doran & Co., 1934.

Jackson, Andrew. *Correspondence,* ed. J. B. Bassett, Vol. V, 1833–1838. Washington: Carnegie Institute of Washington, 1926–1935.

Johnson, Oliver. *William Lloyd Garrison and His Times.* Boston: Houghton, Mifflin & Co., 1894.

Korngold, Ralph. *Two Friends of Man.* Boston: Little, Brown & Co., 1950.

Lader, Lawrence. *The Bold Brahmins,* New York: E. P. Dutton & Co. Inc., 1961.

Lamb, Marth J. *History of the City of New York.* New York: A. S. Barnes & Co., 1877.

Lesley, Susan J. *Recollections of My Mother, Mrs. Anna Jean Lyman.* Boston: Houghton, Mifflin & Co., 1899.

Leslie's History of the Greater New York, Vol. I. ed. David van Pelt. New York: Arkell Publishing Co., 1898.

"Letters of Wendell Phillips to Lydia Maria Child," *The New England Magazine* (new series), V (February, 1892).

Loring, James Spear. "David Lee Child," *Hundred Boston Orators Appointed by the Municipal Authorities, etc.* Boston: Jewett & Co., 1852.

Lossing, Benson L. *History of the City of New York.* New York: George E. Perine, 1884.

Lutz, Alma. *Created Equal, Life of Elizabeth Cady Stanton.* New York: John Day, 1940.

McDowell, Mrs. Katherine Sherwood Bonner. *The Radical Club.* Boston: The Times Publishing Co., 1876.

McKay, Richard C. *South Street: A Maritime History of New York.* New York: G. P. Putnam's Sons, 1934.

Mann, Dorothy Lawrence. *A Century of Book Selling.* Boston: Privately printed, 1948.

Mann, Moses W. "Marm Betty," *Medford Historical Register,* XII (October, 1909).

Markun, Leo. *Mrs. Grundy.* New York: D. Appleton & Co., 1930.

Martineau, Harriet. "The Martyr Age of the United States," *The Westminster Review,* XXXII, 1-59. London: Henry Hooper, 1839.

Massachusetts Anti-Slavery Society Report. Boston: January 24, 1838.

Massachusetts Historical Society Proceedings, Vol. II. Boston: The Society, 1880.

————. Vol. VIII. Boston: The Society, 1866.

May, Reverend Samuel B. *Recollections of Our Antislavery Conflict.* Boston: Fields, Osgood & Co., 1869.

Merchants and Traders Guide and Strangers Memorandum Book. Boston: J. Hancock, 1836.

Minnegerode, Meade. *The Fabulous Forties.* New York: G. P. Putnam's Sons, 1924.

Montez, Lola. *Lectures.* New York: Rudd & Carleton, 1858.

Morison, Samuel Eliot, and Commager, Henry Steele. *The Growth of the American Republic,* Vol. I. New York: Oxford University Press, 1940.

Mott, Frank Luther. *A History of American Magazines.* Cambridge: Harvard University Press, 1939.

National Anti-Slavery Standard, New York, 1841–1850.

New Mirror, Vol. II, New York, October 14, 1843.

New York *Tribune,* May 17, 1842.

Odell, George C. D. *Annals of the New York Stage.* New York: Columbia University Press, 1921.

Ossoli, Margaret Fuller. *Memoirs,* ed. James Freeman Clarke, William Ellery Channing, and Ralph Waldo Emerson. Boston: Phillips, Sampson & Co., 1852.

————. "American Literature," *Miss Fuller's Papers.* New York: Wiley & Putnam, 1846.

Parrington, Vernon L. *Main Currents in American Thought.* New York: Harcourt, Brace & Co., 1927.

Parton, James. *Life of Horace Greeley.* New York: Mason Bros., 1855.

Pickard, Samuel T. *Life and Letters of John Greenleaf Whittier.* Cambridge: The Riverside Press, 1894.

Pollard, John A. *John Greenleaf Whittier*. Cambridge: The Riverside Press, 1949.

Porter, Maria S. "Lydia Maria Child," *National Magazine*, XIV, 161-170.

Portrait and Sketch of Lydia Maria Child in *American Magazine*, LXIX, 370.

Rohan, Jack. *Yankee Armsmaker, The Story of Samuel Colt*. New York: Harper & Bros., 1935.

Rusk, Ralph L. *The Life of Ralph Waldo Emerson*. New York: Charles Scribner's Sons, 1899.

Sargent, Mrs. John T. (ed.). *The Radical Club, Sketches and Reminiscences*. Boston: James R. Osgood & Co., 1880.

Silsbee, M. C. D. *A Half Century in Salem*. Boston: Houghton, Mifflin & Co., 1887.

Smith, Alson. "The Fringe Religions," *American Mercury*, April, 1950.

Snow, C. H. *Geography of Boston*. Boston: Carter & Hendee, 1830.

Some Merchants and Sea Captains of Old Boston. Boston: State Street Trust Co., 1918.

Stanton, Elizabeth Cady, Anthony, Susan B., and Gage, Martha J., (eds.). *History of Woman Suffrage*. Rochester: S. Anthony, 1886.

Stern, Madeleine B. *Life of Margaret Fuller*. New York: E. P. Dutton & Co., 1942.

Stokes, I. N. Phelps. *The Iconography of Manhattan Island*. New York: R. H. Dodd, 1915-1928.

Stone, William L. *History of New York City*. New York: Virtue & Yorston, 1872.

Smith, Mortimer. *Life of Ole Bull*. Princeton, N. J.: Princeton University Press, 1943.

Swedenborg, Emanuel. *Miscellaneous Theological Works*. New York: American Swedenborgian Printing and Publishing Co., 1892.

Swift, Lindsay. *William Lloyd Garrison*. Philadelphia: George W. Jacobs Co., 1911.

Taggard, Genevieve. *The Life and Mind of Emily Dickinson*. New York: Alfred A. Knopf, Inc., 1930.

Thorp, Louise Farrand. "Lydia Maria Child," *Six Persuasive Women*. New Haven: Yale University Press, 1949.

Trial of the Twelve Spanish Pirates, etc. Boston: Lemuel Gulliver, 1834.

Ware, Ethel K. "Lydia Maria Child and Antislavery," *Boston Public Library Bulletin*, October, 1951, and January, 1952.

Weld, Theodore Dwight, Weld, Angelina Grimke, and Grimke, Sarah. *Letters*. New York: D. Appleton-Century Co., 1934.

Wherry, Edgar T. *Wild Flower Guide*. Garden City, N.Y.: Doubleday & Co. Inc., 1948.

Whiting, Lillian. *Boston Days*. Boston: Little, Brown & Co., 1902.

Whittier, John Greenleaf. *Writings*, Vol. V. Cambridge: Oxford University Press, 1888.

Whitton, Mary Ormsbee. *These Were the Women*. New York: Hastings House, 1954.

Willard, Frances E. and Livermore, Mary A. *American Women*. New York: Mast, Crowell & Kirkpatrick, 1897.

Wilson, James Grant (ed.). *Memorial History of the City of New York*, Vol. III. New York: New York History Co., 1892–1893.

Winsor, Justin (ed.). *Memorial History of Boston*. Boston: James R. Osgood & Co., 1880.

Winter, Alice Ames. *The Heritage of Women*. New York: Minton, Balch & Co., 1927.

Wood, Henrietta Danforth. *Early Days in Norridgewock*. Skowhegan, Me.: The Skowhegan Press, 1935.

Wortley, Lady E. Stuart. *Travels in the United States*. New York: Harper & Bros., 1851.

Wines, E. C. *A Trip to Boston*. Boston: Charles C. Little and James Brown, 1838.

Wright, Helen. *Sweeper in the Sky*. New York: The Macmillan Co., 1949.

LETTERS

Child, David Lee. Loring, Ellis Gray. New York Public Library.
——. Parker, General, 1823. Pennsylvania Historical Society.
Child, Lydia Maria. Benjamin, Park, May 30, 1836. Columbia University.
——. Bryant, William Cullen. New York Public Library.
——. Butler, General Benjamin, 1835. Pennsylvania Historical Society.
——. Esler, Mrs. Nathan, 1844–1845. Wellesley College Library.
——. Fields, James T., 1863–1877. Huntington Library, California.
——. Fields, James T. Wellesley College Library.
——. Francis, Convers, October 25, 1857. New York Public Library.
——. Damon family. Privately owned letters of 1874–1880.
——. Fuller, Margaret. Aldis Collection, Yale University.
——. Garrison, William Lloyd, October 28, 1859. Smith College Library.
——. Godwin, Parke. New York Public Library.
——. Greeley, Horace, 1859–1862. New York Public Library.
——. Hopper-Gibbons family. Privately owned letters.
——. Loring, Ellis Gray, 1838–1844. New York Public Library.
——. Miscellaneous letters in the following collections: Boston Athenaeum, 1843–1847; Hoyt Papers, Houghton Library, Harvard University, 1841–1867; Lincoln Collection, Brown University, 1860–1877; The Alma Lutz Collection; New York Historical Society, 1844–1877; Pennsylvania Historical Society; Radcliffe College Library, 1836–1880.
——. New York Society Library, letter to the library, (1855?).
——. Shaw family. New York Public Library.
——. Shaw family, 1863–1879. Wayland Public Library.
——. Silsbee, Marianne, 1845–1880. American Antiquarian Society, Worcester, Mass.
——. Smith, Gerrit, 1836–1872. Syracuse University Library.

————. Tilton, Theodore, 1860–1866. Buffalo Public Library.

————. "Vater" Heinrich, October 19, 1845. Friends Historical Library, Swarthmore, Pa.

————. "Friend" Whittier, 1857–1876. Library of Congress.

Clay, Henry. Child, David Lee, November, 1828. Boston Athenaeum.

Hopper, Isaac T. Child, Lydia Maria, February 11, 1851. Friends Historical Society, Swarthmore, Pa.

Whittier, John Greenleaf. Child, Lydia Maria, May 5, 1876. Wellesley College Library.

MISCELLANEOUS MATERIAL

Child, Lydia Maria. Autograph Album in Medford Historical Society Museum; Baby dress stitched by Mrs. Child, in Medford Historical Society Museum; Gold watch presented to Mrs. Child, in Medford Historical Society Museum; Bible in Medford Historical Society Museum; Last Will and Testament, Probate Court, Cambridge, Mass.

Francis, Convers. Last Will and Testament in Probate Court, Cambridge, Mass.

Hopper house furniture. Privately owned.

Ledger of readers in Boston Athenaeum, 1827–1834.

Miscellaneous mementoes, Wayland, Mass. Privately owned.

Phelps map of New York City, 1846, printed by J. M. Atwood, New York. New York Society Library.

Transfer Deed of Northampton Farm, Register of Deeds, Northampton, Mass.

PERIODICAL BIBLIOGRAPHY

Many of Mrs. Child's "Letters from New York," written for Buckingham's *Boston Courier,* were reprinted in other newspapers such as the *Broadway Journal, The New World,* and the *Tribune.* Others appeared in annuals and gift books. A small percentage of these are listed below; further examples are cited in the text of the book.

Dozens of her poems, often anonymously printed, are in old as well as modern anthologies. For example Bartlett's *Familiar Quotations* contains an excerpt from "Marius Amid the Ruins of Carthage." "The Boy's Thanksgiving Song" which heads the list below is still in children's song books and within the past few years appeared in one of the larger women's magazines.

Mrs. Child's stories fare less well. Falling mainly into reform categories, they make dull and typically Victorian reading. Yet with analysis these tales give a remarkably clear picture of her time, showing the strength of the nineteenth-century surge for humanitarianism and the reformer's stern scorn for weakness, lavender, and old lace. The tales fall roughly into the following categories: Antislavery; Fallen woman and regeneration (prison reform); Material ambition decried; Mysticism (phrenology, second sight, table tapping, etc.); Practicality in everyday life; Strong, faithful sister or wife (feminism); Temperance.

Articles and Aphorisms

"African Character," *The Casket,* 1835.

"Anecdote of Elias Hicks," *The Liberty Bell,* 1839.

"Anecdote of a Musical Genius," *The Rover,* November 6, 1844.

Aphorism, *The Marriage Offering,* 1848.

"Chaos of Opinions," *African Repository and Colonial Journal,* Vol. XIX, 1843.

"Christianity Exemplified," *The Casket,* July, 1846.

"The Eccaloebian in New York," *Rural Repository,* November 9, 1844.

Extracts from "Letters from New York," *The New World,* September 23, 1843.

"Female Affection," *Gems by the Wayside,* 1850.

"Home and Politics," *Western Literary Messenger,* September, 1849.

"Illustration of the Strength of Prejudice," *The Anti-Slavery Record,* May, 1836.

"The Intermingling of Religions," *Atlantic Monthly,* October, 1871.

"The Juvenile Choirs of Harmony," *The Harbinger*, January, 1847.

"The Man that Killed his Neighbors," *The Columbian Lady's and Gentleman's Magazine*, May, 1847.

"Marriage," *Western Literary Messenger*, October, 1849.

"Mistaken Execution for Murder," *The Rover*, November 14, 1844.

————, *Godey's Lady's Book*, September, 1846.

"A New Year's Offering," *Atlantic Souvenir*, 1829.

"Ole Bull," *Anti-Slavery Standard*, June 6, 1844.

"Ole Bull," *The New World*, January 6, 1844.

"Ole Bull," *Gems by the Wayside*, 1850.

"Politeness," *The Lady's Casket*, 1850.

"The Preaching of Whitefield," *The Boston Book*, 1841.

————, *The New World*, July 10, 1844.

"Recollections of Ole Bull," *Columbian Lady's and Gentleman's Magazine*, February, 1846.

————, *Gem of the Season*, 1849.

"Resemblances between Buddhism and the Roman Catholic Religion," *Atlantic Monthly*, December, 1870.

"Service to Others by Forgetfulness of Self," *The Casket*, September 23, 1846.

"Spirits," *Atlantic Monthly*, May, 1862.

"The Synagogue of the Jews," *The New World*, September 30, 1843.

"The Viennese Children," *The Harbinger*, 1847.

Various religious aphorisms, *The Fountain*, 1831.

"Welcome to Ole Bull," *Democratic Review*, September, 1844.

Poems

"The Boy's Thanksgiving Song," *Elementary School Teacher*, Vol. VII, 281-2.

————, *Ladies Home Journal*, Vol. XXIV (November, 1907), 46.

"The Hero's Heart," *Echoes of Harper's Ferry* (Redpath), 348.

"Lines," *The Token*, 1828.

* Dash denotes article appeared in more than one periodical.

"Lines Occasioned by Hearing a Little Boy, etc.," *American Commonplace Book*, 1832.

"Lines to a Departed Friend, Catherine Sargent," *The Liberty Bell*, 1856.

"Lines to a Lady of Great Musical Talent," *American Commonplace Book*, 1832.

"Lines to Those Men and Women Who Were Avowed Abolitionists, etc.," *The Liberty Bell*, 1839.

"Little Bird! Little Bird!" *Merry's Museum*, February, 1872.

"Marius Amid the Ruins of Carthage," *Gift Leaves of American Poetry*, 1849.

————, *Godey's Lady's Book*, September, 1846.

————, *Ladies' Companion*, August, 1841.

"The Parrot," *Merry's Museum*, 1846.

"Pleasant Valley," *The Maine Monthly*, February, 1837.

"Sleep Well, Sleep Well," *National Era*, January 8, 1857.

"Stanzas Occasioned by Hearing a Little Boy, etc.," *The Atlantic Souvenir*, 1829.

"To a Little Girl Walking in the Wood," *Merry's Museum*. October, 1847.

"To a Lady Playing on the Piano Forte," *The Offering*, 1929.

"The Valentine," *The Atlantic Souvenir*, 1828.

"Who Stole the Bird's Nest?" *Godey's Lady's Book*, March, 1871.

————, *Merry's Museum*, December, 1845.

Stories

"Adventures of a Raindrop," *The Token*, 1828.

"Beauty," *The Token*, 1828.

"The Beloved Tune," *Columbian Lady's and Gentleman's Magazine*, November, 1845.

"The Bewildered Savage," *The Union Magazine of Literature and Art*, January, 1848.

"The Black Saxons," *The Liberty Bell*, 1841.

"The Brother and Sister," *The Union Magazine of Literature and Art*, September, 1847.

————, *National Era*, November 11, 1847.

"Charity Bowery," *The Liberty Bell*, 1839.

"Children of Mt. Ida," *Columbian Lady's and Gentleman's Magazine*, April, 1845.

"Chocorua's Curse," *Ladies' Cabinet Volume*, 1832.

————, *Moss Rose*, 1845.

————, *Moss Rose*, 1854.

"Elizabeth Wilson," *The Columbian Lady's and Gentleman's Magazine*, February, 1845.

"Emancipated Slaveholders," *The Liberty Bell*, 1839.

"The Emigrant Boy," *The Union Magazine of Literature and Art*, July, 1847.

"The Fairy Friend," *The Columbian Lady's and Gentleman's Magazine*, March, 1847.

"The Fountain of Beauty," *The Boston Book*, 1837.

"Harriet Bruce," *The Rover*, November 2, 1843.

"Hilda Silfering," *The Columbian Lady's and Gentleman's Magazine*, October, 1845.

"The Hindoo Anchorite," *The Union Magazine of Literature and Art*, April, 1848.

————, *The Gem Annual*, 1855.

"Illustration of the Strength of Prejudice," *Anti-Slavery Record*, May, 1836.

"The Indolent Fairy," *The Boston Book*, 1836.

"Innocence," *The Ladies' Companion*, August, 1838.

"The Irish Heart," *The Columbian Lady's and Gentleman's Magazine*, July, 1845.

"Jan and Zaida," *The Liberty Bell*, 1856.

"A Legend of the Apostle John," *The Columbian Lady's and Gentleman's Magazine*, September, 1845.

"The Lone Indian," *The Token*, 1828.

————, *The Garland*, 1830.

————, *The Garland*, 1839.

————, *The Garland*, 1840.

"Loo Loo," *Atlantic Monthly*, May and June, 1858.

"The Man that Killed his Neighbors," *The Columbian Lady's and Gentleman's Magazine*, May, 1847.

"The Neighbor-in-Law," *The Columbian Lady's and Gentleman's Magazine*, June, 1846.

"The Palace of Beauty," *Dewdrops of the Nineteenth Century*, 1854.

———, *The Oasis*, 1854.

———, *The Oasis*, 1856.

"A Poet's Dream of the Soul," *The Columbian Lady's and Gentleman's Magazine*, September, 1846.

"Poor Chloe," *Atlantic Monthly*, March, 1866.

"The Power of Love," *The Union Magazine of Literature and Art*, May, 1848.

"The Prophet of Iona," *The Dewdrop*, 1852.

"The Recluse of the Lake," *The Token*, 1828.

"The Remembered Home," *The Present*, September, 1843.

"The Rival Mechanicians," *The Columbian Lady's and Gentleman's Magazine*, January, 1847.

"Romance of Real Life," *Dewdrops of the Nineteenth Century*, 1854.

"Rosenglory," *The Columbian Lady's and Gentleman's Magazine*.

"The Self-Conscious and the Unconscious," *The Columbian Lady's and Gentleman's Magazine*, January, 1846.

"She Waits in the Spirit Land," *The Columbian Lady's and Gentleman's Magazine*, March, 1846.

———, *Gem of the Season*, 1849.

"A Simple Story," *The Philipena*, 1848.

"Slavery's Pleasant Homes," *The Liberty Bell*, 1843.

"Stars and Stripes," *The Liberty Bell*, 1858.

"Thot and Freia," *The Columbian Lady's and Gentleman's Magazine*, January, 1845.

"Utouch and Touchu," *The Union Magazine of Literature and Art*, December, 1847.

"Willie Wharton," *Atlantic Monthly*, March, 1863.

"The Young West Indian," *Atlantic Souvenir*, 1828.

Index

Abnaki Indians, 32, 33, 36
Adams, Hannah, 59
Adams, John Quincy, 51, 52, 53, 101, 196
Alcott, Bronson, 114, 116, 168, 304
Alcott, Louisa May, 304
American Anti-Slavery Society, 96, 124
Anthony, Susan B., 264
Anti-Slavery Almanac, 168
Atlantic Monthly, 245, 263, 273, 289, 296

Battis, John, 77
Beecher, Henry Ward, 73, 293
Bell-Everetts, 16, 259, 262
Benjamin, Park, 85, 168
Benzon, Edmund, 149, 177, 186, 190, 192, 199, 235, 241, 306
Boston Atheneum Library, 59, 60
Boston Book, 92
Boston *Courier,* "Letters from New York," 124, 125, 133, 136, 141, 152, 154, 167, 192, 193, 213; published in book form, 165
Boston Ladies' Anti-Slavery Society, 75
Boston Traveler, The, 57
Breckenridge, John, 268
Bremer, Frederika, 192, 212

Broadcloth, Mob, 16, 262
Broadway Journal, 168, 192
Brook Farm, 116, 117
Brooks, Preston, 216–217
Brooks, Van Wyck, 87
Brown, John, 220, 246–254
Bryant, William Cullen, 57, 279
Buchanan, James, 232
Bull, Ole, 178, 180, 198, 213, 293
Burritt, Elihu, 72
Butler, Benjamin, 80

Castle Gardens, 134–135
Channing, Rev. William Ellery, 60, 69, 72, 151
Chapman, Maria Weston, 17, 93, 120, 143, 158, 262
Child, David Lee, early life and education, 44–45; marries Lydia Maria Francis, 50; edits *Massachusetts Whig Journal,* 50–51; opposes Andrew Jackson 51–52; helps found anti-slavery society, 63; defends pirates, 78–80; leaves for Belgium, 91; begins beet sugar experiments at Northampton, 98; turns down editorial chair of *National Anti-Slavery Standard,* 121; replaces wife as editor, 162; resigns, 175; death, 297

Child, Lydia Maria, rescues Wendell Phillips, 17; girls' school in Watertown, 40; *Hobomok,* 41; *The Rebels,* 42; *Evenings in New England,* 42; founds *Juvenile Miscellany,* 45; *Emily Parker, or Impulse, not Principle,* 46; marries, 50; *Frugal Housewife,* 55; *The Ladies Library,* 60; *Appeal in Favor of That Class of Americans Called Africans,* 65; failure of the *Miscellany,* 68; *History of the Condition of Women in Various Ages and Nations,* 83; *Philothea, a Story of Ancient Greece,* 84–85; *The Family Nurse,* 92; *The Evils of Slavery and the Cures of Slavery,* 98; editor of the *National Anti-Slavery Standard,* 122–161; *Flowers for Children,* 164, 190; *Musical Correspondences,* 179; *Fact and Fiction,* 194; *Progress of Religious Ideas,* 222–226; "The Royal Rosebud," 226; *Autumnal Leaves,* 227; Child-Wise correspondence, 250–251; Child-Mason correspondence, 251–253; John Brown, 250; "The Right Way, the Safe Way," 258; *Incidents in the Life of a Slave Girl,* 263; *Looking Toward Sunset,* 278–279; edits *Freedman's Book,* 283, 288; *Romance of the Republic,* 289–290; "Intermingling of Religions," 296; *Aspirations of the World, A Chain of Opals,* 305; death, 308; Phillip's eulogy, 309

Christian Examiner and Religious Miscellany, The, 192
Clay, Henry, 51, 52, 53, 176
Colt, John, 156–157
Colt, Samuel, 157
Columbian Lady's and Gentleman's Magazine, The, 191
Congdon, Charles T., 115
Constitutional Union party, 268
Croton water clebration, 136–141
Curtis, George Ticknor, 48

de Soto, mate of the *Panda,* 81
Devens, Charles, 261, 265
Dial, 117, 167
Dickens, Charles, 152, 153
Dickinson, Emily, 194
Dred Scott Decision, 245
Douglas, Stephen, 220
Dwight, Rev. John S., 105, 111, 116

Emancipation Proclamation, 270
Emerson, Ralph Waldo, 39, 72, 106, 114, 115, 116, 119, 149, 209, 253
Eminent Women of the Age, 295

Fields, James T., 245, 287–288
Folsom, Abigail, 73
Francis, Abby Bradford, 38
Francis, Convers, 21, 22, 29, 38, 39, 273
Francis, David Convers, 19, 21, 25, 26, 98, 104–105, 231
Francis, James, 28, 87, 88, 100
Francis, Lydia Maria; *see* Child, Lydia Maria
Francis, Mary; *see* Preston. Mary Francis
Free Soil party, 202
Fremont, John, 230–232
Fugitive Slave Law, 207, 209

Fuller, Margaret, 45, 47, 60; conversations, 111–120; editor, the *Dial*, 117; hired for New York *Tribune*, 181–189; leaves for Italy, 189; revolutions in Italy, 198, 200; marriage, 205; death, 207

Garrison, Helen Benson, 73
Garrison, William Lloyd, 63, 64, 126, 142, 158, 172, 301; immediate emancipation, 72, 73; champions Women's Rights, 120
Gibbons, James D., 127, 146, 150
Godwin, Parke, 201, 280
"Gorgeous Pedants," 119
Grant, Ulysses S., 293
Greeley, Horace, 72, 182, 183; hires Margaret Fuller, 181; on Dred Scott Decision, 245; attitude toward Reconstruction, 292–293
Greeley, Mary, 172, 181, 186
Greeley, Pikcie, 186, 189
Grimke, Angelina, 72, 83, 106, 107
Grimke, Sarah, 72, 106, 107

Hale, Edward Everett, 68
Hale, Sarah Josepha, 86, 141
Hawthorne, Nathaniel, 116
Hawthorne, Sophia Peabody, 116
Hedge, Frederick, 114
Heinrich, Anthony Philip ("Vater"), 195–196
Higginson, Thomas Wentworth, 69
Hillard, George, 79
Hoar, Elizabeth, 113
Holley, Sallie, 256
Hopper, DeWolfe, 245, 302

Hopper, Isaac Tatum, 72, 124, 190
Hosmer, Harriet, 211

Jackson, Andrew, 51, 52, 53, 54, 80, 81
Jane Eyre, 201
Johnson, Andrew, 281, 294

Kansas emigrants, 229, 230, 236
Kansas-Nebraska Act, 220
King, Augusta, 111
Kirkland, Caroline, 204

Ladies' Companion, The, 153
Lafayette, Marquis de, 42
Leonowens, Anna, 295
Liberator, 73
Lincoln, Abraham, 246, 260, 266, 270, 272, 279, 280, 281
Lincoln, Mary Todd, 272
Locke, John, 170
Longfellow, Henry Wadsworth, 150
Loring, Ellis Gray, 95, 146, 228–229, 240
Lovejoy, Rev. Elijah, 96
Lowell, James Russell, 72, 80, 149, 151, 168
Lundy, Benjamin, 88
Lyman, Mrs., 104
Lynch, Anne Charlotte, 179, 188

McClellan, Edward, 279, 280
Marm, Betty, 21
Marriott, Charles, 157
Marshall, Emily, 50
Martineau, Harriet, 76, 119, 131, 158
Massachusetts Whig Journal, 50, 162
Medford-on-the-Mystic, 19, 20, 26

Mexican, 77, 79
Miller, William, 171
Mott, James, 72
Mott, Lucretia, 72, 83, 93, 94, 120

Nathan, James, 186, 187, 188, 189
New England Anti-Slavery Society, 63
New York Philharmonic Society, 177
Nichols, Mary Gove, 172
Niles' Weekly Register, 65
North American Review, 41, 56
Norman, Amelia, 183–184
Northall, Julia, 204
Noyes Academy, 76

Oasis, 75
Osgood, Frances, 60
Osgood, Lucy, 243, 255
Ossoli, Marchioness ; *see* Fuller, Margaret
Otis, James, "speech" at Faneuil Hall, 42

Page, William, 150, 238
Palmi's Opera House, 177–178
Panda, 77, 78, 79, 81
Parker, Theodore, 39, 61, 72, 114, 116, 168, 169
Parmenter, Louisa, 219
Peabody, Elizabeth, 60, 114, 115, 239
Phillips, Wendell, 15–18, 73, 82, 97, 219, 237, 262, 279, 296 ; converted to Abolition, 69–70 ; and Women's Rights, 120 ; appointed executor of Mrs. Child's estate, eulogy for Mrs. Child, 309

Poe, Edgar Allen, 61, 156, 188, 191
Preston, Mary Francis, 22, 23, 24
Prince Henry the Navigator, 66

Radical Club, 295
Rale, Father, 32–33, 35
Ripley, George, 114
Rogers, Ezekiel, 72
Rogers, Mary, 155
Rogers, Nathaniel P., 126

Sartrain's Union Magazine, 168 204
Sears, Edmund, 243
Seward, William, 260, 272, 276
Shaw, Robert Gould, 276–277
Sigourney, Lydia, 153
Silsbee, Marianne, 86, 197–198, 202, 212, 236
Silsbee, Mary, 212
Sims, Thomas, 208–210, 261, 265
Smith, Gerrit, 98, 144, 283
Smith, Sydney, 195
Soto de, *see* de Soto
Springs, Mr. and Mrs. Marcus, 189, 200
Stael, Mme. de, 42
Stearns, George Luther, 249–250
Stearns, Mary Preston, 256
Stone, Lucy, 238–239
Stowe, Harriet Beecher, 210–211, 219
Sturgis, Caroline, 177
Sumner, Charles, 196, 222, 234–235, 258–259, 265, 296 ; attacked on Senate floor, 229–230
Swedenborg, Emanuel, 47, 49, 171, 172

Tappan, Arthur, 72, 91, 157

Tappan, Lewis, 72, 91, 157
Taylor, Zachary, 201
Thompson, George, 88
Transcendental Club, 111, 114, 115
Tremont Temple, 15
Tyler, John, 139

"Umbrella Girl, The," 152
Uncle Tom's Cabin ; see Stowe, Harriet Beecher
Underground Railway, 148

Van Buren, Martin, 199

Webster, Daniel, 209
Weed, Thurlow, 260
Weld, Theodore, 107
Whitney, Ann, 306
Whittier, John Greenleaf, 18, 39, 61, 72, 157, 158, 226, 240, 253, 271, 279, 301, 302
Willis, Nathaniel Parker, 43, 56, 140, 231, 262–263
Wilson, Henry, 235
Wise, Henry Alexander, correspondence with Mrs. Child, 250–251
Women's Rights, 93, 94, 98, 106, 264, 292
Wright, Frances, 83, 84, 116

B
Child
Baer
The heart is like heaven